African Cooking

African Cooking

by

Laurens van der Post

and the Editors of

TIME-LIFE BOOKS

photographed by

Brian Seed and Richard Jeffery

TIME-LIFE BOOKS, NEW YORK

THE AUTHOR: Laurens van der Post *(far left)* was born in South Africa's Orange Free State, and published his first book about Africa, *In a Province,* in 1932. He has traveled the continent extensively—sometimes on special missions for the British government—and has published several books based on his journeys. *The Lost World of the Kalahari* and *The Heart of the Hunter* deal with the Bushmen of the Kalahari Desert. His other books include *Venture to the Interior* and *The Dark Eye in Africa.* He now lives in London.

THE CONSULTING EDITOR: Michael Field *(left)* is one of America's leading culinary experts. His books include *Michael Field's Cooking School, Michael Field's Culinary Classics and Improvisations* and *All Manner of Food.*

THE FIELD PHOTOGRAPHER: Brian Seed *(far left),* a photographer based in London, spent 10 weeks in Africa for this book. On-the-spot research for much of his travels was by Ann Natanson, Rome correspondent for Time-Life Books.

THE STUDIO PHOTOGRAPHER: Richard Jeffery *(left)* also did the studio work for *Russian Cooking* and *Middle Eastern Cooking.* The still-life materials for Mr. Jeffery's photographs were selected by Yvonne McHarg.

SPECIAL CONSULTANTS: Odette Bery, consultant for South African recipes, worked in that country for two years. She has taught cooking and has served as a restaurant consultant in Boston. Mrs. Mireille Tevoedjre, consultant on West African cooking, is a native of Mali and wife of a staff member of the Dahomeyan Embassy in Washington. Advice on Ethiopian recipes was provided by Haregweyn Abebe of the Ethiopian Mission to the United Nations.

THE COVER: Bread and honey, like this sampling from Ethiopia, are a favored combination of foods in Africa. Both the breads, *yemarina yewotet dabo (top)* and *yewollo ambasha,* are listed in the Recipe Index.

TIME-LIFE BOOKS

EDITOR: Maitland A. Edey
Executive Editor: Jerry Korn
Text Director: Martin Mann
Art Director: Sheldon Cotler
Chief of Research: Beatrice T. Dobie
Picture Editor: Robert G. Mason
Assistant Text Directors: Ogden Tanner, Diana Hirsh
Assistant Art Director: Arnold C. Holeywell
Assistant Chief of Research: Martha T. Goolrick
Assistant Picture Editor: Melvin L. Scott

PUBLISHER: Walter C. Rohrer
General Manager: John D. McSweeney
Business Manager: John Steven Maxwell
Production Manager: Louis Bronzo

Sales Director: Joan D. Manley
Promotion Director: Beatrice K. Tolleris

FOODS OF THE WORLD

SERIES EDITOR: Richard L. Williams
EDITORIAL STAFF FOR AFRICAN COOKING:
Associate Editor: William Frankel
Picture Editor: Iris Friedlander
Designer: Albert Sherman
Assistant to Designer: Elise Hilpert
Staff Writer: Gerry Schremp
Chief Researcher: Sarah Brash
Researchers: Barbara Ensrud, Toby Solovioff, Diana Sweeney, Timberlake Wertenbaker
Test Kitchen Chef: John W. Clancy
Test Kitchen Staff: Fifi Bergman, Sally Darr, Leola Spencer

EDITORIAL PRODUCTION
Production Editor: Douglas B. Graham
Color Director: Robert L. Young
Assistant: James J. Cox
Copy Staff: Rosalind Stubenberg, Florence Keith
Picture Department: Dolores A. Littles, Joan Lynch
Traffic: Arthur A. Goldberger

The text for this book was written by Laurens van der Post, the recipe instructions by Michael Field, and other material by members of the staff. Valuable assistance was provided by the following individuals and departments of Time Inc.: Editorial Production, Robert W. Boyd Jr., Margaret T. Fischer; Editorial Reference, Peter Draz; Picture Collection, Doris O'Neil; Photographic Laboratory, George Karas; TIME-LIFE News Service, Murray J. Gart; Correspondents Ebun Adesioye (Lagos); Maria Vincenza Aloisi (Paris); Margot Hapgood (London); Peter Hawthorne (Johannesburg); Marvine Howe (Lisbon); Ann Natanson (Rome); Adolphus Paterson (Accra); Reg Shay (Salisbury); Abdou Sicé (Dakar); Eric Robins, Edwin M. Reingold (Nairobi); Ato Mogus Tekle-Mikael (Addis Ababa).

Contents

The Recipe Booklet accompanying this volume was designed for use in the kitchen. It contains all the 37 recipes in the chapters plus 83 more. Also included are a glossary of African cooking terms and a shopping guide to stores where ingredients can be purchased. The booklet has a wipe-clean cover and a spiral binding; it can either stand up or lie flat when open.

Introduction: One Man Reads the Many Faces of Africa

This is a very personal book by a very personable man. He is African —born there and bred there—and proud of it, and his pride in his continent and his love for it show through his writing. He is also white, and some may say that shows through too, but he is no white supremacist and although South Africa was his birthplace he has no stomach for the *apartheid* approach to human society. He loves people, he loves food, and he is equally at home with the desert people of the Kalahari, the forest people of Southeast Asia, the sophisticated people who inhabit the world's greatest restaurants—and with all the food that goes with them.

He is, of course, only one man, and let it be said at once that this is only one man's view of a part of Africa—very special, very personal and, of course, far from comprehensive. There is simply too much to African cooking for any one man to know it all. Indeed, the place is so big and so variegated that this is only one of several books in the FOODS OF THE WORLD series to take up the cuisine of Africa. The Mediterranean coastal countries are dealt with elsewhere, and other volumes acknowledge the important culinary debts owed by Latin America, the Caribbean islands and the United States to the people from black Africa who crossed the Atlantic in slave ships. So if it is asked, "How can you cover Africa in one volume?" the answer is that you cannot; it has taken several.

If it were a matter of whose cooking came first, then perhaps this book should lead all others in the field of regional cooking. For it was evidently in Africa that man began his checkered career on earth, and probably in Africa that he first mastered fire—an achievement that the author regards as "the most inspired and greatest of all ideas ever to issue from the mind of man," and that anybody must regard as the crucial first step toward cooking, toward survival, toward civilization.

Africa today has about a fifth of the world's land surface but only about a tenth of the world's population (including a few million Europeans), and some of the world's most splendid scenery. Most of it was never a paradise: afflicted by hunger, disease and tribal wars, its aboriginal peoples were almost always a society on the run. They could never afford to settle down and enjoy the generations of simply staying put that are essential to the development of sophisticated cuisines, and so their systems of cooking remained simple. Their customs—including the culinary ones—and indeed their total cultures had to be handed down by word of mouth. For while they did not lack for languages, speaking some 800 different ones among them, they had no way of leaving written records for their descendants to profit from. Only a few tantalizing clues remain to such peoples' deep and talented past, like the beautiful rock paintings that have survived in a Sahara that once was as green as Eden.

Wherever the outside world of the Arab and the European intruded on Africa, it was for violent purposes of plunder. Raiders, traders and invaders simply helped themselves—to slaves, to ivory and to the helpless continent itself, which they carved into colonial domains in disregard of natural or tribal boundaries. They taught the Africans little (except, perhaps, new dimensions of hatred) and learned little from them. And in this century, as their empires have dissolved, their legacy has been a proliferation of angry nations ill-equipped to endure. In many ways, they have left the "Dark Continent" darker than they found it.

The Africa of this book has had its share of all this. It is immense in itself, stretching all the way from Ethiopia through the sub-Saharan lands of West, East and Portuguese Africa down to the Cape of Good Hope. It is also extremely diverse, but as the author points out, it has interesting common denominators of soil and minerals, of animal and vegetable life, if not of cuisine. For example many of the same animals that are encountered up in Ethiopia, like the greater kudu, are found again thousands of miles south in the Transvaal, on the far side of the great equatorial zone, where they feed on the same kinds of shrubs. The lion and the elephant preside over the wildlife and the great, stark baobab tree, looking "like a carrot planted upside down," stands guard over the landscapes —and provides food—from one end of this Africa to the other.

Since Laurens van der Post knows his continent like a book, it is fitting that he has written this one. Thirteenth child in a family of Dutch and Huguenot descent, he succeeded to a large ancestral farm called Mountain of the Hyenas in the Orange Free State, and his background in the south of Africa runs back 300 years. As a British army officer in World War II he helped return Emperor Haile Selassie to the throne in Ethiopia, blowing up a number of Italian trucks in the process, and his credentials in that country are good. As for the lands in between he likes to say, "I think I have covered more thousands of miles of Africa on my own two flat feet than any other man," and he has found no one to dispute it.

Like every other volume in this series, Colonel van der Post's presents the author's own, personalized view of the subject. His own experiences, opinions and interpretations are here; he does not purport to be, and has not been encouraged to try to be, all things to all Africans. As you read the book you will share in the adventures of a wise and good man who has spent more than six decades getting to know Africa, and who in his seventh decade insists there is great hope for it.

—*Richard L. Williams, Editor,* FOODS OF THE WORLD

I

My Continent: A Personal View

My earliest memories of Africa, and of my life there, center around the large dining table in the home of my Boer grandfather, in the Orange Free State, deep in the interior of South Africa. And almost invariably the scene in this theater of my past is the evening meal. I used to wait for this meal, six decades ago, with the same kind of excitement that I was to experience much later as a drama critic in London, before the curtain rose on the first night of a new work by a friend from whom I expected much. As in a darkened playhouse, the excitement would start when the maids began to light the heavy oil lamps in the long passage that led from the front door on the veranda surrounding the house. At last they came to the dining room, and the biggest lamp of all. In the center of that room was a great table made of an African wood so hard and so dense that a piece of it would sink like iron if it was thrown into water; and over the center of the table, suspended in massive chains from the ceiling, hung an immense oil lamp made of brass that glowed and shone like gold. It took a servant several hours to polish that lamp once a week, and to me it always looked like the sort of lamp that Solomon in all his glory might have hung in his first temple in the Promised Land.

As the 13th of 15 children, I used to stare at the lighting of this lamp as one might witness a miracle. I would watch the shadows roll back into the recesses of the heavy old Dutch furniture and see the lamplight fall, as in a painting by Rembrandt, on the table waiting for its full complement of family and guests. At the same time I would be-

come aware of a subtle scent of spice drifting into the dining room from the kitchen.

The sense of smell is surely the most evocative of all our senses. It goes deeper than conscious thought or organized memory and has a will of its own that the mind is compelled to heed. Since the scent of cinnamon is the first to present itself to my memory of the moment when the great lamp was lit and the great table set and ready, I must accept the fact that my first coherent recollection of the drama of our evening meal begins with the serving of a typical milk soup of the South African interior. What is more, on the nights I remember, it must have been freezing outside because we children had this soup only in winter. I am all the more sure of this because my grandfather and the black ladies who cooked for him knew that there was nothing that pleased young palates more than a milk soup.

Made with the simplest of ingredients, the soup went under the name of *snysels,* which may be translated as "slicelings"—in this case, "slicelings" of a homemade pasta consisting of wheat flour mixed with egg, rolled out as thin as possible, and cut into fine strips. These strips were tossed into a large cast-iron pot of boiling milk, already sugared and richly spiced with sticks of cinnamon. When the strips of pasta rose to the surface, semitransparent but still firm to the tooth, the soup was ready for serving. It would be borne into the dining room in a cloud of aromatic steam, filling the air with that incomparable and unforgettable scent of cinnamon that, more than any other spice, seemed to us the quintessential emanation of the far Far East.

The fragrance of cinnamon would still be adrift in the room when the more acute scent of cloves announced that the main course was on its way. This would be a superbly pot-roasted leg of lamb, a standard dish of the interior. Studded with cloves from Zanzibar, less than 2,000 miles from us as the crow flies, the lamb—itself a product of our farm —was so tender that it seemed to flake rather than cut at the touch of my grandfather's carving knife.

Mixed with the smell of cloves was that of saffron rice and raisins—a dish that was not typical of the interior, but one that had been introduced to the family by my French grandmother. My grandfather served it more as part of a ritual of remembrance of all she had meant in his life than as mere gratification of his own liking for it.

With these varied scents, there came the sharp fragrance of quince jelly, which was always served with our roasts, burning like a maharaja's ruby in its own cut crystal bowl, and tasting as brilliant as it looked. Then, since this was winter, came a dish of dried spotted beans, which we know as governor's beans; centuries ago, presumably, some forgotten governor had first planted them in the vast kitchen garden that his masters, the Dutch East India Company, had made of the Cape of Good Hope. (Their purpose was to provide fresh foods to forestall scurvy among Dutch sailors in the spice trade.) At grandfather's house the beans were cooked in mutton stock and puréed tomatoes and were accompanied by baked pumpkin flavored with nutmeg.

Last of all came a bowl piled high with yellow peaches, turned to burnished gold by the alchemy of the great lamp overhead. These peaches still glow in my memory like an offering of fruit from some sheltered grove of the fabled Hesperides. Like everything else we ate they were the product of our completely self-sufficient farm. They were preserved whole in glass jars in the summer, so skillfully that much of their original savor remained. I have yet to discover, in this technological age of ours, any preserved fruit that could rival those peaches. They brought into the winter night the fullness of the summer gone by and the promise of its return.

The evening meal always ended with a reading from the family Bible —"The Book," as we called it. For this purpose the table was quickly cleared and the Bible was placed on it with some effort, for it weighed no less than 20 pounds. At this point all the servants would enter the room to join in our improvised service. Among them I would see the faces of all the indigenous races of Africa: the Bushman, the earliest inhabitant of the region; his successor, the Hottentot; the tall Bantu who, like us, was an intruder and who lived here by right of previous brutal conquest; and members of the Cape Colored community—that gay and vital breed of men, the product of our own miscegenation with the indigenous peoples of Africa and with slaves brought from India, Java and Sumatra by the Dutch East India Company.

The earliest reading that I clearly remember from "The Book" is the psalm beginning, "The Lord is my shepherd." It was a sentence of particular meaning for the assembly around the table, for now and then the quiet reading and the silence of the veld outside would be broken by the piercing bleats of sheep. Ours was great country for sheep, but we had to fight a daily battle to protect them against all of the flesh-eating animals that threatened them. Every night the flocks were brought in from the field, each defended by at least one shepherd, and were driven into kraals—cramped squares of high stone walls designed to guard them while we slept. All through the night, whenever the jackals or hyenas howled with hunger outside (and they often did; my own farm in the same region is called the Mountain of Hyenas), we would hear the uneasy bleating of some ewe fretting over the safety of her lambs. During our service, it was almost as if the sheep were joining in, calling for the same sure protection, beyond the power of men, that my grandfather found in the 23rd Psalm.

The hymn that followed the Bible reading varied from time to time, but the one that resounds in my memory was a hymn my great-grandfather had sung on his northward march in 1835 from the Cape of Good Hope into the interior. This hymn had become my grandfather's own paean of thanksgiving to God during the wars he fought against British overlords at the cape and later against Bantu tribesmen in the land to the north. Its first verse, roughly translated from the Cape Dutch language in which we sang it, opened with the words: "Rough storms may rage, all round me is night, but God, my God shall protect me."

The hymn ended, the last prayers said and the servants gone, we would leave the table and gather around the blazing fireplace in the dining room. Now one of the most exciting of my childhood experiences would begin, for my grandfather would talk about the past. Often, too, there were present some of the more colorful characters left on the African scene, men who had never lost the instinct for trekking, or wandering, and who continued to move restlessly across our frontiers. From them I heard of the still-wild country that lay farther to the north, beyond rivers with strange names—the Okovanggo, Black Umfolozi, Limpopo, Matetsi, Cunene. At times these fireside talks brought the past so close that I had the feeling I had only to stretch out my hand to touch the hands of the long-dead actors who had played heroic parts in creating our secure life on the veld of the Orange Free State.

Yet I knew even then that, in a larger sense, the journey leading to my grandfather's ample farm had been almost incredibly long and hard. Deep in all human awareness, I believe, is a sense of life itself as a journey. The great stories that form a kind of blueprint of the Western spirit are all concerned with journeys; think for instance of the Hebrews' journey from bondage in Egypt to a land of promise in Palestine, and of the wanderings of Aeneas in search of the place to build the city that became Rome. For my family, this sense of journey had produced a crucial pattern of life. Some 300 years ago, it brought my forebears on my mother's side from Holland to the newly settled Cape of Good Hope. There the family soon had a French branch grafted upon it—a branch brought to Africa by Huguenots fleeing from persecution in France. Significantly, both branches shared a conviction about the inadequacies of the European spirit, and a determination to create a new and better society in the then-unknown wilderness of South Africa.

From that time my family was almost continually on the move, always in the forefront of a slow, relentless push from the southernmost tip of Africa into the unexplored northern interior. The climax of their

Drawn by 16 oxen, an antique Voortrek wagon rumbles over the veld near Johannesburg in a modern rerun of the Great Trek of 1835-1838. In the course of the trek Dutch settlers from the Cape region, impatient with British rule, moved overland to colonize the South African interior and form the Transvaal and the Orange Free State. Their descendants honor their memory in this annual re-enactment.

exodus can be told in a story that sums up all I mean by the sense of journey. The story takes place early in the 19th Century when, for many complex reasons, the Boer pioneers in South Africa came to feel that Europe—the Europe they had found wanting—had caught up with them and reshackled them with the arrival of the British as new masters at the Cape of Good Hope. My people fell back instinctively on a literal interpretation of the idea of life as a journey and abandoned their well-found existence at the Cape of Good Hope to penetrate the interior. There, they thought, they could escape a new bondage to Europe and fashion a world to their own liking.

This episode in African history, which began in 1835 and ended in 1838, is known as the Great Trek. Among those in the forefront of the exodus from British rule was my mother's grandfather. His party, including kinsmen and friends, loaded all that they conveniently could carry in long covered wagons drawn by humpbacked oxen, piled their women and children in the most comfortable places in the wagons, mounted their horses, and confidently set off toward the trackless north.

My great-grandfather's party was one of the smallest in the Great Trek, but also one of the most intrepid, and soon struck off from the main route of migration. The party forded the Orange River, the stream that marked the farthest rim of European awareness of the unknown Africa, and moved across the blue and gold plains of what later became the Orange Free State. The plains were then almost devoid of human beings, for they had been constantly raided and plundered by the fierce African nations of the interior. I remember my paternal grandfather, who traveled as a boy with another party of pioneers, telling me that what impressed him most on the journey was the bleached bones, human and animal, that littered the flat yellow plateau.

For some 400 miles beyond the Orange River, all went so well with

Overleaf: Garnishes add touches of color to the nourishing soups of South Africa. The four soups on the brass stand are *(from left):* a cold, sweet buttermilk soup garnished with cinnamon and nutmeg; curried fish soup garnished with chopped egg; fresh green-pea soup garnished with mint; and a soup made with cucumbers and puréed potatoes garnished with chopped gherkins, scallions and mint. The soup in the foreground contains potatoes and white wine and is garnished with diced bacon and croutons.

my great-grandfather's party that its members developed a false sense of security. When they came to the Vaal River, the next major river to the north, they did not even take the precaution of drawing their wagons into the defensive circle called a *laager,* the normal practice on a march into the wilderness. The travelers settled down almost as if they were on a picnic in familiar country. Yet all the while their movements had been observed by the scouts of one of the most formidable of all the fighting peoples of the interior, the Matabele.

At their leisure, the Matabele had assembled an army of their best warriors to stop any intrusion into what they regarded as one of their vital spheres of influence. During the night they silently crossed the river and set up their most devastating attack formation, in which their *impis,* or organized troops, were arrayed in the shape of a half moon. During an attack, the horns of the crescent could outflank and ultimately surround the target with continual reinforcements from a great mass of warriors held in reserve at the center. Long before dawn, this half moon of an army was in position for attack.

My great-grandfather had no suspicion of the impending disaster. His three children waked before daybreak and made so much noise that he ordered their nurse, a Cape Colored woman, to take them down to the riverbank and amuse them while he and the rest of his company took another hour's sleep. The nurse and her charges—my grandmother, who was only four, my grandmother's sister and little brother—had hardly got to the river when the dawn broke. At the first light, the battle cry of the Matabele shattered the silence of the veld, the horns of the half moon closed around the sleeping wagons, and the whole party was clubbed and stabbed to death.

As soon as she heard the war cries, the nurse gathered the children, dodged with them along the riverbank until she encountered a waterfall and herded them behind the falling water, where they hid all day. By afternoon the Matabele had gone and the last of the fires in the burning wagons had died down. The nurse emerged from her hiding place to find the wagons so thoroughly plundered that there was no food left. Somehow she kept the children alive on bulbs and tubers growing on the veld. Ten days later a patrol of horsemen, scouting far ahead of the main column of lumbering wagons, found the nurse and the children. In one of the wagons following the patrol was the little boy who was to become my grandfather.

This dramatic trek was by no means the only one in which my family was involved, but it was one of the last. When my grandfather and my grandmother were married, they determined to make a stand somewhere, converting the physical pattern of travel into a kind of journey of the mind, expressed in building a new kind of world. They did not settle by the river of the massacre, but doubled back to create a series of flourishing farms near the banks of the Orange River. At one of those farms I ate the dinners described at the beginning of this chapter, and I myself own one of the homesteads to this day.

Growing up on this kind of farm, with this kind of history behind me, I could never think of myself as a European. For me, the old conflicts between white and black and colored had gone, leaving no sense of mistrust or bitterness. One of the first languages I spoke was an African language, Sotho; my nurses were African; my friends on the farm were African children. What fascinated my friends and me was not the lore of Europe so much as the accumulations of myth and legend that the black peoples around us had brought with them on their own long migrations from north to south.

I learned so much from these peoples that at the age of 10 I could have lived off the country, using what my African counselors had taught me about the natural roots and fruits of my region. I did not rely on sandwiches for my lunches at school as children did in the towns. Between classes I went out with my friends, and with our hunting knives we dug up far more exciting food—*krul-uintje,* or curl bulb, and *kalkoentjies,* literally "little turkeys"—straight from the earth of Africa.

Thus, from my earliest years, food was at the center of my experience of South Africa. As I grew up food took its place at the center of my experiences of the wilder, uncleared land that Africans call the bush. Once a year at least the urge to live as the pioneers had done drove my friends and me to make forays into the roughest parts of the country. We never returned from one of these expeditions without feeling strangely renewed, for there is some kind of therapy for the flagging modern spirit in living at one with nature again.

One of the favorite journeys of my youth was the hazardous descent into the gorges of the Orange River, near my home. For days or weeks we would catch fish from the river with homemade nets, and afterward eat the fish wrapped in bacon and roasted on coals at our campfires. Occasionally we would go up into the hills to shoot just enough mountain buck to give us meat for our main meals, while the younger children dug up roots, tubers and truffles to season and accompany it. At dusk we would follow the bees, bright as buttons of gold in the long level light of the sun, on their way to nests cunningly hidden in the deepest clefts and caves of the purple rocks. In the scarlet twilight we would smoke out the nests by piling a leaping fire with special herbs— which, according to our Bushman and Hottentot companions, possessed the unfailing property of putting bees to sleep. The rocks just below the nests would become sticky as flypaper with amber syrup, and we delved deep and high to extract yard-long combs of antique honey, then returned to our camp with buckets full of bee-made dessert for our evening meal.

The whole of Africa was alive for me in these sojourns in the bush, and I was determined to get to know the whole of it as no living man had known it before. The moment I was old enough to be independent, I set out to fulfill what had become a sense of personal mission: to discover the endless Africa that lay to the north.

Before my 20th year, I had already retraced the historical routes of Europeans toward the Far East, traveling from port to port on the eastern coast of Africa up to the island of Mombasa. Along that coast Vasco da Gama had landed repeatedly in the 15th Century, before continuing his voyage across the Indian Ocean to the Far East. I felt that my own course of travel was of vital importance if I was to gain an understanding of Africa in its historical as well as geographical context. After all, Europeans had first used Africa as a mere halfway house on the way to the rich spice trade of the Far East, and I felt I had to know all that those first European journeys implied, what the peoples along the way were like, and what they had contributed to the character of the life I already knew in Africa.

After these early travels I never lost an opportunity to go to other parts of my continent. In my time, I have walked thousands of miles of Africa on my own feet—many more miles, I believe, than any European has ever done. I was too late, alas, to know Africa as it was before Europe came to it; the great era of exploration was already over. But there still remained what I have called some "known unknowns" in the continent. Happily, I was in time to explore some of the greatest of these, notably the Kalahari Desert of southwestern Africa where I traveled for the British government in the first systematic exploration of this area. There I re-established contact with the Bushman, the last representative of the Stone Age man of Africa.

I lived with the Bushman and through him got some inkling of what life was like at the very beginning of civilization. I learned, for instance, what man's first mastery of fire must have meant to him. As I sat down at night to eat the meat of a buck killed by bow and poisoned arrow, listening to lions roaring out in the dark and frightened ostriches booming in reply, I seemed to be in at the genesis of the art of cooking. And on my return to life in various of the world's great cities, I found that my attitude toward food had changed completely. Eating had become something that I could never again take for granted; henceforth, whenever I sat down to a meal, food and the eating of it were invested with some primeval sense of mystery and respect.

Perhaps the most astonishing discovery I have made in some 40 years of exploration of my Africa—a continent that represents more than a fifth of the world's surface—is the underlying unity of its nature. Superficially the *diversity* of African races, languages and bewildering tribal cultures could not be greater. But the more I came to know the land and the peoples of Africa, the more I discovered a deep elemental unity that will one day demand institutions and societies to express it.

This unity would be more obvious to outsiders if it were not for the confusion created by the existence of North Africa. Technically, of course, the northern part of Africa is just as much a part of the whole as is the central or the southern; but in reality, the life and peoples of North Africa, from the hills of the Red Sea to the Atlantic Ocean, belong to the Middle East. North of the Sahara, even the flora and fauna are not African so much as Middle Eastern and Mediterranean. Though my life has taken me again and again to North Africa, I have never ceased to feel an alien there. Traveling southward, I would gain the feeling of being on the way home, to the real Africa, only when the golden dunes of the Sahara went blue on the horizon behind me and I saw my first sentinel-like baobab tree outlined on the quicksilver rim of the land

Opposite: The Bushman of South-West Africa, driven into barren, rugged wastelands by the white man and by more aggressive tribes, sustains himself by scavenging and primitive hunting. The picture opposite shows some of the necessities for his meager diet. The ostrich egg (2) has already been blown out and eaten; it is now being used to carry water. The other items are: (1) jelly, or spiny, melon; (3) caterpillars; (4, 6, 9) desert berries; (5) wild onions; (7) wild dates; (8) wild fruits of the caper family; (10) poisonous beetles, used as a source of poison for arrows.

Continued on page 22

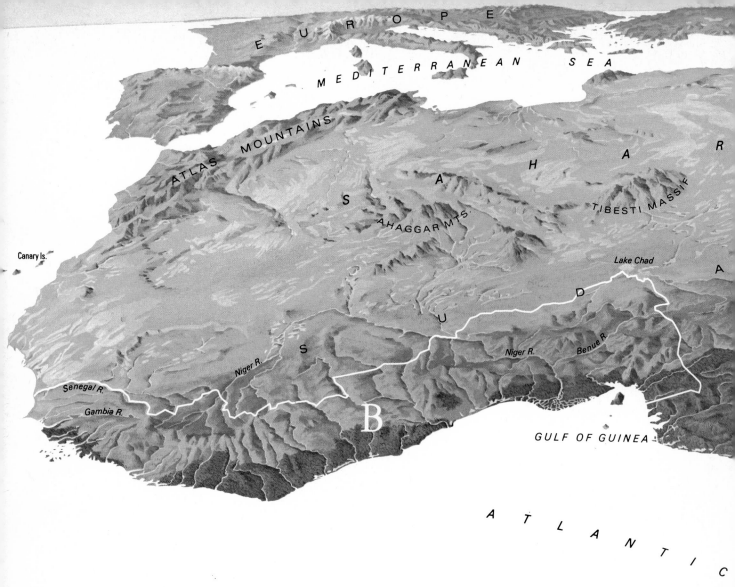

EUROPE

MEDITERRANEAN SEA

ATLAS MOUNTAINS

SAHARA

AHAGGAR MTS.

TIBESTI MASSIF

Canary Is.

Lake Chad

SUDAN

Niger R.

Niger R.

Benue R.

Senegal R.

Gambia R.

B

GULF OF GUINEA

A

ATLANTIC

The Continent Where Man Began: A Place of Extremes

Lying directly athwart the equator, Africa is almost three quarters tropical
or subtropical. High cultures and fine cuisines are to be found there, but in
much of the continent man—who began here—is at best tolerated by nature.
Extremes of topography and climate make agriculture difficult, and some
peoples live in conditions much like those of the hunting cultures of
prehistory. This book concentrates on five sub-Saharan regions that have
developed distinctive and delightful cuisines, each in its way identifiably
African, and marked with the fascination of the continent that produced it.

A Ethiopia

Isolated from the rest of Africa by its steep
escarpments, Ethiopia has kept its old traditions inviolate from European influence.
Most of the country lies on a great plateau,
high enough for its inhabitants to enjoy a
healthy, temperate climate suitable for growing grain and for grazing cattle and sheep.

B West Africa

This region contains the continent's greatest
concentrations of people, living mainly in
moist, hot, river-threaded lowlands. In some
places the forests and jungles have been
opened up for intensive agriculture; palm
trees yield a basic cooking oil; and the coastal
waters are rich in fish and other seafood.

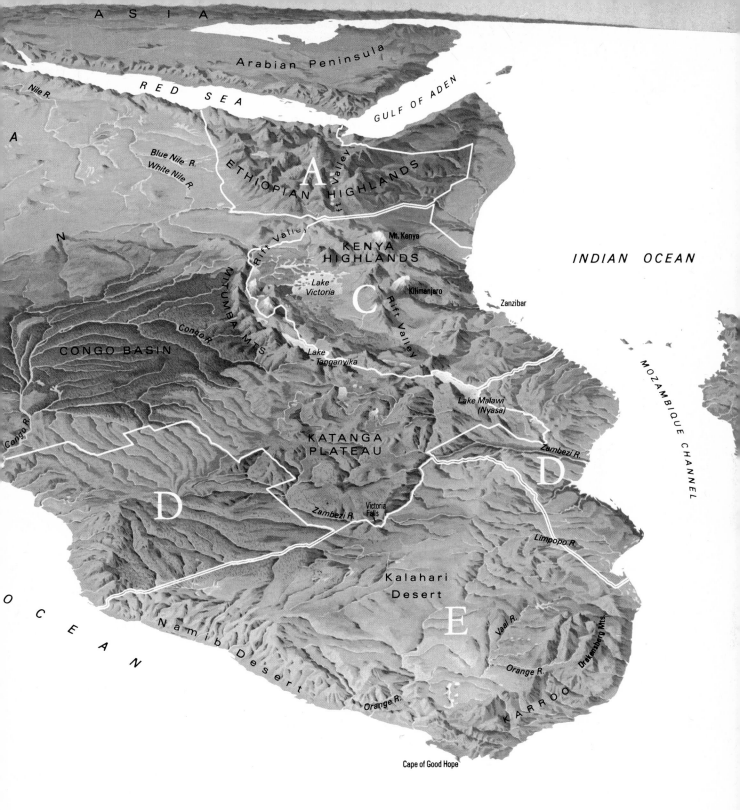

ASIA

Arabian Peninsula

RED SEA

GULF OF ADEN

Nile R.

Blue Nile R.

White Nile R.

ETHIOPIAN HIGHLANDS

A

Rift Valley

Rift Valley

Mt. Kenya

KENYA HIGHLANDS

Lake Victoria

Kilimanjaro

C

INDIAN OCEAN

Zanzibar

MITUMBA MTS.

Congo R.

CONGO BASIN

Lake Tanganyika

Rift Valley

Lake Malawi (Nyasa)

Congo R.

MOZAMBIQUE CHANNEL

KATANGA PLATEAU

Zambezi R.

D

N

Zambezi R.

Victoria Falls

Zambezi R.

D

Limpopo R.

Kalahari Desert

E

Vaal R.

Orange R.

Drakensberg Mts.

OCEAN

Namib Desert

Orange R.

E

KARROO

Cape of Good Hope

C *East Africa*

Hot and dry in its savannas, cool and moist in its highlands, East Africa offers greater climatic extremes than any other region of the continent. Most indigenous peoples here have long been pastoral, but a developing agriculture exists on farms and highland plantations established by Europeans.

D *Portuguese Africa*

The earliest European people to explore the coasts of western and eastern Africa, the Portuguese are now almost the only colonial power left. Angola and Mozambique are underdeveloped agriculturally, although the Portuguese have introduced many fruits and vegetables that flourish in the region today.

E *Southern Africa*

Fertile soil and agreeable climate give South Africa much of the best grazing and cropland south of the Sahara. The Dutch first settled the region, and its culture and cuisine still bear their imprint, but a wide variety of other ethnic strains—European, Asian and African—exist in the south side by side.

ahead. From then on I would know that, no matter where I went, whether east from Cape Verde to Ethiopia or south to the Kalahari and the shimmering hills of Zululand, the baobab tree would keep me company, a mute witness of the oneness of the Africa that is the concern of this book.

It is remarkable how limited a role climate and geographical zones play in the essential nature of Africa. One finds the same animals and plants in Ethiopia as in the bush country of the Transvaal, although the equator, the continent's Great Lakes and its Great Rift Valley lie between. Such differences as there are come mainly from the different kinds of contacts that Africa has had with Europe and the Far East.

What is separable in the unity I have discerned, however, are five distinctive life styles within Africa *(map, pages 20-21)*. To my mind, the existence of these distinctions enriches rather than destroys the embracing oneness of the land.

The first of these life styles appears in the ancient empire of Ethiopia. Some students of Africa place Ethiopia in the same ethnic category as Egypt and Morocco, but Ethiopia is a deeply committed and dedicated African nation. I can say this with confidence: in World War II, as a member of a small British team of officers, I helped to organize the heroic resistance of Ethiopian patriots against their Italian overlords. We went into Ethiopia from Sudan, through an immense stretch of sleeping-sickness country—an era largely unexplored and never occupied by the Italians because it was so unhealthy. This parklike, unspoiled part of Africa is the nearest thing I know to what the continent must have been like before the coming of man. After many weeks we came to the fantastic escarpment of the Ethiopian plateau, a rampart rising like some vast fortress above the hot plains below. When we crossed the last rim of the jagged mountains and saw the lovely highlands stretching endlessly before us, we encountered the first Ethiopians on our journey. They were courteous, dignified, nobly built—and I believed at once what I had read and heard, that Ethiopia was no mere repetition of the Levantine world I had just left behind in the Nile Valley, but the first authentic African civilization.

The next great life style on my continent is that of West Africa. This area is fundamentally the African of the Negro, and its complex contacts with the world of the West may well go back to the days of ancient Carthage in all its glory, enriched by sporadic injections of Arab culture by way of Morocco in the north.

The third style belongs to the Africa centered in Kenya, Tanzania and Uganda and lying east of the Great Rift Valley. This is a country of pastoral Negroid peoples who are less sophisticated than the Negroes of West Africa but who enjoy a healthier climate and are physically stronger and mentally as alert and gifted as any group of human beings on the continent. Their Bantu culture reflects exotic outside pressures: unrecorded but unmistakable contacts with India and the Far East and, above all and unfortunately, contacts with an inferior manifestation of Arabian civilization introduced by Arab slave traders based on the island of Zanzibar.

Farther south lies the world of Portuguese Africa, which achieves its greatest expression in two immense colonies: Mozambique on the east coast of the continent and Angola on the west coast.

Finally, there is southern Africa. Racial, political and economic stresses have begun to pull at the region in recent years, but it remains a definable cultural mix because of the amalgam of Dutch, French and British influences that have dominated it from the middle of the 17th Century to the present day.

Each of these five life styles includes its own distinctive cuisine. Yet food is a key not to the disparity but to the unity of the continent. Just as my first memory of Africa sharpens into focus around food, my most recent memories of my continent are also profoundly concerned with food. Some months ago I badly injured my right arm and was told by my doctors that, if I ever meant to use it for writing again, it would have to be rested for many months. This enforced ease seemed a wonderful opportunity to revisit the whole of Africa. I would see again the lands I had explored for 40 years of my life; I would see what Africa was achieving now that so many influences of European colonialism were vanishing. I intended, once I could write again, to set down my appraisal of this new emergent Africa. But everywhere I went I found myself too profoundly depressed by what I saw to write dispassionately about it. In an Africa that is so much at one in its deepest nature, millions of human beings are involved in divisive conflicts, killing one another from Mali to Zanzibar and The Congo on a scale that even the reviled former imperialists would never have permitted. The political and social scene in Africa seemed to me eroded and bankrupt, and I instinctively rebelled against joining in any form of activity so negative and destructive.

All this may be part of the price Africa must pay before it can enjoy ultimate unity. But I was certain that I could not further this unity by entering into the ideological conflicts and rivalries that are tearing the continent apart. I came to believe that embattled Africa could best be regenerated by a profoundly nonpolitical reassessment of common aims and ideals—a rediscovery of the overriding values of the dignity of man and the reverence for life.

Then I wondered, often in desperation, what in the world all the warring systems, countries, tribes and races still had indisputably in common. Oversimple and childlike as it may seem, one answer that popped up unbidden from my imagination was *food*. If I did what has never been done before—if I wrote about the food of Africa as a whole, about African man and his ways of eating and cooking from the Stone Age Bushman to the sophisticated gourmet in Addis Ababa or Capetown—perhaps I could render some service and at least pay homage to my troubled continent. In a way, I would be doing what my grandfather did at those meals at his homestead, when he assembled all the races around his table every night. In a small way, too, I could recall for my readers the fact that all men are one in their needs and searchings, that whatever sets them apart is evil and whatever brings them peaceably together is good. This is what I have tried to do in the chapters that follow.

To serve 6

1 cup red wine vinegar
2 teaspoons sugar
¼ teaspoon ground ginger
6 whole cloves
¼ pound slab bacon, rind
    removed, cut into strips about
    ¾ inch long and ¼ inch wide
1 large onion, peeled, cut crosswise
    into ⅛-inch slices, and separated
    into rings
A 5½- to 6-pound leg of lamb,
    trimmed of excess fat, but with
    the fell (the parchmentlike
    covering) left on
½ cup seedless raisins
2 garlic cloves, peeled and cut into
    small pieces
2 teaspoons salt
½ teaspoon freshly ground black
    pepper
2 tablespoons vegetable oil
2 cups boiling water
2 tablespoons apricot jam
1 tablespoon flour
2 tablespoons cold water

Mock Leg of Venison *(South Africa)*
MARINATED AND LARDED BRAISED LEG OF LAMB

Starting a day ahead, combine the vinegar, sugar, ginger and cloves in a deep bowl and stir until the sugar and ginger are completely dissolved. Drop in the bacon strips and onion rings, and turn them about with a spoon until they are well coated. Marinate at room temperature for at least 30 minutes.

To lard the lamb, remove the bacon from the marinade. With a small, sharp knife, cut slits about 1 inch long and 1½ inches deep on all sides of the leg of lamb, spacing the slits about 2 inches apart. One at a time, spread each slit open and insert 2 or 3 raisins, a piece of garlic and a bacon strip. With your fingers, rub the salt and pepper all over the surface of the leg.

Place the leg of lamb in a glass or enameled dish or pan large enough to hold it comfortably and pour the marinade and onion rings over it. Cover with foil or plastic wrap and marinate the lamb at room temperature for at least 12 hours, turning it over and basting it with its marinade every 3 or 4 hours. If you prefer, you may marinate the lamb in the refrigerator; in that case let it stand for at least 24 hours, turning it over two or three times.

Preheat the oven to 400°. Remove the leg of lamb from the marinade and pat it completely dry with paper towels. (Reserve the marinade and the onion rings.)

In a heavy casserole equipped with a tightly fitting lid and large enough to hold the lamb comfortably, heat the oil over moderate heat until a light haze forms above it. Brown the lamb in the hot oil, turning it frequently with tongs or two wooden spoons and regulating the heat so that the leg colors richly and evenly without burning. Add the marinade, onions and 2 cups of boiling water, and bring to a boil over high heat.

Cover the casserole securely and cook the lamb undisturbed in the middle of the oven for 1 hour and 15 minutes if you prefer the lamb rare or for as much as 2 hours if you like lamb well done as the South Africans do. Transfer the leg to a heated platter and drape foil over it to keep it warm while you prepare the sauce.

With a large spoon, skim as much fat as possible from the liquid remaining in the pan and discard the cloves. Bring the liquid to a boil over high heat and, stirring occasionally, cook briskly, uncovered, until it is reduced to about 2 cups. Stir in the apricot jam and reduce the heat to low. Make a smooth paste of the flour and 2 tablespoons of cold water and, with a wire whisk or spoon, stir it gradually into the simmering liquid. Cook, stirring frequently, for about 5 minutes, or until the sauce thickens lightly. Taste for seasoning.

To serve, carve the lamb and arrange the slices attractively in overlapping layers on a large heated platter. Serve the sauce separately from a bowl or sauceboat. Mock leg of venison may be accompanied by separate bowls of stewed sweet potatoes *(opposite),* red cabbage (made with quinces or apples) and yellow peach pickle *(Recipe Index).*

Red cabbage, sweet potatoes and peach pickle accompany this South African mock leg of venison (pot-roasted lamb).

Stewed Sweet Potatoes *(South Africa)*

Combine the sugar, flour and salt in a small bowl and stir them together. Place about one third of the sweet potatoes in a heavy 3- to 4-quart saucepan, overlapping the slices to cover the bottom of the pan completely. Sprinkle the potatoes with about one third of the sugar mixture and dot the top with 1 tablespoon of the butter bits.

Cover the first layer with another third of the sweet potatoes, another third of the sugar mixture and 1 tablespoon of butter. Then arrange the remaining sweet potato slices on top, and sprinkle them with the rest of the sugar and butter bits.

Tuck the cinnamon under the top layer of potatoes and pour the water down the side of the pan. Bring to a boil over high heat, cover tightly, and reduce the heat to low. Slide the pan back and forth occasionally to prevent the bottom layer from scorching, and simmer the potatoes for 45 minutes, or until they are soft but still intact.

With a slotted spoon, transfer the potatoes to a heated bowl and moisten them with about ½ cup of the cooking liquid. Serve at once.

To serve 6

¼ cup light-brown sugar
1 tablespoon flour
1 teaspoon salt
2 pounds sweet potatoes, peeled and sliced into ½-inch-thick rounds
3 tablespoons butter, cut into ¼-inch bits
3 one-inch pieces of stick cinnamon
½ cup water

25

II

The Ancient World of Ethiopia

A young priest of the Ethiopian Church bears an ornate filigree cross in a solemn religious procession in Gondar. Ethiopia's adherence to Christianity dates back to 340 A.D. A separate branch of the faith, Ethiopian Christianity is related to Egypt's Coptic Church but distinct from Western Catholicism and Eastern Orthodoxy.

The great historian Edward Gibbon dismissed the history and the culture of Ethiopia with the words: "The Ethiopians slept for nearly a thousand years, forgetful of the world, by whom they were forgotten." Nothing could have been farther from the truth. Wiser—if less famous —historians always knew that Ethiopia was in some way crucial to the history of Africa, and through the centuries artists and poets of the Western world never lost touch with the mystery of that land, at least in their imaginations. (Its other name of Abyssinia derived from Habesh, as it is still called in the Arabic-speaking world, after the Habashat tribe of Arabs who entered the country from Yemen across the Red Sea sometime before 500 B.C.) In southern Africa, 3,000 miles away, we were always intensely aware of the fabled kingdom to the north, and we were certain that our history would have been utterly different had it not been for the long, persistent pull of both a known and a mythical Ethiopia on Mediterranean and European minds.

We knew that the main reason for our presence in southern Africa was the European search for a route to the spice trade of India and the Far East, and we knew also that this search had been stimulated in part by the belief that somewhere down in Africa there existed a land of immense riches. The 15th Century Portuguese explorers thought that this land and Ethiopia were one, that this opulent realm was a Christian country ruled by a king called Prester John, and that they could deal profitably with this king on their voyages. These beliefs of the Portuguese were fantastic, of course, but they had very profound effects on African history,

Landlocked until 1950 when the former Italian colony of Eritrea was joined to it, Ethiopia now has a seacoast and easier access to the outside world but is still culturally and geographically unique. It is literally a land of bread and honey —the bread from vast fields of sorghum, millet and wheat, the honey from myriad hives of both wild and domesticated bees. Coffee may have originated in Ethiopia; wild coffee trees abound on the hillsides of Kaffa and Harar.

and on my own youthful dreams of exploring the whole of my continent.

As a young man I tried hard to get into Ethiopia, but the means and the opportunity evaded me until the outbreak of World War II. In a sense the delay was providential. Had I gone to Ethiopia earlier I would have gone by a contemporary route: by ship to the port of Djibouti on the Red Sea, then by rail to Addis Ababa. The exigencies of the war compelled me to make my way to Ethiopia by one of the most fascinating routes that a traveler can take.

I went into Ethiopia from the north, leading a camel train of troops down through an all-but-empty bush country where the Italian overlords of Ethiopia rarely ventured. Our point of departure for this journey was the Blue Nile in Sudan and—for the purposes of this book—it could not have been more happily chosen. There the Africa of the Mediterranean abruptly ends and the true Africa begins. Behind us lay a great plain, flat, bleached, stretched out as on a rack under a crackling sun; before us were upthrusts of strange hills studded with deep cracks. Vegetation blanketed the earth with a lushness that seemed almost wasteful after the desert we had left. There were the long yellow tasseled grasses of Africa, resounding like the strings of aeolian harps in the evening air, scores of varieties of acacia, soaring fever trees, banyan and thorn-tipped scrub. Above all there was the baobab tree, perhaps the strangest tree that nature ever invented.

It is not a tree to everyone's liking: the explorer David Livingstone said that it reminded him of a gigantic carrot planted upside down. But in my country we call it the "cream of tartar tree" because we make a crude baking powder from its seeds; we dry the flesh of its fruit as a welcome addition to our cooking; and on many a hot and waterless day in the bush I have placed baobab seeds under my tongue, and their astringent flavor helped keep my thirst away. And because it grows everywhere south of the Sahara, the baobab tree has always symbolized, for me, the oneness of Africa.

In our long slow progress through the bush, we found the ground ever more broken, the upheavals of earth ever steeper and more pronounced. Finally, weeks after the start of our journey, the great escarpment of Ethiopia itself loomed on the horizon. Around us there began to appear columns of rock and walls of stones like the ruins of great cities, their tops tumbled and reduced to boulders in the bush below. I remembered a letter home from a British soldier who had accompanied a 19th Century expedition into Ethiopia: "They tell me Ethiopia is a table land. If it is they have turned the table upside down and we are scrambling up and down the legs." When we clambered at last over the last blue rim of rock and stood upon the tableland of Ethiopia proper, it was clear that we had entered a new world. With breathtaking suddenness, we were plunged into the midst of Ethiopian civilization.

That civilization derives much of its unique character from the great escarpment. Like a deliberate wall thrown around the land, it defends Ethiopia from natural and man-made invasions. Its very height provides one of the healthiest climates on earth, along with variations of rainfall and sun, a fertile soil and potential abundance. In such a region man

could achieve the degree of complexity and the freedom from hunger and disease that are the basic elements of civilization. Most of Ethiopia lies between 7,000 and 10,000 feet above sea level, with mountains rising above the plateau to even greater heights; one part of the tableland, the cold, wind-swept Simyen Mountains, reaches to 15,000 feet. At the same time Ethiopia has perhaps the world's deepest and most labyrinthine systems of gorges and river cuts outside the Grand Canyon of the United States. The contrasts one encounters in traveling through the country are spectacular. "At one moment," I wrote home during my travels, "I seem to be walking scalded in a land of fire and steam, the next combing thunderclouds out of my hair."

Many explorers have spoken of Ethiopia as a barbarous and cruel country. Yet it seemed far from barbaric to me as I traveled thousands of miles through it in the next few months after my arrival. True, the houses, compounds and villages were of a relatively primitive and tentative kind. In the Gojjam, a remote province that was one of the four kingdoms of ancient Ethiopia, the buildings were of the beehive pattern one encounters all through Africa right down almost to the Cape of Good Hope. The first house I entered stood in a clay compound, and I had to stoop to get through the low entrance. When my eyes grew accustomed to the dim light I saw that the thatched roof of the hut was pillared by

Two shepherds drive their modest flock along a hillside rich with *maskal* daisies, so called because they bloom at the time of the Maskal festival *(page 48)*. Crowning the hill a few miles outside the city of Gondar are the ruins of an 18th Century royal retreat, one of many ruined palaces that stud the Ethiopian plateau.

29

the trunk of a tree. A side of the tree had been hacked out and a bed of clay had been built into it. My mind went back to Homer's description of Odysseus' first night with Penelope after his return to Ithaca, in a room with a great bed also built into a tree. The only real difference was that while Homer called Odysseus' home a palace, we products of the 20th Century would dismiss it as a hut.

I was not surprised that the first offerings of food I tasted in this setting were Homeric too. My host, the chief of a small band of highlanders, made me sit on his only chair—a low, crude oxhide affair—as if it were a throne. His wife then came forward, with great dignity, and bowed to me with the elegance common in a land where the ancient arts of courtesy are rigorously practiced from youth to the grave. Her dark features revealed a beauty I had seen hinted at occasionally in the faces of early Byzantine murals or in the mosaics of the time of Constantine the Great. She seated herself behind her husband and summoned someone in a low, clear voice. Almost immediately a tall young boy, delicately made and in his way as beautiful as his mother, appeared with a large earthenware jar. He handed the jar to my hostess, who removed its stopper and poured some liquid into her husband's hand. He tasted it with the air of a gourmet sampling his favorite wine in some fashionable restaurant, and grimaced at the liquid as if it were not good enough to offer to a guest. The little ritual was an example of good and courtly manners—but it was also a survival from an age when hosts did not hesitate to use such occasions for poisoning their enemies and could only prove their good faith by tasting their offering first.

The young boy (whom I already thought of as a page, because the scene made such an epic impression on me) now presented each of us with an earthenware drinking vessel. Elsewhere in Ethiopia I was to see far more impressive vessels, notably some small silver decanter-shaped bottles with narrow necks that are among the most beautiful traditional objects to be seen in wealthy households. But for all their beauty, these so-called *bereles* did not make the liquid they contained more welcome or more tasteful to me than on this occasion.

It was my first taste of the Ethiopian honey wine called *tej,* a drink that corresponds roughly to the mead of the ancient Britons and the hydromel of the ancient Greeks. The only thing necessary to complete the Homeric sense of the occasion would have been a libation poured on the ground for pagan gods, and if Ethiopia had not been a Christian country I am sure that this is precisely what my host would have done. It was extraordinary how far back in time the smoky flavor of the *tej* took one's taste. Coming as I did from the thirst and the heat of a long march under an equatorial sun, I found it bliss on my tongue. It warmed me through like the finest of wines; but my palate knew, the moment it encountered the ancient flavor, that this drink was far, far older than wine.

After the *tej* came an offering of curds and whey, accompanied by millet bread in wicker baskets. The baskets were beautifully woven and the wickerwork decorated with abstract patterns in rich, earthy colors. Such baskets are among the proudest possessions of an Ethiopian housewife, and even in the poorest of households I was impressed by the skill and sense of beauty that went into their making. The bread that came out of the baskets was round and flat, resembling thick pancakes rather than the foodstuff we call bread; it was, in fact, bread as it might have been made in the beginning. Finally, there was honey in the comb, lifted out of another wicker basket covered with a tightly fitting lid to keep the flies away. The honey was sweet, of course, but the sweetness of that Ethiopian honey had a razor edge, as if the flowers and pollen that had gone into its making had in some alchemical way absorbed and resolved all the tensions and contradictions that had pushed the Ethiopian earth so high above bush and desert plain.

I could not resist holding my slab of honey for a moment against the brilliant light that glowed at the hut's entrance like a sheet of gold silk. The honey was dark in color, yet so translucent that it might have been made of prehistoric amber. I noticed then that my round of millet bread was purplish in color. I folded my honey into the bread as a miser might fold a piece of gold into a packet before tucking it safely away. To this day I can recall the tart, fresh taste of the mead and the curds and whey, the subtlety of the honey that made my welcome in the humble hut so royal, and the purplish bread that made it so real. There are certain English words and phrases that can never be improved upon because they contain ultimate evocations and completely and forever convey everything they are meant to convey. Among them I have firmly placed from that day: "milk, bread and honey."

These three foods—and *tej*—were offered to us everywhere in the Gojjam. Beyond this province, in areas too treeless and flowerless for bees to survive, *tej* is replaced by a kind of beer called *talla,* made out of wheat, barley or Indian corn and flavored by an indigenous hop called *gesho*. I remember lying in huts at night during the rainy season—the compounds outside crowded with sheep and goats, mules and oxen, and the huts themselves filled with hens and chickens and other livestock—listening to the roar of the rain. My bed would be made of dried clay with a built-in clay hump at the end for a pillow. In the lulls between one thunderclap and another I would hear the brew of beer in a vat by my head gurgling like a witch's cauldron, and I would be oddly reassured by the sound. If *tej* is one of the earliest alcoholic drinks of classical man, *talla* is one of the first feeble alcohols of Africa. I believe that on a hot day I would probably prefer *talla* to *tej,* while on a cold night or during a great feast my mouth would water for *tej*.

Throughout the Gojjam, however, it was always *tej,* not *talla,* that would be offered to me by the village chiefs. There was hardly a compound that did not have a grove or a single, wide-spreading tree on which beehives were hung from leather slings. The hives themselves were long cylinders rather like slender wine vats or African drums, and the trees from which they were hung were held in almost mystical esteem. I got into serious trouble with one group of villagers because I was compelled to destroy one of their oldest and biggest honey trees. Our guns and medicines were running out, and I had to find a flat piece of earth to make an airstrip where planes could land with fresh supplies. The only suitable land had an enormous honey tree standing in the middle of it. It

The origins of beekeeping in Ethiopia are lost in the remote past and, though honey is more in demand today than ever before, apiary techniques still stem from centuries-old traditions. Here a farmer in the Gojjam, "the province of honey," charms a swarm into a pair of man-made straw hives by smoking the hives with a fragrant incense. Attracted by the scent, the bees will gather together; when a sufficient number have assembled, the farmer will place the hives in a tree. After a year or more, depending on rain and other factors, he will get his first honey.

had to come down, and when it fell I thought the villagers were going to start their own private war with me.

My experiences of hospitality in the Gojjam were often rounded off with Ethiopian coffee. Ethiopians claim that coffee originated in their country, and that it derives its name from an Ethiopian place called Kaffa, where it grows wild to this day. Like their honey, their coffee has for me an intense, almost passionate flavor, again as if all the contradictions and tensions of their native earth had gone into forming the character of the bean. I remember my excitement in one twilit hut when, long before the coffee itself was passed around, I knew it was being brewed by the scent that began to infuse the dim air. I know of no more evocative smell than that of coffee, unless it is the smell of fresh bread coming warm out of a brick oven at dawn to join all the pure dew scents of nature refreshed and renewed in the night.

We had no sugar in the Gojjam to sweeten our coffee. Instead, we would place a bit of dark honey under the tongue; then, taking a mouthful of coffee, we would hold the liquid under our palates until it and the honey were one, and then swallow the whole. This old way of drinking coffee is one of the best I know. I recommend it to anybody who would fully savor Ethiopian food—or, for that matter, any food.

Another memorable eating experience I had in Ethiopia was made of sterner stuff and took place in a sterner setting. As part of my military mission, I had particularly to make contact with an Ethiopian patriot, a certain *dejasmatch,* an aristocratic title that can be translated as "one, who in war, camps near the door of the Emperor's tent." This *dejasmatch* was a man who had never surrendered to the Italian occupiers of his country. He told me that in nearly 20 years, for reasons of personal safety, he had never made his bed in the same place twice. He was one of the last few living reminders of how the Ethiopians throughout their long history have fought desperately to maintain themselves and their feelings of separate identity in Africa. In the process they developed a scorn for personal safety and a courage in battle greater than that of any of the many peoples I have encountered in war. With this came a passionate recklessness and disregard for human life—as well as an instant suspicion of foreigners and a certain instinctive cunning. What is surprising is that the Ethiopians also retained qualities of great nobility, tenderness, dignity, good manners and religious faith, making them the paradoxical and contradictory individuals who puzzle many outsiders to this day. The same paradoxes seemed to me to be present even in their foods and their cooking and to account partly for their love of extreme flavors, from the sweetness of Ethiopian honey, for example, to the fierceness of *berberé (Recipe Index),* a volcanic red-pepper mixture.

Paradoxes were present also in the personality of this intrepid *dejasmatch.* In the blue of the Gojjam he rode toward me on his horse, looking like some legendary figure; a white cloak, yellow with dust, fell from his shoulders to the stirrups. The first meal I had with him started, as was customary, with *tej* and bread. But the main course was raw meat, passed moist and still half warm from one guest to another. Each man would take the edge of the meat firmly between his teeth and then, slicing up-

Opposite: An Ethiopian-style stuffed whole honeycomb tripe served with a turmeric-flavored sauce makes both a decorative conversation piece and a savory main course at any table.

32

Continued on page 37

In Amharic, the official language of Ethiopia, *berberé* is the name of the fiery pepper seasoning used in a wide range of Ethiopian dishes. The seasoning contains a variety of things besides pepper. Those used to make a version of *berberé* suitable for American kitchens are shown at left:

1 Mixed paprika and red pepper
2 Salt
3 Ginger root
4 Onion
5 Garlic
6 Cloves
7 Cinnamon sticks
8 Nutmeg
9 Cardamom pods and seeds
10 Allspice
11 Black peppercorns
12 Crushed fenugreek
13 Coriander seeds
14 The *berberé* paste

At right, in the first stages of making her own *berberé,* Mrs. Wolde Emanuel picks over a tray of red peppers that have been drying for three days in the sun.

Lishan Sefu's Universal Seasoning

When Berhanu Wolde Emanuel, a civil servant in the Ethiopian city of Gondar, was about to marry Lishan Sefu *(above),* he made inquiries about the quality of her *doro wat,* or chicken stew. The report was good; in fact, it turned out that she was something of a perfectionist. For example, she insisted on preparing her own *berberé* seasoning for her *wat,* and making *berberé (Recipe Index)* is no simple matter. Red peppers must be dried in the sun and pounded in a mortar; ginger and garlic are ground separately, along with a whole procession of spices both familiar and arcane. It is a long, trying process, but *berberé* is the pivot of the Ethiopian cuisine, the universal seasoning for everything from a rich man's delicacy to a poor man's chunk of bread—not to speak of the Wolde Emanuels' *doro wat.*

What rice is to a Japanese, or tortillas to a Mexican, *injera* is to an Ethiopian. Made of teff, a flour milled from a specially high grade of millet, *injera* cooks like a giant pancake on a covered ceramic griddle. The cook pours the batter in a spiral fashion, starting at the outside *(left)*. Then she covers the griddle with a lid, sealing the edges with a damp rag. In a matter of minutes the *injera* is done.

Inside her *tukul,* a round straw-thatched hut, Zentalem Desta cooks a supply of *injera* over a eucalyptus-wood fire. Most families make enough to last them three days at a time, and her husband, parents and small child can consume about 25 pieces of *injera* in that period.

ward with a sharp knife, would cut off a mouthful, narrowly missing the tip of his nose in the process. The few women who were there sat immediately behind the men, and young boys stood wrapped in yellow and white shawls, tall and candlelike in the background.

At this meal I had my first encounter with *berberé*. The mixture includes the most potent of all Ethiopian peppers, and every district and household has its own way of preparing it. On this occasion my *berberé* was a paste consisting of powerful pepper, dried and finely powdered, and mixed with many spices and herbs, and blended with a little water. One would dip one's red meat into the red paste before eating it; and if one must eat meat raw, it is surely best done in this way, for the sauce gives the impression of being hot enough to cook the meat right on the tongue. *Berberé* soon became one of my favorite tastes, and I welcomed its presence in certain Ethiopian beef and chicken stews, in which it appears as an essential ingredient.

Apart from helping me to get through my first banquet of raw meat, *berberé* gave me my first inkling of the essential role played by spices in the more complex forms of Ethiopian cooking I was to encounter later. In this respect the Ethiopian concept of cooking seemed to me related to that of India and of Indonesia, particularly Java; I suspect that there may have been far more contact between Ethiopia and the Far East than the history books indicate. Certainly, it was remarkable how easy Ethiopian food was on the tongue for someone who, like myself, had already learned to like Indian and Javanese cooking.

I particularly found this to be true in the case of the national dish of Ethiopia, a stew called *wat*, in which all manner of spices play an essential part. *Wat* comes in various forms; the most delicate and appealing, to me, is chicken *wat*, or *doro wat (Recipe Index)*. But there are meat *wats* as well, and on the shores of Lake Tana, the source of the Blue Nile, I have eaten a fish *wat*. And as both chicken and meat are forbidden on the numerous fast days imposed upon all Ethiopians, there are also vegetable *wats* based upon lentils, beans or chick-peas. The finest of all vegetable *wats*, a complex matter called *metin shuro*, is made from powdered dried peas, lentils, chick-peas, beans, onions and fresh ginger.

In a well-to-do and well-run household *wat* is a very complicated affair. Consider, for example, a chicken *wat* that I once ate in the northern Ethiopian city of Gondar. It was made with powdered ginger, ground black pepper, powdered cardamom, minced onion, lemon juice and hard-boiled eggs. Even that was not the end of the story, for the real catalyst of the mixture was a tablespoon of *berberé* containing dried fenugreek, coriander, cumin, fennel seed, red and black pepper, onions, garlic, sacred basil, cardamom and ginger. In one form or another *berberé* is kept handy in most Ethiopian kitchens, though not always in so heady a mixture as this. Still, any list of the spices commonly used by Ethiopian cooks would have to include not only those I have enumerated but also bishop's weed, rue, mint, cloves, cinnamon, turmeric and nutmeg. Even the butter used in cooking a favorite *wat* has such spices worked into it as ginger, garlic, cinnamon, turmeric, bishop's weed, sacred basil and crushed cardamom seeds, and a good Ethiopian housewife usually has an earthenware container of *niter kebbeh,* or spiced butter oil *(Recipe Index),* standing ready for use in some recess of her kitchen.

Obviously, the *wat* is not suited to every palate; one visitor to Ethiopia spoke of a variety "so fierce that it practically makes the ears bleed." A gentler alternative stew, which never contains *berberé,* is the *alecha. Alechas* in their various forms are favored by many European and American visitors in Ethiopia precisely because they are not so incendiary as *wats,* and they are delicious in their own right. The most popular base for an *alecha* is chicken, possibly because in his secret warrior's heart the Ethiopian male really prefers all other meats raw—as if in transforming them by cooking he runs the risk of depriving them of some element of masculinity. All the same, I have eaten excellent well-done beef *alechas* all over the country, and have especially enjoyed a tripe *alecha.*

Indispensable to the enjoyment of a *wat* or an *alecha* is bread. Normally Ethiopians use neither forks nor spoons; instead, they dip bread, always held in the right hand, into their spicy dishes to soak up the liquids, or wrap a solid ingredient in bread and lift it to their mouths. This habit, too, links them to the Indians. But bread by itself plays a far greater role in Ethiopian than in Indian cooking, and in this respect Ethiopian custom is nearer European or American.

There are many kinds of Ethiopian bread; in a single area one may find three or four different varieties simultaneously. The country's climate and fertile soil make it possible for farmers to grow excellent wheat, barley and millet. (Oats are also grown, but the grain has never been popular among Ethiopian farmers, and in some areas is even destroyed as a weed.) So the traveler may encounter wheat, barley and various millet breads, occasionally flat as pancakes and unleavened—like the kind I encountered in my Homeric meal in the Gojjam—but usually shaped into a rough kind of loaf. The most refined of all breads is a thin, round bread called *injera (Recipe Index),* made of finely ground teff, the finest, subtlest and most delicate member of the millet family. To make *injera,* teff flour is combined with water in a batter, which is allowed to ferment for three to four days, and is then poured on a flat clay griddle. The Ethiopian housewife covers her *injera* with a raised lid the moment it spreads out into the normal-sized round. A round of *injera* takes barely five minutes to cook over a hot wood fire.

Eating *injera* as I first did, warm from the fire, I took to it at once. The very appearance of the bread was enormously attractive. During the brief period of baking on the griddle, bubbles of fermentation break through the pale-gold batter as on a pancake, leaving the surface as pitted as a full moon. *Injera* generally has a faintly sour, provocative, yet soothing flavor —making it the perfect complement to the fiery spices that go into the making of a *wat*—while its pitted surface is the ideal vehicle for carrying the food, sauce and all, from the dish to one's mouth. Indeed one secret of truly enjoying both *injera* and *wat* lies in abandoning knife and fork. Eating thus in an Ethiopian household at night, with a cold rain falling heavily outside and the thunder continuous and loud, a meal of *tej, injera* and *wat,* finished off with coffee and honey, seemed to me the perfect answer to the storm.

Opposite: The spicy chicken stew called *doro wat,* made of chicken and hard-cooked eggs simmered with *berberé* and other spices, is one of Ethiopia's national dishes. Here it is accompanied by side dishes of *yegomen kitfo,* or collard greens and buttermilk curds, and rice—but an Ethiopian diner probably would forgo the rice for *injera (page 36)* from the covered basket at top.

The distinctions between breakfast, lunch and dinner are neither as clearly defined nor as rigid in Ethiopia as they are in Western countries. An Ethiopian countryman rarely eats more than two cooked meals a day and often only one, contenting himself between hot meals by munching bread and strips of cured meat. Dried meat is, in fact, a foodstuff one encounters throughout Africa. The Ethiopian sets about drying his meat very much in a way that I have seen it done in the jungles of Java and Sumatra. He cuts the meat into long strips, rubs it well with salt and (if he has any) with black pepper, but always and above all with a little *berberé*. He then hangs the meat to dry in a clean, cool place for about a fortnight. It will keep for months, is a light, nourishing and easy ration to carry about, and can always be taken out of store when other forms of nourishment fail.

An Ethiopian has other ways of satisfying his hunger when he finds it impossible to prepare a complete cooked meal. There is, for instance, roasted-barley flour, dampened, salted, rolled between the fingers into large round pellets and swallowed with *talla*. There is barley, wheat or chick-peas roasted whole when nothing else is available. And there is almost always, as everywhere else in Africa, curds and whey, made more palatable in Ethiopia by a subtle wood-smoke flavor that seems to penetrate deep into their substance. My memories of my first meals in Ethiopia are so perfumed with this smell of aromatic wood smoke, always present in most Ethiopian households, that I find the food cooked in Western kitchens not half as good.

For lighter between-meals eating, there is a snack called *dabo kolo,* which is a sort of cross between scone and biscuit. It begins with wheat flour made into a thick dough by stirring water into it drop by drop. When the dough is smooth, *berberé* is sometimes stirred into it. About half a pint of cooking oil is added; then the dough is thoroughly kneaded and rolled into strips about a quarter of an inch thick. Finally it is cut into small rounds and roasted until brown. In Ethiopian cities, *dabo kolo* is now often served at cocktail parties, but it tastes best to me on its own, when one is hungry and deprived of other foods.

Another flavorsome snack called *chiko,* good for breakfast, tea or cocktails, contains roasted barley and the spiced butter oil of Ethiopia. Pounded barley is dried in the sun, pounded again and winnowed to remove the husks. It is then roasted on an *injera* griddle and once again pounded and winnowed to remove the rest of the husks. The residue, finely ground, is mixed with the spiced butter oil to form a thick paste that can be stored in a cool place indefinitely.

Such snacks are especially important because of the variability of Ethiopian meals. In the average household, the main meal is eaten sometime toward evening or, on special occasions, in the middle of the day. But actually there is no fixed routine. I have had substantial *wats* and *alechas* for breakfast, though more conventional breakfast foods do exist—bread; eggs, usually eaten hard-boiled or sucked raw; curds and whey; and several kinds of porridge.

Another difficulty in defining the pattern of Ethiopian eating is the elaborate system of fasts that the Ethiopian form of Christianity imposes

Continued on page 46

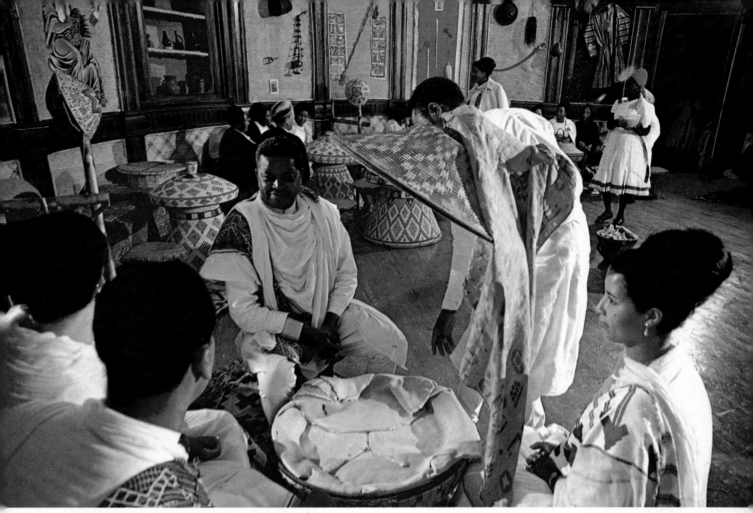

A waiter at the Addis Ababa Restaurant whips the
wicker cover off a basket table spread with rounds of
injera bread. The *wat,* or stew, will be poured over
the *injera,* and the diners will eat it with their fingers,
tearing off pieces of bread as they go along.

In Addis Ababa, a Place Where One Can Eat as the Ethiopians Eat

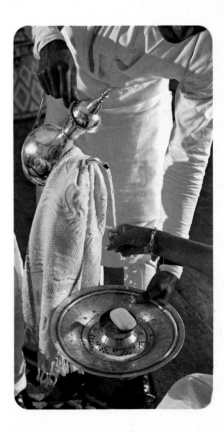

In the center of Ethiopia's capital city, not far from Haile Selassie Square, is
the Addis Ababa Restaurant. In design, it is an elegant adaptation of the
ubiquitous Ethiopian thatched hut called a *tukul,* and in this exotic ambiance
tourists can try Ethiopian cooking at its best. A meal at the Addis Ababa
offers not only a cuisine but a whole culinary tradition. Eating in Ethiopia is a
highly ritualistic experience, from the washing of hands *(right)* that precedes
a formal dinner to the service of coffee in ornate cups at its close. The Addis
Ababa makes the most of all this. Even the equipment is distinctive—layers
of *injera* bread, draped over the circular basket table, serve as both tablecloth
and plate and are consumed along with the food ladled over them.

Opposite and at top left, a well-to-do couple of the Amhara tribe enjoys beef *wat* at the Addis Ababa. A nice point of Ethiopian etiquette involves choosing a particularly attractive morsel, wrapping it in a bit of *injera* bread and popping it into your companion's mouth. Along with their *wat* the couple drinks *tej,* a powerful honey wine, or mead, from narrow-necked carafes called *bereles*. Even the use of a *berele* calls for a special knack; if the vessel is not tilted at exactly the right angle the *tej* will not flow out of it. As in the West, the traditional conclusion of a dinner is coffee. At its peak of refinement, Ethiopian coffee is served unsweetened, after being spiced, boiled and reboiled into a concentrated richness that smells faintly of cloves. At left below a serving woman fills cups with coffee from the typical black *jebena* (jug).

Overleaf: In honor of provincial leaders of the Ethiopian Women's Welfare Association, who were dining at the Addis Ababa, the management staged a special program of dances and songs from different regions of the country. To start the program a soloist sang a "desperate lament," accompanying himself on a one-stringed fiddle; then the group of dancers shown in the pictures performed a fast-moving folk number from the northern province of Tigre.

upon the land. I have never encountered a country where fasting is so complicated, frequent and exacting. The Ethiopian is expected to fast as many as 200 days of the year; the clergy are supposed to fast no fewer than 250 days. For the farmer, a fast day means that he has nothing at all to eat or drink until midday, though he may have been hard at work in his fields since sunrise. Even after midday, milk, meat, eggs, animal fat and fowl are forbidden on a fast day, so that he has to get along on such foods as cereals, peas, beans and lentils.

The rigors of fasting have had at least one advantage, however: they compelled Ethiopians to invent vegetable substitutes for meat as no other culture in Africa has done. I have already mentioned their fine vegetable *wats,* and in the region of Eritrea on the Red Sea, where Ethiopian contacts with the outside world have been strong, farmers have learned to grow such "foreign" vegetables as tomatoes and to put these in stews. And I have eaten beans and peas, both fresh and dried, cooked not only in the universal manner but in purées—mixtures with vegetable oil and *wat*-like sauces thoroughly beaten into them until they had the airy consistency of a fine French soufflé. Eaten with bread and *talla,* these purées make a meal that leaves no room for hunger.

Another excellent fasting dish is *yeshimbra assa (Recipe Index),* or "chick-pea-flour fish," of which there are several versions. One that I enjoy—a specialty of the Tigre region—contains chopped red onions, *berberé,* oil, *wat* spices, chick-pea flour and salt to taste. The onions are browned, then a little water is added along with the *berberé* and the oil. More water goes into the mixture, then the spices; the pot is covered and the mixture is allowed to boil. Meanwhile, the cook prepares a thick mixture of pea flour and a little water, from which she molds small cakes in the shape of fish, then fries them in oil. These "pea-flour fish" are dropped into the mixture in the pot and cooked gently until done.

Modern communications and the intermingling of cultures have had their effect upon the eating habits of Ethiopia. Nevertheless, traditional ways of cooking still have so firm a hold on the country that I cannot see them ever vanishing altogether. Indeed, I am amazed every time I return to Ethiopia by the fact that I can eat exactly as I first ate there some 30 years ago. In many respects, the scene seems hardly to have changed at all. The farmer still breaks his rich soil with a wooden plow hitched to sturdy humpbacked oxen, their heads bowed under the yoke. At harvest time the same oxen tread out the wheat on clay threshing floors. At the end of the day tall highlanders still toss the trampled wheat with wooden shovels, so that the fitful puffs of evening air will blow away the pale yellow chaff, while their women crowd around with wicker sieves for the final winnowing of the grain. Down in the valleys and in the fertile northeast, there are modern irrigation systems to support the cotton, citrus and sugar crops, but up on the vast tableland, at the evening meal in the beehive huts, the sweetening still comes from honey. The food and the flavors that make food a delight in Ethiopia come out of one of the deepest wells of the past, worth preserving as long as there are flowers to cull and bees for making honey.

All this and more was in my mind recently when I returned to Addis

Ababa on the eve of the Ethiopian Good Friday. Cavalcades of people on horses and mules, their servants and retainers trotting at their sides, were converging on the capital to take part in the greatest of all Easter observances. Those who passed near me, men and women, bowed in greeting from their saddles with the greatest of grace and elegance, the women invariably accompanying the bow with a smile. Both the purpose and the manner of their journey charged the air with a Chaucerian quality, as if I were witnessing an Ethiopian "Canterbury Tale" in the making.

Even more remarkable than the mounted processions were the herds of cattle and sheep being driven to the capital by tall herdsmen wrapped in shawls of white. Wherever I looked, these flocks and herds were moving toward the city. For days, Addis Ababa's newspapers had prominently displayed instructions and details of the hours and the routes laid down by the authorities for controlling the movements of these animals toward the marketplaces. The concourse of livestock I saw was only a small part of a much greater number required to assuage the hunger that all Ethiopia experiences at the end of the eight-week-long Lent, the most rigorous of the national fasts. These thousands of animals, following their herdsmen in perfect trust toward the slaughter, somehow symbolized the role that fasting continues to play in the life of Ethiopia.

I have another recent memory that in quite another way symbolizes all that Ethiopia is. Not long ago I was one of some thousand guests summoned to the imperial palace for a banquet, part of the ceremonies celebrating the 25th anniversary of Emperor Haile Selassie's return from exile. This dinner was preceded by a staggering display of fireworks in the imperial gardens. Deep in the Ethiopian spirit, as in the spirit of men as far apart as the Chinese and the Spanish, there is a belief that loud noise and fire will turn evil away. This particular display was conducted with such violence that it shattered windows in the palace.

As for the dinner itself, I do not think there is any surviving royal household or governmental organization, however powerful, that could have organized a banquet on such a scale with greater elegance and dignity and with such vivid pageantry. Casting about in my mind for adequate parallels, I thought of Versailles under King Louis XIV, Le Roi Soleil. At this Ethiopian banquet, for instance, there was a footman for every two guests at the table. Each footman stood behind his allotted chairs in a tailcoat of bright-green velvet, faced with gold brocade, trimmed with gold braid at the hems, and glittering with gold buttons. Completing their costume were a white satin waistcoat and knee breeches, and white silk stockings above black patent-leather pumps bearing silver buckles. When the food appeared the footmen served it with hands covered by white gloves. Between courses, groups of young men and women, each in the traditional dress of his or her own province, danced the dances and sang the songs of Ethiopia.

The menu was not long, but it was superbly chosen. Perhaps by design, the imperial kitchen had contrasted the best of French food with the best of Ethiopian. For every European course there was an Ethiopian course to match it. For every European dish, there was a vintage French wine to accompany it and the European wine list ended appropriately, in

Continued on page 52

47

Processions and Bonfires to Honor the True Cross and a Byzantine Queen

The most brilliant festival in Ethiopia is an echo from the deep past of Christian legend. Maskal commemorates the miraculous discovery of the actual Cross on which Christ was crucified, a deed supposedly performed in the Fourth Century by the devout Queen Helena, mother of the Roman Emperor Constantine. According to the Ethiopian version of the story, she journeyed from Rome to Jerusalem in search of the relic. Upon her arrival she burned incense and prayed for guidance, and the column of smoke rising from the incense mysteriously bent over and pointed to the spot where the Cross was buried. Overjoyed, Helena set a huge bonfire as a sign of thanksgiving, a fire so big that Emperor Constantine, way back in Byzantium, was able to see its glow. Today, 16 centuries later, the Maskal festival celebrates all of these events with processions, feasting and—appropriately—bonfires.

48

Maskal (the word means cross in Amharic) begins late on the afternoon of September 26 with great processions of priests and lay dignitaries in every Ethiopian city and town. Carrying crosses and incense, they march through the streets until they arrive at a huge *demera,* or bonfire, standing ready to be lit. All day long men and boys have been adding sticks and poles to the pile. After circling it three times, the clerics will bless it. At left, beneath ceremonial umbrellas, a procession bound for the *demera* moves in stately array through the capital of Addis Ababa. The young priests below are celebrating Maskal in the ancient city of Gondar.

Chief among the Maskal celebrants is the Lion of Judah, Emperor Haile Selassie himself. At left, as dusk falls over Addis Ababa, he lights a huge straw torch called a *chibo* as he prepares to ignite the towering *demera* in the background. When the bonfire is burning, he will take his place on a raised throne to watch a parade of torchbearers *(above)*, followed by priests, military troops, brass bands and floats bearing electrically lit crosses.

the French manner, with the best of dry champagnes. I myself did not have a single European dish or a sip of European wine during the entire long evening. Instead I drank the ancient Ethiopian mead, the *tej* I had first tasted at the start of my wartime journey so long ago. In the cut-glass goblet before me it had the sparkle of a golden Rhine hock, but I would not have exchanged it for any wine in Europe. Instead of French bread I had *injera* at its subtle best. Instead of hors d'oeuvre of caviar and pâté I had a superb little crisp Ethiopian pastry filled with succulent Ethiopian mixed seafood, fresh from the Red Sea. Those guests who chose the European menu went on to roast turkey, while I enjoyed a great chicken *wat* made with barley, eggs and a whole host of tingling spices. The European-style dessert was a cake; mine was a dish of superb native strawberries. The comparison between French and Ethiopian cooking could have been an awkward one. Yet so far as I was concerned, the national dishes, climaxed with coffee from the Emperor's native province of Harar, more than held their own. If I had harbored any fears that modernization would deprive Ethiopia of what is good in Ethiopian cooking, they vanished that night at the banquet in the imperial palace.

Following a custom that has existed since Ethiopian history began, the Emperor remained seated at the head of the main table while all his guests stood and departed. Outside the palace, above the chatter of farewells and the noise of automobiles moving off, I heard the howling of hyenas, insatiable as they massed in the hills to begin their scavenging in the city right up to the gates of the palace itself. For a moment I felt that I was in a camp in the interior rather than in the capital. But when I looked back into the hall there was the Emperor still in his chair, alone, calm in a world and time of his own, as if posed on the pedestal of a monument to himself. Cities, even the greatest of them, are perhaps no more than camps that must be struck when they have served their brittle purpose, but those who pitch these camps always leave behind some essential part of themselves. And the Emperor seemed to be affirming that some part of the old, old Ethiopia, which has endured against all the odds of Africa and fate, would remain even when he got up to leave the great hall empty, its lights extinguished.

Doro Wat *(Ethiopia)*
CHICKEN STEWED IN RED-PEPPER SAUCE

To serve 4

Pat the chicken dry with paper towels and rub the pieces with lemon juice and salt. Let the chicken rest at room temperature for 30 minutes.

In an ungreased heavy 3- to 4-quart enameled casserole, cook the onions over moderate heat for 5 or 6 minutes, or until they are soft and dry. Shake the pan and stir the onions constantly to prevent them from burning; if necessary, reduce the heat or lift the pan occasionally from the stove to let it cool for a few moments before returning it to the heat.

Stir in the *niter kebbeh* and, when it begins to splutter, add the garlic, ginger, fenugreek, cardamom and nutmeg, stirring well after each addition. Add the *berberé* and paprika, and stir over low heat for 2 to 3 minutes. Then pour in the wine and water and, still stirring, bring to a boil over high heat. Cook briskly, uncovered, for about 5 minutes, or until the liquid in the pan has reduced to the consistency of heavy cream.

Pat the chicken dry and drop it into the simmering sauce, turning the pieces about with a spoon until they are coated on all sides. Reduce the heat to the lowest point, cover tightly and simmer for 15 minutes.

With the tines of a fork, pierce ¼-inch-deep holes over the entire surface of each egg. Then add the eggs and turn them gently about in the sauce. Cover and cook for 15 minutes more, or until the chicken is tender and the dark meat shows no resistance when pierced with the point of a small knife. Sprinkle the stew with pepper and taste for seasoning.

To serve, transfer the entire contents of the casserole to a deep heated platter or bowl. *Doro wat* is traditionally accompanied by either *injera* or spice bread *(Recipe Index)*, but may also be eaten with Arab-style flat bread or hot boiled rice. *Yegomen kitfo (Recipe Index)* or plain yoghurt or both may be presented with the *wat* from separate bowls.

A 2½- to 3-pound chicken, cut into 8 serving pieces
2 tablespoons strained fresh lemon juice
2 teaspoons salt
2 cups finely chopped onions
¼ cup *niter kebbeh (below)*
1 tablespoon finely chopped garlic
1 teaspoon finely chopped, scraped fresh ginger root
¼ teaspoon fenugreek seeds, pulverized with a mortar and pestle or in a small bowl with the back of a spoon
¼ teaspoon ground cardamom
⅛ teaspoon ground nutmeg, preferably freshly grated
¼ cup *berberé (page 56)*
2 tablespoons paprika
¼ cup dry white or red wine
¾ cup water
4 hard-cooked eggs
Freshly ground black pepper

Niter Kebbeh *(Ethiopia)*
SPICED BUTTER OIL

To make about 2 cups

In a heavy 4- to 5-quart saucepan, heat the butter over moderate heat, turning it about with a spoon to melt it slowly and completely without letting it brown. Then increase the heat and bring the butter to a boil. When the surface is completely covered with white foam, stir in the onion, garlic, ginger, turmeric, cardamom, cinnamon, clove and nutmeg. Reduce the heat to the lowest possible point and simmer uncovered and undisturbed for 45 minutes, or until the milk solids on the bottom of the pan are a golden brown and the butter on top is transparent.

Slowly pour the clear liquid *niter kebbeh* into a bowl, straining it through a fine sieve lined with a linen towel or four layers of dampened cheesecloth. Discard the seasonings. If there are any solids left in the *kebbeh,* strain it again to prevent it from becoming rancid later.

Pour the *kebbeh* into a jar, cover tightly, and store in the refrigerator or at room temperature until ready to use. *Kebbeh* will solidify when chilled. It can safely be kept, even at room temperature, for 2 or 3 months.

2 pounds unsalted butter, cut into small pieces
1 small onion, peeled and coarsely chopped
3 tablespoons finely chopped garlic
4 teaspoons finely chopped fresh ginger root
1½ teaspoons turmeric
1 cardamom pod, slightly crushed with the flat of a knife, or a pinch of cardamom seeds
1 piece of stick cinnamon, 1 inch long
1 whole clove
⅛ teaspoon ground nutmeg, preferably freshly grated

Yataklete Kilkil (Ethiopia)
FRESH VEGETABLES WITH GARLIC AND GINGER

To serve 6

One at a time, peel the potatoes and trim them into oval shapes, dropping them, as you proceed, into a bowl of cold water to prevent discoloration. Then with a small, sharp knife, cut out narrow V-shaped wedges ¼ inch deep at ½-inch intervals all around the length of the potatoes and return them to the water as each one is done.

When you are ready to cook the vegetables, first drop the potatoes with a slotted spoon into enough lightly salted boiling water to cover them completely. Add the carrots and string beans and let the vegetables boil briskly, uncovered, for 5 minutes. Then drain them in a large colander and run cold water over them to stop their cooking. Set them aside in the colander to drain completely.

In a heavy 4- to 5-quart casserole, heat the oil over moderate heat until a light haze forms above it. Add the onions, green pepper and chilies and, stirring frequently, cook for about 5 minutes, until the vegetables are soft but not brown. Watch carefully for any sign of burning and regulate the heat accordingly. Add the garlic, ginger, salt and pepper, and stir for a minute or so.

Add the reserved potatoes, carrots and string beans, and the scallions to the casserole, and turn them about with a spoon until the vegetables are coated with the oil mixture. Reduce the heat to low, cover partially, and cook for about 10 minutes, or until the vegetables are tender but still somewhat crisp to the bite.

To serve, transfer the vegetables to a heated bowl with a slotted spoon. In Ethiopia *yataklete kilkil* is traditionally served during Lent as a main course but it may be served as an accompaniment to any main dish.

6 small boiling potatoes, each about 3 inches long

3 large carrots, scraped, cut lengthwise into quarters and then crosswise into 2-inch lengths

½ pound fresh green string beans, trimmed, washed and cut crosswise into 2-inch lengths

¼ cup vegetable oil

2 medium-sized onions, peeled, cut lengthwise in quarters, then separated into layers and cut into ½-inch pieces

1 large green pepper, seeded, deribbed and cut into strips about 2 inches long and ½ inch wide

2 whole fresh hot chilies, each about 4 inches long, washed and stemmed (*caution: see page 76*)

1 tablespoon finely chopped garlic

2 teaspoons finely chopped fresh ginger root

1 teaspoon salt

½ teaspoon white pepper

6 large scallions, including the green tops, trimmed, cut lengthwise in half and then crosswise into 2-inch lengths

Yemiser Selatta (Ethiopia)
LENTIL SALAD WITH SHALLOTS AND CHILIES

Place the lentils in a sieve and wash them under cold running water. Then drop them into enough lightly salted boiling water to cover them by 2 to 3 inches. Reduce the heat to low, cover the pan partially, and simmer for 25 to 30 minutes, or until the lentils are tender but still somewhat firm to the bite. Drain the lentils in a sieve or colander and rinse them under cold running water to cool them quickly. Then drain them thoroughly and set them aside.

Combine the vinegar, oil, salt and a few grindings of pepper in a deep bowl and beat them together with a whisk. Drop in the lentils, shallots and chilies, and turn them about with a fork until they are well mixed. Taste for seasoning and let the salad marinate at room temperature for at least 30 minutes, stirring gently from time to time.

To serve, mound the lentil salad attractively on a small platter or in a shallow bowl.

Yemiser selatta is traditionally served during Lent either alone or with *injera* bread or to accompany such dishes as chick-pea flour "fish" (*Recipe Index*) and fresh vegetables with garlic and ginger (*above*).

To serve 4 to 6

1¼ cups (about ½ pound) dried lentils

3 tablespoons red wine vinegar

2 tablespoons vegetable oil

1 teaspoon salt

Freshly ground black pepper

8 large shallot cloves, peeled and cut lengthwise into halves

2 fresh hot chilies, each about 3 inches long, stemmed, seeded, and cut into strips about 1 inch long and ⅛ inch wide (*caution: see page 76*)

An array of Ethiopian Lenten dishes includes *yemiser selatta,* a salad of lentils seasoned with green chilies and shallots; chick-pea flour "fish" (which is simmered in the red-pepper sauce); and sautéed vegetables.

To serve 12 as a first course or 6 as
a main dish

¼ cup *niter kebbeh (page 53)*
½ cup very finely chopped onions
3 tablespoons very finely chopped
  green peppers
2 tablespoons very finely chopped
  fresh hot chilies *(caution: see
  page 76)*
1 teaspoon very finely chopped,
  scraped fresh ginger root
½ teaspoon very finely chopped
  garlic
½ teaspoon cardamom seeds,
  pulverized with a mortar and
  pestle or the back of a
  spoon, then rubbed through a sieve
1 tablespoon strained fresh lemon
  juice
2 teaspoons *berberé (below)*
2 teaspoons salt
2 pounds beef fillet or top round,
  trimmed of fat and cut into ⅛-
  inch dice or coarsely ground
12 medium-sized Italian frying
  peppers (optional)

To make about 2 cups

1 teaspoon ground ginger
½ teaspoon ground cardamom
½ teaspoon ground coriander
½ teaspoon fenugreek seeds
¼ teaspoon ground nutmeg,
  preferably freshly grated
⅛ teaspoon ground cloves
⅛ teaspoon ground cinnamon
⅛ teaspoon ground allspice
2 tablespoons finely chopped onions
1 tablespoon finely chopped garlic
2 tablespoons salt
3 tablespoons dry red wine
2 cups paprika
2 tablespoons ground hot red
  pepper
½ teaspoon freshly ground black
  pepper
1½ cups water
1 to 2 tablespoons vegetable oil

Kitfo *(Ethiopia)*
RAW CHOPPED BEEF WITH SPICES

In a heavy 8- to 10-inch skillet, melt the *niter kebbeh* over low heat. As
soon as the *kebbeh* is warm, add the onions, chopped green peppers, chilies, ginger, garlic and cardamom. Stir for 1 to 2 minutes, until the
seasonings are heated through and the *kebbeh* begins to splutter.

With a rubber spatula, scrape the *kebbeh* mixture into a deep bowl.
Then set it aside at room temperature for 15 minutes or so to cool. Stir in
the lemon juice, *berberé* and salt. Add the beef and toss the ingredients
together thoroughly. Taste for seasoning.

Mound the *kitfo* on a platter and serve it at once, accompanied, if you
like, by *injera* or spice bread *(Recipe Index)* or by Arab-style flat bread.

You may also serve the *kitfo* stuffed into raw Italian frying peppers.
Without removing the stem, slit each pepper lengthwise from about ½
inch of the top to within about 1 inch of the narrow bottom end. Make a
crosswise slit 1 inch wide at the top of the first cut and gently scoop out
the seeds. Carefully cut out as much of the white membranes or ribs as
you can without piercing the skin of the pepper. Wash the peppers inside
and out under cold running water and pat them completely dry with
paper towels. Then stuff the peppers with the *kitfo,* dividing the meat
evenly among them, and serve immediately.

Berberé *(Ethiopia)*
RED-PEPPER AND SPICE PASTE

In a heavy 2- to 3-quart saucepan (preferably one with an enameled or
nonstick cooking surface), toast the ginger, cardamom, coriander, fenugreek, nutmeg, cloves, cinnamon and allspice over low heat for a minute
or so, stirring them constantly until they are heated through. Then remove the pan from the heat and let the spices cool for 5 to 10 minutes.

Combine the toasted spices, onions, garlic, 1 tablespoon of the salt and
the wine in the jar of an electric blender and blend at high speed until
the mixture is a smooth paste. (To make the paste with a mortar and pestle or in a bowl with the back of a spoon, pound the toasted spices, onions, garlic and 1 tablespoon of the salt together until pulverized. Add
the wine and continue pounding until the mixture is a moist paste.)

Combine the paprika, red pepper, black pepper and the remaining tablespoon of salt in the saucepan and toast them over low heat for a minute or so, until they are heated through, shaking the pan and stirring the
spices constantly. Stir in the water, ¼ cup at a time, then add the spice-
and-wine mixture. Stirring vigorously, cook over the lowest possible heat
for 10 to 15 minutes.

With a rubber spatula, transfer the *berberé* to a jar or crock, and pack
it in tightly. Let the paste cool to room temperature, then dribble enough
oil over the top to make a film at least ¼ inch thick. Cover with foil or
plastic wrap and refrigerate until ready to use. If you replenish the film
of oil on top each time you use the *berberé,* it can safely be kept in the refrigerator for 5 or 6 months.

An Ethiopian favorite, raw beef with a hot *berberé* dip, is shown at top
and far right; in a milder alternative, chopped meat is seasoned with
onions, lemon juice and spices to make a *kitfo* stuffing for green peppers.

III

New Cuisines for New Nations

At Bida in northern Nigeria, market-bound Nupe women bear enameled washbasins full of yams and other salable produce, topped by woven straw covers to discourage flies.

The Great Rift Valley of Africa is not only a dramatic line of demarcation slashed by nature in the earth, but also a dividing line in the mind of African man. East of the Rift Valley, much of the land tends to be high and open—and the people who inhabit it seem to me to resemble it in spirit, being straightforward and uncomplicated. West of the Rift Valley lies a great deal of lowland and rain forest: *Afrique Noire,* the land of the blacks. I find this a somewhat more sophisticated land, with a more acute sense of history than that of the East. The western region has an original tradition of art, including the impressive wood carvings and masks of Nigeria and Ghana and the great bronzes of Benin, as serenely dynamic as any sculpture of ancient Greece.

This Africa of the West has few hard-and-fast political, social or natural frontiers to contain it. In the 19th Century imperialist scramble for the continent, boundaries were ignorantly drawn, unnaturally dividing members of the same tribes and clans against one another. These arbitrary lines are already being redrawn as new nations divide up the land all over again; I believe that in another generation the map of western Africa will surely differ as much from the map of today as a contemporary map of Europe differs from its pre-1914 version.

Some sense of the sheer size of the region can be gained when one remembers that the old French West Africa alone comprised almost two million square miles, and the Belgian Congo another million. Over this vast area the population, though comparatively large for Africa, has always been thinly spread. In all of West Africa there are no more than 60 million people. Yet their variety is enormous: in Cameroon alone there are more than 80 different tribes, and in the area once controlled by the French more than 200 different languages are spoken.

In the last analysis one can only map out *Afrique Noire* in terms of one's own experience. For me, Africa west of the Rift Valley begins in the Congo basin, goes on into Cameroon and Nigeria and follows what used to be known as the Slave Coast into the countries that border the Gulf of Guinea: Dahomey, Togo, Ghana, Ivory Coast, Liberia, Sierra Leone, Guinea, Portuguese Guinea and finally sprawling Senegal, which surrounds the enclave of once-British Gambia. I exclude much of the northern parts of the states from Nigeria to Senegal; I also exclude Mauritania, Mali and Upper Volta, regretfully turning my back upon cities of legend and myth like Timbuktu and upon such modern cities as Kano in Nigeria, where pilgrims making their journey to Mecca arrive by plodding camel and transfer to jet airplane.

The West of Africa has been in touch with Europeans far longer than the East; the Portuguese worked their way down the coast to Cape Verde in 1445 and by the middle of the 16th Century had sailed up the great rivers of the interior. But exploration was not the main objective of later Europeans. Wherever there was a harbor or a river inlet, the Portuguese, French, Dutch and English trafficked in slaves. Most of the Negro population of the West Indies, of South America, and of the United States are descended from people who came originally from West Africa. Long after slavery was abolished in Africa, a savage policy of exploitation kept thwarting Negro progress. Always, the European tendency was to run the colonies not for their own sakes but for what could be extracted from them. In matters of food, Europe taught Negro Africa little that was good, and learned precious little from it.

In the realm of food, in fact, Europe flatly rejected all that it *could* have learned from West Africa. I have my own vivid recollections of how this rejection worked. In The Congo, for example, 10 days before the country was granted its independence in 1960 I was staying in the capital of Leopoldville (now Kinshasa) at a Belgian hotel named after the Flemish painter Hans Memling (who, whatever his great merits, could hardly claim any association with Africa). Like every Belgian house or restaurant I knew, the hotel was air-conditioned; the very air of Africa was rejected. And I was offered not the food or the drink of Africa, but the wines and dishes served every day back in Brussels. An efficient air service supplied the Belgians with produce that was picked in Belgium in the afternoon and delivered to The Congo the following morning. It was easier to get snails *à la bourguignonne* than an honest African yam or sweet potato; easier to get a Nuits St.-Georges than a glass of palm wine or African beer—the beer that had been such a joy at the end of my long dusty journey in Ethiopia.

On another occasion, only a few months ago, I stopped at the western extremity of the continent, Dakar, the capital of Senegal. Dakar, an air-transportation crossroads, is a boom town, proliferating malignant concrete cells of itself and equipped with every conceivable modern convenience. As in The Congo, the food I encountered here was strictly Eu-

ropean. Even in the interior, my impression did not change. Some 150 miles from Dakar, I came one hot afternoon to a little French inn on the outskirts of a provincial town. It was called The Baobab, because at this point, where the sands of the Sahara run out, a baobab tree stood like a botanical immigration officer on the frontier of the real Africa, checking the passports of all entering vegetable matter. I was too late for lunch, and the French guests of the inn were enjoying their postprandial nap, but the drowsy French proprietor offered me a snack—a bottle of Alsatian wine, crisp white French bread, fresh Normandy butter from a refrigerator and a board of a dozen French cheeses.

In the depths of the bush, to be sure, the story is usually different. There, meat is a luxury; sheep, goats and cattle are forms of currency and eggs are the small change of the housewife, not likely to be squandered on mere eating. The African farmer often lives on milk, curds and whey, and dishes of green vegetables, peas, beans and cereals; for nourishing bulk, he may turn to starchy tubers like cassava, yams and sweet potatoes. But his ingenuity in drawing on the plants of plain and forest is impressive. Everything that his struggle for existence has taught him is the least bit nutritious, goes into his cooking. The baobab tree, for instance, is treasured for both the seeds and the flesh of its fruit. The seeds are dried, crushed and ground to serve as flavoring in stews. The flesh is dried, stamped into a fine powder and used to thicken sauces and gravies, adding a tart flavor of its own. Nor is the baobab the only unexpected blessing that appears at the tables of the African poor. In each locality there are numerous wild fruits and leaves that are used in all manner of ways by the housewife in her cooking.

With cultivated staples, the West African is equally ingenious and sometimes almost reverential. Along much of the west coast the yam is

Long known for the goods (grain, ivory, slaves and gold) it supplied to trading ships from Europe, West Africa now consists of a series of Atlantic coastal nations, most of them independent. The region is the most densely populated in sub-Saharàn Africa and contains some of the continent's greatest cities —Freetown, Abidjan, Accra, Lagos, Dakar. Low-lying coastal terrain predominates, with some higher, drier plateau land upcountry.

61

not only a food of vast importance but also a kind of symbol. The yam has helped many West Africans to survive. Accordingly, his gratitude to it is so great that eating it is almost a religious exercise. Yam feast days are common; they are celebrated at their best, I think, among the Ashanti of Ghana, where yam dishes figure in the ceremonies that accompany birth, death, marriage and recovery from accidents or disease. On these occasions the Ashanti will eat yam in any of a number of ways, often accompanied by an egg sauce, because egg is for him an immemorial symbol of fertility and triumph. (An old African saying, which might well have originated among the Ashanti, goes: "The sun is but an egg that hatches great things.")

Elsewhere, Indian corn holds first place in the emotions and among the dishes of the people. One great Ghanaian harvest festival, picturesquely called "Hooting at Hunger," commemorates the time when the Ga tribe migrated to the coast of Ghana and prayerfully sowed Indian corn for the first time. (The crop was a success.) Hooting at Hunger is celebrated with colorful costume and pageantry and, above all, with *kpekple,* a farina prepared from Indian-corn meal and eaten with a fish-and-palm-nut stew. Neither the yam nor corn is indigenous to the land, but the Africans have gratefully made both their own.

Another foreign but first-line reinforcement of the yam is cassava, or manioc. (Found in most tropical and subtropical areas of the world, cassava goes by a multitude of names; generically it is the tuber from which tapioca is made.) Cassava leaves are used in cooking, but it is the flour of the tuber that helps give bulk to the West African diet. The form in which cassava flour is considered most delectable is a slightly fermented one known in Ghana as *gari.* It is especially popular among the Ewe tribe, and one has only to mention *gari* to an Ewe abroad to spur in him an acute attack of homesickness.

Traditional West African ways of preparing food are interesting, but if they and the ways of the cook in Europeanized cities were the only alternatives, I would have to judge the West African concept of cooking invalid in 20th Century terms. The traditional cuisine I find monotonous; the urban style is too tamely European. Fortunately, West Africa offers a third alternative. A rapidly expanding indigenous middle class is now developing a new approach to what Africa can offer and European methods refine. The best meals I have eaten on my recent travels in the region have invariably been served in the homes of this new class. For these people cooking, after the long centuries of deprivation, is still a voyage of discovery. Their approach to it has a kind of morning freshness, their taste is exhilarating and exploratory and their inventiveness lively. And their meals stimulate not only the palate but the mind as well; some of the best conversations I have ever heard have taken place over food eaten with West African friends.

I find great hope for the future of African cooking in the fact that the most stimulating food in West Africa comes from this rapidly expanding middle class. Great as the contributions of the peasant and the aristocrat may be to the art of cooking in its beginnings, it has always seemed to me that the middle classes are the real developers and consolidators of taste

in the modern world. (It is no accident, I think, that one cannot eat better in France than in the *cuisine bourgeoise.*)

As an example of this new spirit, consider what is being done with the basic yam. The white yam of West Africa is a formidable-looking tuber; it has been called the potato of Africa, but there have never been potatoes like it—not even those giants displayed at British agricultural fairs, where the exhibitor is concerned less with quality than with the sheer size of his entry, and would if he could grow vegetables that weigh a ton. The yam in its full glory has to be seen to be believed, and one of the best places to see it is at a rural West African market, where the vegetables are so big that a single one proudly carried off on a housewife's head can surely satisfy the needs of an entire family.

The traditional way of preparing yams is to boil, peel and then slice them or pound them to a paste called *fufu (Recipe Index)*. But on the sophisticated West African tables of today I have had them served as delicious croquettes, crisp and browned in palm or peanut oil. I have had small balls of mashed yams served deep-fried, as the French serve potatoes *dauphine,* but with ingenious additions: the housewife will sometimes work a crushed pepper into her yam purée or grate fresh nutmeg over the freshly cooked mixture. I have had yams parboiled, cut in paper-thin slices and fried in palm oil so that they become a kind of potato chip—one that goes extremely well with grilled chicken and fried fish

On her way to exchange some eggplants for cash, a heavily laden woman follows an overgrown track leading from the village of Cheggo to the market town of Tamale, two miles away. The scene is northern Ghana, the time late summer, after the harvest: the millet stalks in the village patch *(left)* have already been stripped of their ears.

63

Many West African markets are filled with exotic and—to the uninitiated—apparently inedible foodstuffs. It pays to look more closely. The Ghanaian woman in Kaneshie Market in Accra *(above)*, for example, is selling a kind of gargantuan gastropod called a forest snail. Roasted on coals in West African style and eaten with a sauce of palm oil, parsley, salt and pepper, it bears comparison with its French relatives. The Senegalese boy in Dakar's great Tilene Market *(opposite)* offers a variety of vegetables, both familiar and unfamiliar. They include a group of small West African eggplants (which are *supposed* to be green); sweet cassava, which is an African staple; and exactly the same kind of juicy cherry tomatoes that grow in many American gardens.

or meat. I have had them cooked with palm nuts, boiled in milk, inserted in chunks into ragouts and stews. In some middle-class homes I have had them done as a sort of *pommes de terre à la lyonnaise,* cooked between layers of finely sliced onions, grated cheese and bread crumbs. Finally, I have eaten yams baked and sweetened with sugar and cinnamon sticks, as an accompaniment to a cut of venison.

Even more inventive is the new West African approach to the banana and to the plaintain, the senior member of the banana family. Both bananas and plantains are often served as a salad with a lemon mayonnaise. But this is only the beginning of what I found in West Africa. Some West Africans make plantain *fufu,* or mix plantains with ground peanuts to make cakes, meringues, tarts and syrups. They make delicious croquettes of them that go well with a dish of smoked or sun-dried fish. They eat them as sweets, fried with a touch of cinnamon and grilled slices of orange, or topped with hot chocolate sauce. They make banana and plantain purées, whipped with eggs into a delicious sort of custard. They even make a powerful banana wine.

The peanut (or groundnut) is equally versatile. It has become as much an essential of the region's cooking as the nut of the palm. The palm nut, however, is cultivated mainly for its oil, while the peanut not only yields oil but also is eaten for its own sake. Along with such elementary forms as the salted nut and pounded peanut "butter," the peanut appears on West African tables as the principal ingredient of a score or more different kinds of sauces. Such a sauce may consist of pounded peanuts boiled and thinned with water and blended into thick soups cooked from fish, fowl or meat; or it may be flavored with crushed pepper and poured over grilled shrimp or prawns.

The people of Cameroon have a particular flair for using peanut extracts with prawns and shrimp. They start out with absolutely superb raw materials: while all the rivers and coasts of West Africa yield prawns in abundant quantities and of an unusual size, Cameroon prawns seem to me to be unequaled, and it is interesting that the very name of the country comes from the Portuguese word for prawns: *camarões.* In Cameroon I have had the good fortune to eat prawns deliciously grilled on wooden skewers placed over fragrant coals of wood, served with a peanut sauce that was sharpened and uplifted by the addition of finely crushed peppers, chopped onions and wild herbs.

Peanut sauces are an indispensable ingredient of the best West African stews, and they go particularly well with chicken. In Ghana, Nigeria and Sierra Leone, roast chicken is rarely served without such a sauce, and a humble chicken stew is redeemed of potential drabness by its presence. On my most recent journey through West Africa, one of the best dishes I ate was a chicken-groundnut stew *(Recipe Index)* made with tomatoes, onions, peppers, a judicious touch of garlic and a generous amount of peanut flour. The secret of the dish, my hostess told me, was that great care was taken in removing the excess peanut oil that rose to the surface as the stew simmered. Served with boiled rice or *fufu,* hard-boiled eggs, the youngest of eggplants, fried plantains, pineapple cubes, fresh diced papaya and grated coconut, the dish was a feast in itself.

Like its American relative, eggs and hominy grits, *gari foto,* a West African dish of scrambled eggs and manioc meal with tomatoes and onions, makes an excellent breakfast or brunch. Red beans may be served on a platter with the *gari foto,* as shown, or separately as a side dish.

The coconut is almost as important a food source in West Africa as are peanuts and palm nuts. Most Europeans and Americans know the coconut best in the form of various confections. Africans, too, enjoy it in macaroons, fudge, pralines, tarts and fondants. But more significantly, they use coconut as an accompaniment to a main course. In Dahomey in the home of a fellow African writer, I ate roast chicken flavored with onions, pepper, turmeric and garlic and served with boiled rice and a sauce made from the pulp of coconuts cooked in their own milk. The sauce was an integral part of the dish, for it was poured into the roasting pan and the chicken was basted with it for the last 15 minutes before serving, so that when the dish came to the table, chicken, sauce and spices were completely at one.

More simply, the liquid pressed from the shredded meat of the coconut is often used directly in the cooking of plain rice, and the two go together happily. In Nigeria and Ghana I have eaten coconut rice as a delightful accompaniment to shellfish of all kinds. And from Cape Verde to The Congo coconut milk or flesh—or both pulped together—produce variations of taste and savor for all sorts of soups, stews and roasts, both fish and meat. The *frejons,* or bean purées, of Nigeria would be unthinkable without the inclusion of coconut milk; on many occasions sugar is added and the purée is eaten as a sweet. Sometimes *frejons* are made exceptionally thin by the addition of two or three times the normal amount of coconut milk; such a mixture may be chilled and served as a thickish but thirst-slaking refreshment in the heat of the day.

Besides such novel uses of staple footstuffs there are fascinating cooking methods being employed in West Africa. Fish and meat, for example, are often cooked together. In one characteristic method, diced meat is combined with smoked or salted fish that has been carefully boned and flaked. Both are browned in oil, then are joined with chunks of yam, onions, tomatoes, diced chilies and herbs, and the whole is simmered in a mixture of oil and water. When the meat is sufficiently tender, the dish is ready. If it proves too watery for the housewife's taste, she will thicken it with mashed yam, sweet potato purée or even a *frejon.* The variations of such thickeners are endless, from purées of black beans to grated coconut pulp and plantain mashes. Each house performs as its own conductor in orchestrating the theme, which one encounters from Dakar in Senegal to Brazzaville in The Congo Republic.

The sea and the rivers of West Africa are singularly blessed with fish, a source of food whose full potential is only just beginning to be recognized, and it is a sign of the times that fish barbecues are a growing fashion among my West African friends. West African fish—notably the tilapia and the carp—tend to be fleshier and more substantial than those that swim in European waters, and lend themselves more readily to grilling or roasting in the open.

I have pleasant recollections of sitting beside a hospitable fire in the soft West African night, watching my hostess roast a 15-pound fish on wooden coals and getting hungrier by the minute as the smells of wood smoke, fish and the palm oil used for basting grew stronger in the air. Her basting oil was spiced with crushed herbs, pepper, onions and garlic, although combinations and additions vary from one household to another. The fish itself had deep incisions cut into it right down to the bone, so that it seemed to glow in the fire like an illuminated tribal design. From time to time the spiced oil and its herbs were ladled over the fish while a metal scoop with a long handle was held underneath the grill. In this way, most of the juices released by the basting could be gathered and set aside as the basis for a fine hot sauce to be served with the rice or the yam *fufu* that accompanied the finished dish.

Unlike fish, beef and mutton are scarce in West Africa—and when available, seem to come from animals that have been trained all their lives as long-distance runners. Even chicken is rarely tender enough for roasting or grilling straightaway. The most common way of handling tough meat and poultry in West Africa is the universal one of preparing it in stews or casseroles, but the best method of tenderizing I found was marinating. In Senegal, an entire class of marinated fish, chicken or meat

Two Muslim gentlemen enjoy a cup of mint tea in the courtyard of the old slave market on Gorée Island, off the coast of Senegal, near Dakar. The building behind them, now a museum containing objects connected with the slave trade, is a grim reminder of the activity that for centuries was the main occupation of Gorée. Largely Arab before the coming of European colonists, the island today has a mixed population, with Muslims once again predominating.

Large lumps of sugar cut from a loaf are placed in the teapot to steep along with the mint tea.

is known as *yassa,* and Senegalese lemon-based marinades stand up well to the competition of wine and vinegar, both of which are readily available in the onetime French colony. Again, the variations of the marinade from home to home are endless, but the minimum for a roasting chicken or its equivalent in fish or meat would be the juice of four lemons, along with finely diced onions, shredded hot peppers, salt and pepper. The chicken, meat or fish is cut up and soaked in the marinade for a period of time that depends on the nature of the raw material and the taste of the cook. One must guard against letting the tart taste of the lemon become too dominant, for lemons are used so much in West Africa that they can easily tyrannize the palate. For fish, in which toughness is seldom a problem, the period of soaking in the marinade is rarely more than 15 minutes; for chicken, of course, the process takes a longer time, and for beef or mutton, longer still.

A meal I had with some Senegalese friends, at which I ate a marvelous chicken *yassa,* is particularly worth mention here because it sheds some light on the advances that have occurred in West African cooking. We began with a kind of Senegalese *quiche.* The pastry was remarkable for its extremely light texture; the filling was a finely flaked smoked tuna, to which had been added some browned chopped onions, ground grilled peanuts, diced peppers and fresh tomato purée. A whisked egg was folded into the filling at the last minute and the whole was baked in a very hot oven for about 20 minutes. I loved it.

Now we came to the *yassa au poulet (Recipe Index).* The bird had been boned and cut up into sections, rather as a Chinese cook might have done. Then, since even the best roasting chickens of Africa are comparatively tough, the pieces had been thoroughly beaten with a rolling pin to begin their tenderizing. My hostess told me that in the cool season, after the pounding, the chicken is often wrapped in pawpaw leaves and left overnight in a stage of preparation that makes the flesh still more tender and gives it a subtle herb flavor as well. On this occasion, however, she had transferred the chicken straight from the pounding board to a marinade of lemon juice, onions, chilies and black pepper. She had left it to soak in this marinade for about half an hour, then had grilled it until it was crisp and brown. During the grilling, she had browned the onions from the marinade separately in oil, then put them back in the marinade; to complete the dish, she simmered the chicken in the pungent marinade for a quarter of an hour.

Our chicken *yassa* was served over white boiled rice that had been emptied from the saucepan, pressed into a greased bowl, and turned out onto a hot serving dish. I shall never forget the taste of the final mixture. The oil, the onions, the peppers and the chicken had so transformed the lemon juice of the marinade that it was no longer the separate, arrogant flavor that is the lazy cook's favorite camouflage, but had become part of a greater whole, and the succulent rice acted as a perfect absorbent for it. The meal ended with a fruit salad assembled from very thinly sliced bananas, diced fresh pineapples and guavas, served in half of a hollowed-out pineapple shell and topped by a very cold custard that had been flavored with vanilla bean.

Continued on page 72

Life on the Seashell Island of Fadiouth

Though the island of Fadiouth is separated by only a few hundred yards of shallow lagoon from the Senegalese mainland, its people are closely associated with the sea. The surface of the island itself is not soil or sand but a mass of seashells that crunch underfoot. The people make their living from—and, to a large extent, subsist upon—the abundance of oysters, clams and fish that the sea yields. Until a long wooden causeway was built recently, the only way of getting from the island to the mainland was by a seagoing dugout pirogue *(left)*, a primitive but efficient vessel that every inhabitant of the island learns to use for travel, for fishing and for moving freight. The very air of Fadiouth is touched by the sea —a fish market in the main street casts its scents on the breeze every morning, while all day long shellfish, most of them clams, dry on mats in the sun.

A husband and wife gather oysters in the Fadiouth lagoon at low tide as their small son plays in the stern of the family pirogue. The villagers "farm" oysters, planting oyster spawn on the bed of the lagoon, later harvesting the mature "crop" on a cooperative basis. Restaurants and markets located in Dakar, 85 miles northwest along the coast, buy up most of the oyster crop.

A woman of Fadiouth uses calabash containers to winnow millet, on a small nearby island that serves the village as a granary.

A few of Fadiouth's superabundance of seashells, which completely cover the island, are used by the villagers for decoration. In the picture at right the shell-studded bricks of a house rise from a similarly adorned curbstone. Split fish, laid directly on the shells embedded in the street, are drying in the sun; clams will be spread out to dry on the straw mat.

Obviously, the cooking of West Africa has traveled a long way upward from the days when families gathered for their meal huddled round a common pot in a smoke-filled hut. The change is reflected in a summary of my notes on the food I ate during a journey through West Africa a few months ago. To start with, there was a breakfast dish that is common in the interior of Dahomey, a porridge made of small pellets of millet flour cooked in water and continually stirred. When the pellets expand and are about to congeal, the saucepan is removed from the fire and the mixture is allowed to cool slightly. The water is then poured off, some dark-brown sugar flavored with vanilla is poured over the porridge, curds and whey are added, and the whole is stirred together before serving. On the hot morning when I ate this dish I found it wonderfully light and tangy, and could think of only one possible improvement on it—substituting some Ethiopian honey for the sugar.

Another breakfast dish I recorded was one I had a number of times on the Ivory Coast—eggs baked over mashed yam. The yam, already hot and browned when the eggs were added, was spread about half an inch thick. Salted, dusted with ground chilies and glazed with a thin film of palm oil, the dish was placed in a hot oven until the eggs were done to taste. In a country with no bread of its own the combination seemed just right for starting a hard working day.

Then in Conakry, in Guinea, I had omelets made with fresh crushed peppers, green or red according to the diner's taste, beaten into the eggs. (The fiery red peppers were used sparingly, the sweet green peppers far more generously.) More elaborate, and the best omelet variation I discovered in Guinea, was an interesting combination of sweet peppers, tomatoes and eggs. The tomatoes had been peeled and sieved, and only the pulp was used. Green sweet peppers, finely chopped, were added to the tomatoes, and the mixture was gently cooked in a little palm-nut oil. It was then whisked with the eggs and poured into a pan smoking with a thin layer of hot oil. Unlike its predecessor, this omelet was turned over like a pancake so that it came to the table browned on both sides as a sort of African Spanish omelet. Its hearty texture and flavor made it a welcome dish not only at breakfast but at any other meal of the day. Still other omelets appeared as sweets at the end of a meal, sometimes folded over cubes of fresh pineapple that had been browned in palm oil or over sliced and similarly browned bananas and plantains. On some occasions the delicious sweet omelets were filled with the flesh of the papaya or the guava, with added sweetening supplied by dark sugar flavored with vanilla, cinnamon or nutmeg.

A number of luncheon dishes also came as a surprise. At the beach cottage of friends in Ghana, for example, I came across a fascinating concoction that I can only call a fish tartare. I was used to *sashimi,* raw fish eaten with piquant sauces in Japan, but had never guessed that the Africans had anything like it—yet I was told that on the West Coast, where one can get fish straight from the sea at dawn, it is now a favorite dish. A red snapper was soaked and filleted, sliced and salted, then spread out in a deep flat dish, covered with fresh lemon juice and left to soak until lunch time. The lemon juice worked its alchemy on the fish: when the

Continued on page 76

Calalou aux fruits de mer (Recipe Index), a stew of spinach, lamb and seafood, is served with cornmeal cakes.

At Winneba on the Gulf of Guinea, a fleet of pirogues, each marked with its purchase price, awaits the turning of the tide.

How to Handle Hot Chilies

Hot chilies are cousins to the familiar green bell peppers, but they require special handling. Their volatile oils may make your skin tingle and your eyes burn. While working with the chilies, wear rubber gloves if you can and be careful not to touch your face. To prepare chilies, rinse them clean under cold running water. (Hot water may cause fumes to rise from dried chilies, and even these fumes can irritate your nose and eyes.) Cut or break off the stems if you wish to leave the seeds (the hottest parts of chilies) in the pods. If a chili is to be seeded, pull out the stem and the seeds attached to it, then break or cut the pod and brush out the remaining seeds with your fingers. In most cases the ribs inside are thin, but if they seem thick and fleshy you may cut them out with a small, sharp knife. Follow the instructions in the recipes for slicing or chopping chilies. After handling hot chilies it is essential to wash your hands thoroughly with soap and water.

juice was poured off, the fillets had the opaque look that is characteristic of parboiled fish. The red snapper was then rinsed in fresh cold water and served with a seasoning of oil, chilies, thyme, wild parsley and grated coconut. It was accompanied by a refreshing salad of raw grated vegetables, served with a dressing made with coconut milk, lemon, peanut oil, salt and black pepper.

Another seafood experience was the fish *imojo (Recipe Index)* that I ate in Ghana. There are very few natural harbors on the country's seacoast; every day, the fishermen have to paddle their dugouts through a savage surf to get to their most productive fishing ground. But their catches include some of the finest fish of Africa and fish *imojo* depends for its success on the freshness of the catch. A fish that has been cleaned and washed is salted and seasoned with garlic, simmered gently in a saucepan and allowed to cool. It is then boned, flaked and placed in a serving bowl. An equal quantity of fresh shelled prawns, cooked separately, is added to the dish, along with a dressing made of lemon juice, ground red peppers, some finely chopped tomatoes, onions and a clove or two of garlic. The secret of the dish, I was told, is that the prawns are soaked in the same dressing for two hours before being added to the fish. I had my fish *imojo* garnished with slices of sweet green peppers and surrounded by some diced half-ripe papaya.

In Sierra Leone, incidentally, prawns of the kind used for a fish *imojo* are abundant and large. I ate them with sweet peppers, onions and tomatoes, all cooked together in a small amount of palm oil and served with fried plantains, baked sweet potatoes or plain boiled rice. The dish went best, I think, with the rice, which beautifully absorbed the fine flavors of the spices and the rich textures of the tomatoes and oil.

I have left for last one of my favorite dishes. It is Jollof rice *(Recipe Index),* named after the once-powerful Wollof tribe of West Africa, and it is made with chicken or meat or both combined. The dish is generally agreed to be native to Sierra Leone but has spread over much of West Africa, and is now so firmly established that it is the food of choice in many middle-class homes on Sundays. Even hotels and restaurants, despite their internationalist prejudices, often include it in their menus. Cooked with appropriate skill and solicitude, it is, I think, one of West Africa's finest offerings, a delight for anyone who has no fear of occasionally taking on generous amounts of hearty food.

As always in West African countries, there are many excellent versions of the dish, but all of them are intricate and lusty. The general concept goes something like this: The meat or chicken is rubbed well with lemon, salt and garlic, and is allowed to stand in a covered bowl for an hour or two. Tomatoes and onions are cut into the most delicate of rings, while additional tomatoes are pressed through a sieve and mixed with additional onions and some crushed red peppers. The meat or chicken is cooked in two stages. It first goes separately into a cast-iron pot containing about two cups of water and a tablespoon of palm oil. A close-fitting lid is set over the pot and weighted down—I remember that in the household where I first encountered Jollof rice the lid was clamped down with an old-fashioned flatiron. When the chicken or meat is just tender the stock is drained off into a separate bowl.

A cup and a half of oil is now heated until a characteristic faint blue haze appears above it, and the chicken or meat is browned in it to a rich dark color. The sieved mixture of peppers, onions and tomatoes is simmered in the same oil, and supplemented with a fresh tomato purée made of half a dozen large peeled and seeded tomatoes seasoned with thyme, garlic, bay leaves and lemon juice. The rice for the dish, added in an amount that varies with the taste of the cook, is sautéed in just enough oil to brown it, then the reserved stock is added to it a little at a time and stirred continually over low heat. When all the stock has been absorbed, the grains of rice are nearly soft, and at that point the sliced onions and tomatoes are added to the purée mixture.

Finally, the meat or chicken and all its accompaniments—including the cooked rice—are set in the cast-iron pot, the cover is replaced firmly and the dish is simmered and steamed for five minutes. Jollof rice is often eaten with hard-boiled eggs, but I remember that the first time I ate the dish the only accompaniment served, or needed, was a delicious spinach-like green made of sweet-potato leaves.

My most recent memory of Jollof rice comes from a small restaurant on a spit of sand that bars the long Atlantic swell from breaking into the spacious harbor of Freetown, the capital of Sierra Leone. I remember the occasion vividly, because the whole of the new Africa seemed to come to a focus in that single meal. I arrived at my destination just as the sun went down in the spectacular kind of sunset one seems to get only on my continent. The sun on the edge of the purple Atlantic seemed thrice its normal size; its color was a bright scarlet and, as always in tropical climes, it was in a hurry to set. Indeed, it seemed to plunge into the sea with such speed and violence that the immense thunderclouds piled high in the turquoise-blue sky appeared to be caught up into a kind of whirlpool of valedictory light. The lovely green mountains fringing the coast, which gave Sierra Leone its name because they seemed to the early Portuguese explorers to rumble with thunder like an angry lion growling in the jungle, were quickly lost in darkness and almost immediately festooned with garlands of electric light.

Hard by the little restaurant where we sat down to eat under a fringe of palms lay the huge yacht of the President of desperately impoverished Liberia. The ship had run aground during a recent state visit, and though it was undamaged, no attempt appeared to have been made to salvage it. Beyond the grounded yacht stood a casino where diamond miners from the interior came to gamble away their money. Atop a hill near the casino stood the skeleton of a very large concrete hotel on which building had stopped some three years before. On one side of the spit of land lay the smooth black waters of the harbor, a lagoon of reflected light; on the other side the long Atlantic rollers, with not a single spot of land between Freetown and the coast of Brazil to break their rhythm, made music like an offstage chorus.

Whenever the foaming surf retreated, and before it was resurrected in another great comber, the sands shone like a mirror, and I walked across *Continued on page 82*

Beneath an umbrella denoting rank, a chief parades through Odumasi-Krobo preceded by a "talking" drum on a man's head.

Carved statuettes atop golden maces illustrate local legends.

With Pride and Thanks

Local pride and religious rejoicing are knit together in the Nmayem, a festival held at the end of September in the Ghanaian city of Odumasi-Krobo. In one of its aspects Nmayem is a harvest festival, offering thanks to the gods who have blessed the land with a crop of millet; it is also a tribal gathering that celebrates the unity of the Ga Adangbe people. In Odumasi-Krobo, Nmayem is something like the Fourth of July and Thanksgiving in one. Among the attractions of the festival are appearances by various chiefs in their regalia, considerable dancing and merrymaking, and feasting that continues for a week.

A priestess, her face rubbed heavily with white clay as a symbol of purification, holds bunches of unthreshed millet.

Is That make-up you wearing

Overleaf: Borne in a brilliantly colored palanquin, a tribal chief moves through the streets toward the *durbar,* or official gathering, where he will join other chiefs at the high point of the seven-day Nmayem festival.

them after ordering my dinner; Orion and Aldebaran hung so low in the sky that I felt as if I were treading them almost underfoot. There is no land in the world in which one so quickly forgets the sun and takes so happily to the starry night as in this land of West Africa.

Back at my table the smell of the sea and the warm breath of grass and jungle on a terrace under palms evoked the entire continent at its best. My imagination quickened with intimations of the wonder that could still be worked in so relatively untouched and beautiful a setting with such responsive human beings. The quickening was all the keener because this was the last night of a journey through Africa, and I knew that in less than 24 hours I would be back again in the busy world of London. I felt an extra compulsion to eat nothing but the food of Africa, in a kind of ritual of farewell.

I began with a large avocado pear filled with some flaked and delicately smoked West African fish, covered with a sauce of African inspiration. The waiter, as dignified and impeccable in appearance and behavior as a royal steward, told me that the sauce began with the yolks of hard-boiled eggs, sieved and stirred vigorously with a little milk until they were of a smooth mayonnaise consistency. Some lemon juice and peanut oil, a little sugar (just enough to appease the lemon) and grated nutmeg were stirred into the sauce, and the finished dish was criss-crossed on top with the finest of sliced pimientos. It made so good an hors d'oeuvre that I had two helpings.

For my main dish I had Jollof rice; it was made with chicken in much the way I have already described, except that instead of sweet-potato leaves for a vegetable I was served some large slices of baked pumpkin. The pumpkin had been dusted with dark-brown sugar and cinnamon and had been baked with palm oil. Just before serving, a fresh lime was squeezed over the pumpkin, and its tartness provided a perfect check to the rich sweetness of the dish.

I ended the meal with a pineapple fritter *(Recipe Index)*. When I saw the word "fritter" on the menu I admit my palate recoiled; for nobody can move about the English-speaking world as much as I do and not live in terror of this cliché of its hotel and restaurant kitchens. But the headwaiter gently insisted on the dessert, and as all the other dessert dishes on the menu were international I took his advice. The pineapple slices, he told me, were soaked in a local rum for an hour or two before cooking. The cream in which they were then immersed was made of equal quantities of sugar and sago flour. Whole eggs and additional egg yolks were worked into the flour, and milk that had been boiled with vanilla bean and allowed to cool was then added until the mixture became a smooth cream. The cream was slowly brought to a boil; when it thickened heavily, butter and ground roasted peanuts were stirred into it. The pineapple slices were dipped into the cream, then into a fritter batter and fried in oil. When they became deep brown they were sprinkled with a mixture of sugar and cinnamon and then with a dash of rum. The result, with its fascinating gamut of flavors running from tart fruit to the richness of peanuts to the mingled sweetness of vanilla, sugar and rum, can be described only as the best fritter in the world.

There was not a European on the staff of the establishment, from chef to waiters—all were men of Africa, of a class that had emerged into the world some 30 years before from round beehive huts in the remote interior. A large party of Russians and I were the only European diners in the restaurant; all the others were West Africans.

I had felt like a glutton when I ordered a second helping of my hors d'oeuvre, but I felt much less greedy when I saw that the Russians were asking for repeats of *every* course twice and even three times. I was not surprised when they clamored again and again for more pineapple fritters, for all Russians are chronically starved for fruit. Not many years before, I remembered, I had stopped at a Far Eastern station of the Trans-Siberian Railway. A rumor went round that the dining car had some bananas and pineapples for sale, and a crowd of eager villagers appeared, broke into the car and cleaned it out of these fruits. I thought of that incident when I left the Freetown restaurant. The Russians were well into their third round of pineapple fritters, and they looked as if they would never leave. For all I know they are still at their table—and if I were there I would hasten to join them.

Barbara Baeta, one of Ghana's leading culinary experts, opened her own catering service in Accra in 1968 and an invitation to one of her dinners is highly prized. Here Barbara, at far left, and her guests are about to partake of a Baeta buffet at Jimmy Moxon's Black Pot Restaurant. The meal centers on a tureen of West African peanut stew. Supplementing it are dishes of rice, oranges and papaya, papaya and pineapple, tiny eggplants and boiled okra. The large bowl on the left contains *gari foto,* a West African blend of cassava meal, eggs, tomatoes and onions. Watermelon *mokette* and pineapple delight *(right rear)* are the desserts.

To serve 6

A 5- to 6-pound chicken, cut and
  chopped into 12 or more pieces
1 tablespoon salt
1 tablespoon ground ginger
½ cup peanut oil
1 cup finely chopped onions
5 medium-sized firm ripe tomatoes,
  coarsely chopped and puréed
  through a food mill
¼ cup tomato paste
½ cup dried ground shrimp, if
  available *(see Recipe Booklet
  Glossary)*
1 teaspoon finely chopped garlic
¼ teaspoon finely grated, scraped
  fresh ginger root
½ teaspoon ground hot red pepper
½ teaspoon white pepper
6 cups boiling water
¼ cup coarsely crumbled dried
  small fish, if available
  (see Recipe Booklet Glossary)
2 whole fresh hot chilies, each about
  3 inches long
  (caution: see page 76)
1 cup peanut butter and 1 cup cold
  water beaten to a smooth paste
12 large fresh okra, washed and
  stemmed, or 12 frozen okra
6 hard-cooked eggs

GARNISHES
½ cup finely chopped onions
1 cup finely diced fresh pineapple
½ cup coarsely chopped unsalted
  roasted peanuts
Diced tomato salad *(below)*
Spiced okra *(opposite)*
Avocado salad with ginger
  (opposite)
Fried plantain cubes *(page 86)*
Diced ripe papaya *(page 86)*
Yam *fufu (page 86)*

DICED TOMATO SALAD
2 large firm ripe tomatoes
1 tablespoon fresh lemon juice
¼ teaspoon ground hot red pepper
½ teaspoon salt

Chicken-Groundnut Stew (West Africa)
STEWED CHICKEN WITH PEANUT-AND-TOMATO SAUCE

Pat the chicken completely dry with paper towels. Combine the salt and ground ginger, and rub the mixture evenly over each piece of chicken.

In a heavy 5- to 6-quart casserole, heat the oil over moderate heat until it is very hot but not smoking. Brown the chicken in the hot oil, 3 or 4 pieces at a time, turning the pieces frequently with tongs and regulating the heat so that they color richly and evenly without burning. As they brown, transfer the pieces to a plate.

Discard all but about ¼ cup of the oil remaining in the pan and drop in the chopped onions. Stirring frequently and scraping the browned particles from the bottom of the pan, cook the onions for about 5 minutes, until they are soft and translucent. Watch carefully for any sign of burning and reduce the heat if necessary.

Add the puréed tomatoes, tomato paste, ground shrimp (if available), garlic, ginger root, red pepper and white pepper. Raise the heat to high and stir until the mixture comes to a boil. Then reduce the heat to low and simmer uncovered for 5 minutes.

Stirring constantly, pour in the boiling water in a thin stream and add the dried fish (if available) and the whole chilies. Return the chicken and any liquid accumulated around it to the casserole, and turn the pieces about with a spoon until they are evenly coated. Cook uncovered over low heat for 15 minutes.

Stir in the peanut-butter paste and the okra, and continue cooking uncovered for about 1 hour, or until the chicken is tender and the dark meat shows no resistance when pierced with the point of a small, sharp knife. Add the hard-cooked eggs and simmer for 4 or 5 minutes, or until the eggs are heated through.

Serve the stew at once, directly from the casserole or mounded attractively in a heated bowl or deep platter, accompanied by as many of the garnishes as you like.

In West Africa, chicken-groundnut stew is often presented with *fufu* alone or with only two or three of the fruit or vegetable accompaniments. The *fufu* can be arranged on top of or around the stew, or served on a separate plate. Other garnishes are usually served in individual bowls or arranged separately on a large platter.

DICED TOMATO SALAD: Drop the tomatoes into a pan of boiling water and let them boil briskly for about 10 seconds. Run cold water over them and, with a small, sharp knife, peel them. Cut out the stems, then slice the tomatoes in half crosswise. Squeeze the halves gently to remove the seeds and juice, and chop the tomatoes as fine as possible.

In a small serving bowl, combine the lemon juice, ground red pepper and salt, and stir until well mixed. Add the tomatoes and toss together gently but thoroughly. Let the salad marinate at room temperature for about 30 minutes before serving.

Tightly covered, the salad can safely be kept at room temperature or in the refrigerator for 1 to 2 hours.

SPICED OKRA: In a small heavy saucepan, combine the water, onions, garlic, ground red pepper, white pepper and salt, and bring them to a boil over high heat.

Drop in the okra and cook briskly, stirring gently from time to time, for about 15 minutes, or until almost all of the liquid in the pan has evaporated and the pieces of okra are tender but still intact.

Transfer the entire contents of the saucepan to a sieve or colander and run cold water over it to set the color and stop the cooking. Place the okra in a small serving bowl and let it cool before serving.

Tightly covered, the okra can safely be kept at room temperature or in the refrigerator for 2 to 3 hours.

AVOCADO SALAD WITH GINGER: Cut the avocado in half. With the tip of a small knife, loosen the seed and lift it out. Remove any brown tissue-like fibers clinging to the flesh. Strip off the skin with your fingers, starting at the narrow, or stem, end. (The dark-skinned variety does not peel as easily; use a knife to pull the skin away, if necessary.) Cut the avocado into ½-inch cubes.

In a small serving bowl, combine the lemon juice, ginger and salt, and stir until they are well mixed. Add the avocado cubes and toss gently but thoroughly.

Let the salad marinate at room temperature for at least 30 minutes be-

SPICED OKRA
2 cups water
1 tablespoon finely chopped onions
¼ teaspoon finely chopped garlic
¼ teaspoon ground red hot pepper
¼ teaspoon white pepper
½ teaspoon salt
¼ pound large fresh okra, washed, stemmed and each cut crosswise into 3 pieces

AVOCADO SALAD WITH GINGER
1 large ripe avocado
1 tablespoon strained fresh lemon juice
½ teaspoon ground ginger
½ teaspoon salt

Fufu (mashed yam balls) lend distinction to chicken-and-peanut stew; the garnishes include vegetables, fruits and nuts.

fore serving. Tightly covered, the salad can safely be kept at room temperature or in the refrigerator for 1 to 2 hours.

FRIED PLANTAIN CUBES: Peel the plantains and cut them in half lengthwise. Scoop out the seeds by running the tip of a teaspoon down the center of each half, then cut the plaintain into ½-inch cubes. Mix the ginger, red pepper and salt in a bowl, drop in the plantain, and turn the cubes about with a spoon until they are evenly coated with the seasonings.

In a heavy 10- to 12-inch skillet, heat the oil over moderate heat until a light haze forms above it. Fry the plantain in the hot oil in two or three batches, turning the cubes gently with a slotted spoon or spatula, for about 5 to 8 minutes, or until they are browned on all sides. As they brown, transfer the cubes to paper towels to drain.

Serve the fried plantain while it is still warm, or at room temperature if you prefer.

DICED RIPE PAPAYA: In a small serving bowl, combine the papaya, lemon juice and chilies, and toss them together gently but thoroughly. Serve at once or cover tightly and let the papaya marinate at room temperature or in the refrigerator for up to 2 hours before serving.

FRIED PLANTAIN CUBES

2 medium-sized firm ripe plantains
½ teaspoon ground ginger
¼ teaspoon ground hot red pepper
1 teaspoon salt
1 cup peanut oil

DICED RIPE PAPAYA

1 small ripe papaya (about 1 pound) peeled, seeded and cut into ½-inch cubes
1 tablespoon strained fresh lemon juice
1 tablespoon fresh hot chilies, seeded and cut into strips ⅛ inch wide and 1 inch long (*caution: see page 76*)

To make about ten 1½-inch balls

1½ pounds yam (*see Recipe Booklet Glossary*)
2 cups water
2 teaspoons salt

Fufu (*West Africa*)
YAM PASTE BALLS

With a sharp knife, slice the yam crosswise into ½-inch-thick rounds and then peel each slice, cutting ⅛ to ¼ inch deep into the flesh to remove all the skin. As you peel the yam, drop the slices into a bowl of cold water to prevent discoloration.

Combine the yam, water and salt in a heavy 2- to 3-quart saucepan and bring to a boil over high heat. Reduce the heat to low, cover the pan tightly, and cook for 30 to 45 minutes, or until the yam is tender enough to be easily mashed with a fork.

Drain the yam slices in a large sieve or colander. Then purée them through a food mill set over a large, heavy earthenware or metal bowl.

Using an up-and-down motion, pound the yam vigorously with a large pestle or the smooth side of a wooden kitchen mallet. After four or five strokes, dip the pestle or mallet into cold water to keep the yam moist as you pound and to prevent it from sticking to the pestle. Repeat for about 10 minutes, or until the yam forms a compact but slightly sticky paste.

To shape the *fufu* into balls, fill a mixing bowl with cold water and set it beside a large, flat plate. Sprinkle a little water on the plate and moisten your hands lightly. Lift up about ¼ cup of yam paste and roll it between your palms and across the plate until it is a smooth, firm ball and its surface appears shiny and somewhat translucent. (Moisten your hands and the plate again from time to time if necessary.)

Arrange the yam *fufu* balls attractively on a platter and serve at once, or cover them tightly with foil or plastic wrap and set them aside at room temperature for up to 2 hours before serving.

In West Africa *fufu* is also made from cassava, cocoyam or plantain and is a standard accompaniment to spicy soups, stews and sauces such as chicken-groundnut stew (*page 84*) or *mokoto* (*Recipe Index*).

Banana fritters (*top*) are an easy-to-make West African dish, while pineapple fritters (*bottom*) are a more complex, sophisticated dessert.

To serve 6 to 8

1 pound uncooked medium-sized
  shrimp (about 21 to 25 to the
  pound)
1½ pounds halibut or haddock
  steaks, cut about 1 inch thick
1 quart water
1 cup coarsely chopped onions
2 medium-sized bay leaves,
  crumbled
6 whole black peppercorns
1 tablespoon salt
2 medium-sized firm ripe tomatoes,
  peeled, seeded and finely chopped
  (see diced tomato salad, page 84)
½ cup finely chopped onions
¼ cup finely chopped sweet red
  bell pepper
½ small sweet green bell pepper,
  seeded, deribbed and cut into
  strips about ⅛ inch wide and 1
  inch long
2 tablespoons finely chopped fresh
  parsley
1 tablespoon finely chopped fresh
  hot chilies *(caution: see page 76)*
1 tablespoon finely chopped garlic
⅓ cup strained fresh lemon juice
¼ cup olive oil
2 tablespoons tomato paste
Freshly ground black pepper

To serve 4

4 hard-cooked eggs, the yolks
  rubbed through a sieve and the
  whites finely chopped
¼ cup milk
¼ cup strained fresh lime juice
¼ teaspoon sugar
½ teaspoon salt
⅓ cup vegetable oil
2 tablespoons olive oil
½ pound smoked whitefish
2 large ripe avocados
12 strips of fresh red bell pepper or
  canned pimiento, each cut about
  ¼ inch wide and 2 inches long

Fish Imojo *(West Africa)*
FISH-AND-SHRIMP SALAD

Shell the shrimp. Devein them by making a shallow incision down their backs with a small, sharp knife and lifting out the black or white intestinal vein with the point of the knife. Wash the shrimp under cold running water and drain them in a sieve or colander. Wrap the fish in a double thickness of cheesecloth and set the fish and shrimp aside.

Combine the water, coarsely chopped onions, bay leaves, peppercorns and salt in a heavy 3- to 4-quart casserole. Bring to a simmer over high heat, add the cheesecloth-wrapped fish and reduce the heat to low. Simmer uncovered for 5 minutes, then drop in the shrimp and simmer for 5 minutes longer.

With kitchen tongs or a slotted spoon, transfer the fish and shrimp to separate plates. Strain the stock through a fine sieve set over a bowl and reserve; discard the seasonings.

While the fish is still warm, lift it out of the cheesecloth and, with your fingers or a small knife, remove the skin and bones. Flake the fish coarsely with a table fork. Cut the shrimp into ½-inch pieces and combine the fish and shrimp in a large serving bowl.

Add the finely chopped tomatoes, onions, sweet red and green peppers, parsley, chilies and garlic, and turn them about with a spoon until all the ingredients are well mixed.

In a small bowl, beat the lemon juice and olive oil together with a wire whisk or a fork until they are blended. Stirring constantly, add ⅔ cup of the reserved cooking stock, the tomato paste and a few grindings of black pepper. Taste for seasoning.

Pour the sauce over the fish mixture and toss together gently but thoroughly. Let the salad marinate at room temperature for about 30 minutes before serving.

Avocado Stuffed with Smoked Fish *(West Africa)*

In a deep bowl, mash the egg yolks and milk together with a spoon or table fork until they form a smooth paste. Add 1 tablespoon of the lime juice, the sugar and the salt.

Then beat in the vegetable oil, a teaspoon or so at a time; make sure each addition is absorbed before adding more. Add the olive oil by teaspoonfuls, beating constantly. Stir the remaining lime juice into the sauce and taste for seasoning.

With your fingers or a small knife, remove the skin from the fish and pick out any bones. Drop the fish into a bowl and flake it finely with a fork. Add the chopped egg whites and the sauce, and toss together gently but thoroughly.

Just before serving, cut the avocados in half. With the tip of a small knife, loosen the seeds and lift them out. Remove any brown tissuelike fibers clinging to the flesh.

Spoon the fish mixture into the avocado halves, dividing it equally among them and mounding it slightly in the center. Arrange 3 strips of sweet pepper or pimiento diagonally across the top of each avocado and serve at once.

Avocado stuffed with smoked fish *(top)*, *pâté africain (center)*, and fish *imojo (bottom)* appeal to eye and palate alike.

Banana Fritters *(West Africa)*

In a deep mixing bowl, stir the flour and sugar together and, with a wire whisk, beat in the eggs one at a time. Whisking constantly, add the milk, about ⅓ cup at a time, and continue to beat until the batter is smooth and elastic enough to stretch like a ribbon from the beater when it is lifted up out of the bowl.

Peel the bananas, chop or slice them coarsely, and drop them into a shallow bowl. With the tines of a table fork, mash the bananas to a smooth purée. Stir the purée into the batter and let the mixture rest at room temperature for about 30 minutes before frying.

Pour oil into a deep fryer or large, heavy saucepan to a depth of 2 to 3 inches and heat the oil until it reaches a temperature of 375° on a deep-frying thermometer.

For each fritter, ladle about ¼ cup of the banana batter into the hot oil. Deep-fry 2 or 3 fritters at a time, leaving enough space between them so that they can spread into 3- to 4-inch rounds or oblongs. Turning them once or twice with a slotted spoon, fry for about 3 minutes, or until the fritters are a rich golden color on all sides. As they brown, transfer them to paper towels to drain.

While the fritters are still warm sprinkle them lightly with confectioners' sugar and serve at once.

To make about 20 fritters

1½ cups all-purpose flour
6 tablespoons sugar
3 eggs
1 cup milk
4 or 5 medium-sized ripe bananas
  (about 1 pound)
Vegetable oil for deep frying
Confectioners' sugar

IV

In the Highlands of East Africa

Looking like a dream of winter above the everlasting heat of the Tanzanian grasslands, Mount Kilimanjaro soars to more than 19,000 feet above sea level. On the plain below, grass, brush and umbrella trees compose a typical East African landscape.

Like West Africa, East Africa is huge. Kenya is bigger than France, Uganda is the size of West Germany, and Tanzania, the largest of the region's three major nations, is bigger than Kenya and Uganda put together. Like West Africa, too, the region contains a bewildering variety of humanity: there are literally hundreds of peoples. But at this point the resemblances between West and East Africa almost disappear.

The Europeans who lately controlled East Africa came there barely a hundred years ago. At that time, I believe, the diet of the average East African consisted largely of millet meal, sorghum, bananas and milk (usually in the form of curds and whey). To these he added Indian corn from America; he soon made cornmeal so basic a part of his fare that millions of Africans now eat it in the belief that it is something inherited from their own earliest beginnings.

The great paradox of the East African diet, even today, is the almost total absence of meat. East Africa is unquestionably the greatest game area on earth, and a land where cattle have been bred and husbanded for centuries. But cattle, sheep and goats are traditionally regarded as a form of capital and currency rather than as a source of food—except insofar as the cattle provide milk. Nilotics such as the Masai lived almost entirely upon the milk and the blood of their cattle.

It was almost inevitable, then, that the great transforming influences upon East African cooking came from communities of foreign settlers, who tended to repeat and reinforce the patterns of cooking they had brought with them from their homelands. The earliest of these influences

91

Near Bagamoyo, in Tanzania, a herdsman of the Wakwavi tribe tends his longhorn cattle. Typical of the tall, handsome peoples of the East Coast, the Wakwavi are closely related to the famous Masai tribe and, like them, subsist mainly on a diet of milk and blood drawn from the living cow. Drought in the highlands has forced this man and his herd from their usual pastures down to the Serengeti Plains.

was Arab, exercised for a thousand years before the coming of the Europeans. It was strongest in the coastal areas, which became Arab colonies and once had great Arab harbors and prosperous cities, now reclaimed by the jungle. Forty years ago, when I first visited East Africa, this influence was still pronounced. It is less so today, but valuable traces of it remain.

In Tanzania, the largest East African state, the great foreign influence should have been German, because the first missionaries to establish themselves there were German and until 1920 it was a German colony. In 1926, when I first sailed into the capital, Dar es Salaam, I saw a neat, orderly little city of white-walled houses with red-tiled roofs clustered round a church spire like chickens round a hen. It might have been a village lifted straight from Germany and transported by magic carpet to a world of glistening jungle and radiant palm. In the clubs and hotels ashore one drank German beer and schnapps and could eat dishes like hasenpfeffer, cooked in the Germans' incomparable way with game and venison. But when I was in Tanzania a few months ago, neither in Dar es Salaam nor anywhere else could I find a trace of German influence at table. When the German rulers left, the impulse to continue their ways of life and cooking soon declined.

The place of the Germans was taken by the British, who followed them into Tanzania, and by the Indians whom the British employed. Already firmly entrenched in the highlands of Kenya, supported by a middle class of Indian artisans and civil servants, the British became all-powerful in East Africa, and British and Indian concepts of food took charge of the modern East African kitchen.

By chance, one of my earliest experiences of East African food was in the oldest of the three basic traditions—the Arab. I first came to the offshore island of Zanzibar and the coast of East Africa the way history came to them, from the East. My ship, a Japanese tramp, came upon the island at dawn. We had company: all round us were dhows, their white sails trimmed, rigid and aslant. The scene looked, I am certain, very much as it must have looked when Vasco da Gama first broke into those waters some 400 years before.

We rounded the land, a tall feather of palm in its cap, and the sun shot up, the sky flashed like a mirror, and there was a little Arab city, tidy and compact at the rim of the harbor front. We were the only modern ship in the roadstead. On the sea there was nothing in sight but the dhows, their sails pecking like white doves at the troubled water farther out between the island and the invisible mainland. We dropped anchor, and when the rattle of the chains ceased I suddenly realized that a subtle perfume was coming out from the coral shore, the gleaming white warehouses and the fronds of palm. It took me a good moment to realize it was the scent of cloves.

Zanzibar and its sister island of Pemba made their history out of trading in slaves and spices. Now the slaves were long gone but the spices remained, and after breakfast I walked with the captain of my ship through a market knee deep in cloves, their scent so charged on the air that it was stifling. The dark narrow streets beyond the warehouses were lit by the white robes of a new kind of man: part Arab, part African, and still so identified with his Asian origins that he wore the white Arab *kuffiyyah* on his head and a curved dagger like a crescent moon at his waist.

My sense of the Arab roots of the place became still more intense when I accompanied my Japanese captain to a meal with the old Sultan who ruled the island. First of all, the banquet was an all-male affair. The only hints of a feminine presence were occasional glimpses round dark corners of saffron-colored faces with large black eyes made larger and darker by a liberal use of kohl; but the moment the women caught my eye they vanished with a pronounced start. What was more important, the food was far from European and of a kind that I had never encountered before. It was the cooking of the island at its best.

The foundation of the meal was rice, served with fish, mutton and roasted chicken—and the savor of the rice is still with me. All that escapes me is its Zanzibari name, but I remember being told that it was rice cooked in an ancient Persian manner and that the Sultan, who claimed descent from the aristocracy of Persia, always served this rice at state banquets like a heraldic badge of the ancient origin of his house.

Less than a year ago I found to my amazement that the Sultan's method of cooking rice was still alive—in Kenya. The person mainly responsible for its resurrection is a young German chef in Nairobi, who has been to Zanzibar and has cooked in Iran as well. According to him,

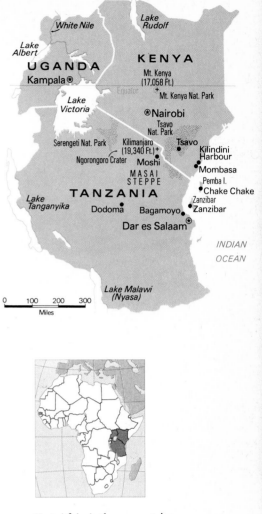

East Africa's three countries, Uganda, Kenya and Tanzania, until recently were colonial holdings of Great Britain. It is in the lovely highlands, where European settlers built their estates, that foreign influence survives most strongly. Despite the abundance of game, the peoples native to the region somehow have never been great meat eaters, living instead on corn and other grains, and on the milk and blood of their prized livestock.

93

Starkly outlined against an East African grassland plain *(opposite)*, a fantastical old baobab tree looks about as useful as a permanently grounded witch's broom. But the baobab is in fact one of the world's most versatile trees. Its gourd-shaped fruit is edible (the peddler above is hawking a cluster of them); its leaves are widely used for making soup and a kind of spinachlike relish; ashes of baobab wood contain enough chlorides to be used in place of salt; the pods and seeds can be steeped in water to make a drink, or roasted and eaten; and the fat trunk is usually full of water, a lifesaver to a dehydrated hunter. What is more, a hollow baobab makes a livable hut.

the only elements essential to the success of the dish are time and patience, a rice made up of completely unblemished grains, a water with a substantial content of chalk—and a wood fire.

This young Nairobi chef would have his assistants select each grain of rice specially some 12 hours before the dish was to be cooked. Any grain in the least bit damaged or misshapen was rejected, and when the collection was complete the rice was thoroughly washed twice. It was then placed in a flat dish and covered with water, and layers of clean white linen were pressed over the dish to protect it from dust. On top of the linen was laid some coarse salt, both to hold the linen firmly in place and to impart its own savor through the damp cloth to the grains. Two hours before cooking, the rice was taken from the dish and washed again, quickly boiled until it whitened, and drained once more. It was then arranged in layers in a large iron pot, each layer separated from the next by small lumps of butter, until the pot was about three quarters full. Finally, the rice was covered again with several folds of dry cloth, to seal in the steam that rose in the cooking process.

The cooking was done over a wood fire, with the heat coming not only from underneath the pot but also from live coals placed on the lid. The great secret was that the rice cooked at a constant temperature. The German chef said that in Iran a dedicated cook would not allow even an earthquake to distract him from attending to this phase of the operation in person. Patiently squatting by his fire, he would watch the flame, at one moment encouraging the heat by fanning the coals with a palm leaf, at another damping it down with a dash of water, and constantly renewing the live coals on the lid. After an hour or so the lid would be removed and one would see that the rice had risen to the brim, white and light as snow in the middle, faintly browned at the sides. It was ready to be served, steaming and fragrant. It seems poetic justice that the dish should still be living in East Africa. It is one of the finest accompaniments I know to almost all other foods, for it brings out the taste not only of beef and mutton, fowl and fish, but also of vegetables.

Finally I must add a word about the Sultan's chicken. The skin of that chicken had first been pricked all over with a sharp needle and the bird was basted in a very hot oven with butter, then finished off in a cast-iron pot with a mixture of water and pomegranate juice in quantities just sufficient to prevent it from burning. When the chicken was cooked to crisp perfection, the remaining pomegranate juice and water were thickened with minced fried walnuts.

There is another dish that I associate with Zanzibar. It is eaten to this day on the East African coast in areas that once were part of the vanished Sultanate, and I call it "Zanzibar duck" *(Recipe Index)*. The duck was first pricked and browned in the oven to get rid of excess fat. It was then set in a casserole along with stock made from the minced liver of the duck, a cup of stock and a dozen cloves. The casserole was firmly covered and cooked gently for at least two hours. At that point the duck was removed; the juice of a lemon, some salt and a finely chopped red pepper were added to the juices in the pot, and the sauce was thickened with cassava flour. We ate it with plain rice.

From Zanzibar our ship followed the way of history to the island of Mombasa and its harbor of Kilindini. An old fort stood there to mark our course, with the pink and white plaster of its walls burning faintly among banana groves and palm on the edge of the sea. (Today, you have to search for it among the luxury hotels of the proliferating city.) Mombasa looked so unprepossessing that I preferred to live in the tidy Japanese world of our cargo ship and was happy to take the first train to the uplands of the interior. The first-class compartments of our train were almost entirely occupied by members of the Nairobi rugby club, who had been playing a match against their rivals in Mombasa. I was amazed that men could play the game in the heat of the equator when they would never dream of doing it in the mild English summers of their homeland but always confined it to the winters. The incident reflected both the profound nostalgia of the European in Africa and his determination to bend Africa to his ways.

The journey was memorable, too, because it was my first experience of how the British ate in Africa. There were no dining cars and the train was halted for dinner at a siding called Tsavo, deep in the bush. This siding had a little fame of its own. Some years before, an Indian stationmaster at Tsavo, clocking in for duty one evening, found his platform in possession of a pride of lions. He locked himself in his office and tapped out a telegram to Nairobi in the immortal words: "Beg to report man-eating lions in possession of station. Kindly send instructions."

Happily, the lions were not in possession of the station the evening I was there—but they were roaring in the night round about us and at some moments talk was impossible. We sat, grimly silent in the cramped station dining room, at tables crowned with ketchup, salt, pepper and vinegar, and bottles of Worcestershire sauce made, as the labels informed us, from "a recipe by a nobleman of the county."

On that evening I felt no incentive to laugh at the bottle of sauce on my table, just as I had no desire to make fun of my rugby-playing companions. There was something profoundly ambassadorial about the bottle, standing erect on a stained railway tablecloth like a representative of the English kitchen. I could almost see the American tomato ketchup stretching out a hand to the British Worcestershire sauce and gravely saying, "Dr. Livingstone, I presume." Our meal started with a brown meat consommé, strongly flavored with Bovril, followed by fried fish and fried sweet-potato chips, boiled beef, dumplings, onions and carrots; it was rounded off with rice pudding and stewed prunes. There was obviously no concession to Africa in this way of eating.

Fortunately, there were other things than food to think about. At dawn I was at the window of my compartment looking out on one of the most beautiful parts of Africa. The country was high, wide and handsome, open to the sky and molded to distance and uncluttered space. The jungle of the coast had vanished, the tangled bush around Tsavo had gone; the world had been taken over by yellow grass and a flawless blue horizon. Away to the south there was the outline of Kilimanjaro, under snow and blue as a mountain in a Japanese woodcut. Snow is commonplace in Europe and America, but here on the equator it was a miracle. Soon, far

96

Continued on page 100

In a lookout post at the Ngorongoro Crater Lodge, a tourist can enjoy the double delight of animal spotting and tea.

In the Little World of Ngorongoro, a Wealth of Wildlife

"At noon we suddenly found ourselves on the rim of a sheer cliff and looked down into the oblong bowl of Ngorongoro, the remains of an old crater. Its bottom was grassland, alive with a great number of game; the western part was occupied by a small lake." Thus did Oskar Baumann, a 19th Century Austrian explorer, record the first sight by a white man of one of the gems of East African topography and wildlife. In a region that contains the world's greatest array of wild animals *(see overleaf),* with game parks set up by a half dozen governments, Ngorongoro, in Tanzania, remains exceptional. Its grassy floor, 12 miles across and walled in by 2,000-foot slopes, is the home of thousands upon thousands of game animals, from gazelles to zebras, lions to rhinoceroses, waterfowl to wild dogs. Tourist lodges on the lip of the crater make it possible to watch the animals without disturbing them. Like many of East Africa's game parks, however, Ngorongoro is not reserved for the exclusive use of wildlife and tourists. Masai cattle raisers have lived in and around the crater for over a century, and it belongs to them, too.

Zebras' stripes stand out in sunlight, but make the animals almost invisible at dusk, when leopards hunt.

A baby rhinoceros revels in a roll in the dust.

An elephant cocks his slightly ragged ears in alarm.

Supremely confident of her strength and security, a lioness lounges.

Giraffes roam open grasslands, but feed chiefly on the upper leaves of the acacia and mimosa trees.

Cattle egrets take to the air in a flutter and sweep of wings.

Being contemplated by a hippo is a sobering experience.

An eland may weigh over half a ton.

away to the northwest in the sparkling morning air, there appeared the mitered summit of East Africa's second mountain giant, Kenya, not with a crown but with a bright feather of snow in its cap.

Bare as it seemed at first, the land was full of game. Like the mountains, the animals were out in the open for inspection by the human eye. Even at the time I first saw it, some 40 years after the coming of the European and his destructive guns, the land seemed to be bursting at its blue seams with animal life. Elephants in compact family huddles; inquisitive giraffes, sometimes almost looking in our train windows; vast herds of harlequin zebras; elands with white, dew-laundered socks in patent-leather shoes; gazelles, with their white tails lashing the shining air and their skins a flicker of flame in the yellow grass—all were there, literally in thousands, to watch our progress toward Nairobi.

In such a land, with such a wealth of raw material, one would have thought that Europeans and Indians in Africa would have become the world's greatest masters in the art of cooking game. In sad fact, it is almost incredible to see what unimaginative use they made of their unique opportunity. They cooked game much as they cooked beef, mutton and fowl at home, and they considered a great deal of the natural material unsuitable for their table.

The colonial rulers of East Africa might have evolved something startlingly original out of African raw material if it were not for four overriding factors. One was their nostalgia for their homelands, exemplified by the out-of-season rugby players and Worcestershire sauce on my journey to Nairobi. Second, there was the failure of the aboriginal East African society to use its own foodstuffs in ways that were attractive to Europeans. Third, the Europeans found favored conditions of climate and soil in the highlands of East Africa, and came to believe that they could resurrect a life that had become impossible in the Europe they left behind. Finally, the Europeans were never isolated in East Africa as the Portuguese and the Dutch had been in southern Africa because fast steamships and railways already existed when they arrived there, and the airplane was about to bind them even more closely to the countries of their origin. (When I first visited the region, Kikuyu mothers in search of new names for their children often called them "Airplane.")

The British set about realizing their dream of a new-old life with astonishing energy and persistence, suffering almost unendurable hardships in the process. They started by importing cereals, vegetables and fruit from Europe and India. Later, they brought tea from the East and began to grow African and Middle Eastern coffee. At vast expense, they brought domestic animals from Great Britain—cows, bulls, sheep, horses and the rest—and aimed at being the first gentlemen farmers of Africa.

It is a fact that in respites from the battle to establish a world of their own the British kept up their courage by playing polo, hunting in scarlet coats on horseback and establishing racecourses as elaborate as Epsom Downs. More extraordinary still, they brought their love of fishing with them and rounded off their dream of a squire's life by stocking their African rivers with trout. To this day there is not a highland stream in Kenya, Uganda or Tanzania that has not been stocked. The world of the colonists was not a literary world and books were scarce, but I do not think I have ever seen as many copies of Izaak Walton's *Compleat Angler* as I have seen in the homes of East Africa. Trout appears as a matter of course in the most unlikely circumstances and is eaten as if it were native to the land. I remember walking some years ago into the White Rhino Hotel on the slopes of Mount Kenya to find the bar crowded with fishermen telling tall tales. The Mau Mau revolt was about to burst on the land, the air of Kenya was charged with impending disaster, and the future was volcanic with momentous change—but the minds of these men were entirely concerned with fishing. Their longest discussion of the evening was concerned with deciding whether they had been told the truth or merely had their legs pulled by an angler who claimed that his fly had hooked a passing bat and that he had been almost overcome with superstitious awe when he found his reel unwinding rapidly and the line vanishing into space.

Despite their extravagances and their hardships, the British came through to achievements that were meaningful not only to Kenya but to East Africa as a whole. In animal husbandry, for example, they eventually met with complete success. Kenya was the first African country north of the Limpopo River to produce beef that I would compare favorably with the best of Europe and the Americas. The beef is slightly darker and the marbling somewhat different, but the taste and tender texture seem to me as good or better. Along with cattle, the highlands of Kenya produce pigs as fine as those of Great Britain. And the dairymen of East Africa produce their own equivalents of the best-known European cheeses, from Cheddar to Camembert and Gorgonzola.

Kenya's achievements in cattle breeding were matched by its progress in agriculture. In time, all European vegetables and fruits became readily available, and a cook could work routinely with such delicacies as strawberries, raspberries and asparagus. As with animals and vegetables, so it was with flowers. Everywhere they went the English grew roses, hollyhocks, sweet Williams, larkspur, carnations and gladioli as lovely as any in Britain. With all this and more, it is not surprising that the European went his own way in East Africa.

What was more important was the fact that he trained the Bantu of East Africa to be his cooks and domestic servants. He translated *The Kenya Settlers' Cookery Book,* his one and only cookbook, into Swahili for them, and it had already run through 12 editions when independence came to the region. By the time of independence the 60,000 Europeans in East Africa had homes that were run entirely by African males. Thus, though the European and his Indian ally are fast being eliminated from the economic life of the land, there are great numbers of European-trained African cooks at work everywhere in the new East Africa. Their influence must inevitably be profound. And since they were trained by men who came from homes in which the standards of service were high, they themselves have acquired standards that seem to me higher than anywhere else on the continent. I rarely arrive at an East African airport or walk into an East African hotel without being impressed by a high order of cleanliness and service.

Continued on page 104

On a New Kind of Safari with a Nonhunting Hemingway

The safari land of East Africa is fantastically rich in wildlife but old-style safaris and hunters, heedless of animal life, were threatening this abundance. Today sophisticated conservation techniques are being developed and used by men who scarcely a generation ago might have spent their lives as "white hunters" searching for trophies. Patrick Hemingway, son of the writer, was a professional hunter for eight years; now he teaches wildlife management.

Shooting for his party's table, Hemingway draws a bead on a Thomson's gazelle with a .30-06 Springfield. The time is dawn.

Pat Hemingway periodically takes a group of his students from the College of African Wildlife Management near Moshi in Tanzania into the field for practical lessons in surveying, wildlife supervision, biology and marksmanship. Safari tradition does not call for roughing it in the bush, and on this occasion Hemingway's nine-year-old daughter Mina accompanied him. Preparing luncheon, the safari cook (*left*) gives the carrots a final stir, watched by some Masai tribesmen. The main course, "Tommy saddle," or roast saddle of Thomson's gazelle, was prepared over another fire. Except for the rough grass and bright sun, the luncheon (*right*) might have taken place in the Hemingway dining room. A connoisseur of game cookery, Hemingway has been conducting a campaign to teach local people how to kill and use wild animals without destroying the ecological balance of the area.

Unaware of a hidden cameraman, two Thomson's gazelles forage on the dry brush-covered grassland of the Ngaserai Plain.

It is heartening to report that these Bantu cooks are already making a brave beginning in the ingenious use of their native foods. On the coast, for example, some of these cooks now make the most of the unique harvest of crustaceans and fish provided by the coral seas. The giant crabs, the small dark oysters that compensate for their lack of size with an assertive taste and a character of their own, the king prawns, shrimp, crayfish, magnificent sea bream and scores of other creatures—all are beginning to get the civilized treatment they have so long deserved. There is, for instance, a shrimp pâté I ate recently in the rooftop restaurant of a new hotel in Dar es Salaam. It was a Dar es Salaam completely transformed from the transplanted German village I first sailed into four decades earlier. The harbor, a landlocked lagoon ringed with jungle and palm, was full of modern ships, one of them anchored almost within a stone's throw of my table. Forty years earlier I would have been imprisoned in a cramped dining room behind mosquito nets, but now I was dining beneath the stars in a world of sparkling light. Instead of a lethargic European, who would have fed me in a take-it-or-leave-it way, there was an alert Tanzanian headwaiter, who recommended the shrimp pâté as proudly as if he were referring to his national flag. The shrimp themselves were chopped fine and seasoned with chopped African parsley, grated nutmeg, and finely minced shallots and red peppers, and the mixture had been baked for about an hour in a medium oven.

In Mombasa I began a recent meal with a king-prawn soup, made with what I consider the most generously fleshed prawns in the world. The prawns had first been shelled and cooked in a casserole with some finely chopped onions and chilies and a dash of peanut oil; then they were covered with water and simmered for about three quarters of an hour. The mixture was strained through a sieve and the cooked prawns were mashed with a mortar and pestle before being returned to the cooking liquid. Finally, the soup was thickened with a roux of *mazena* flour and flavored with saffron. It was a delicious introduction to the main course, a chicken done in the Zanzibar way.

I am glad to report, too, that the cooking of game animals is taken more and more seriously in East Africa. The gazelle, impala and other wild African equivalents of the sheep; the eland, kudu and buffalo, which represent the cattle of the natural scene—these have always figured, in a somewhat crude and obvious way, in the standard Kenyan cuisine. But other worthy species of wild animals are beginning to be explored. The zebra, the unprepossessing warthog, the hippopotamus and even the elephant can be eaten. There are men who claim that elephant meat is as good as any other if properly treated, and I have often seen my own bearers go wild with excitement when I have had to shoot a rogue elephant. They would eat elephant meat as if it were caviar—partly because their traditional diet is so deprived of meat—and would sit over their fires feasting the night through like Roman emperors. I myself have tried elephant, and found it edible but no more. It seems to me the African equivalent of whale meat, and I consider both whale and elephant of too giant a texture to be truly palatable. A stronger case might be made for selected portions of the elephant. A great African favorite of the curiosity-seeking

European cook has always been the tip of the tongue and the pads and lower joint of the foot, and I have eaten and enjoyed cold elephant trunk in aspic—but I still do not believe that the elephant will ever play a serious role in the cooking of Africa, let alone the rest of the world.

The hippopotamus has perhaps the finest natural lard of any animal in the world; as a child, I knew great hunters who assured me that hippopotamus lard was so sweet and tasty that one could eat it raw. There is the surrealistic giraffe, too. I do not know what giraffe meat tastes like, but I do know that the marrow of giraffe bone is one of the oldest and most sought-after delicacies in Africa. The warthog, if properly treated, could play the role on the future African table that wild boar played in historic European cooking and still plays in Germany, Poland, Belgium and southern France. But the greatest contribution to the East African table will surely come from the antelope world.

One would have expected that organizers of luxury safaris, which are conducted on a far greater scale in East Africa than in any other part of the world, would have been pioneers in the cooking of venison. They started, after all, by taking great and privileged personages—most of whom must have had reasonably cultivated palates—into the wilds, where they were charged with the responsibility of feeding them as well as they could. But safari cooking, even at its best, has rarely been more than an imitation of international hotel fare cooked in a wild setting. I have been on safaris on which one was expected to down cocktails before dinner, then eat six courses, all accompanied by champagne. The ingenuity that made this possible was impressive, but hardly justified the indifferent result. I am afraid that my strictures still apply to safari cooking, but in the homes of Europeans born in Kenya, and in some East African hotels and restaurants, a real transformation has taken place.

A few examples will illustrate the point. Only recently I had both impala and Thomson's gazelle that were truly delicious. The steaks were cut like *tournedos* from the back of the gazelle and left to stand for 12 hours in a marinade of dry red South African wine and wild gooseberries. Then the steaks were well peppered and salted, dusted with flour and browned in butter; when brown they were coated with a fiery native banana gin called *waragi* in Uganda. (I sometimes wonder whether the name is a corruption of the Arab *arak*.) Finally, more butter and more berries, either strawberries or black currants, were simmered with the steaks until done. In the finished dish, the flavors of strong meat, marinade, spirits and fruit joined in a succulent blend.

I have also had kudu steaks, marinated in a similar manner but served in a sauce made of the natural juices of the steaks along with butter, *waragi,* wild honey and cream. The sauce was added at the last moment, and simmered until it was reduced to a creamy texture. Wild gooseberries or cultivated strawberries were then added to the whole, and the dish was served with either Kenya rice or minced pistachios. The strawberries of Kenya, incidentally, go beautifully with game. They have a more precise flavor than any strawberries I have ever encountered in Europe and serve the same function for any heavily roasted meat or venison that red currants do in Europe or quinces in South Africa.

As he has done every day for years, Major Alfred Herbert MacIlwaine works a wet fly through the waters of his own stocked pond in search of trout. Thanks to devoted anglers like him, nearly every highland stream and lake in East Africa now has a stock of trout, mainly browns.

Continued on page 108

Bearing a brace of guinea fowl, his cased Morocco 12-bore over-and-under shotgun slung on his shoulder, Gostling returns home from a successful foray in the field. An official of the Kenya Automobile Association and editor of its publication *Auto News,* he spends most of his spare time hunting. Other fowl bagged for his luncheon included a yellow-necked francolin ("most delicate in flavor," his guests reported) and lesser bustard.

A Gourmet Huntsman's Luncheon in Kenya

Lance Gostling and his wife live in a pleasant house on the outskirts of the cosmopolitan modern city of Nairobi, but no frontiersman ever had the hand and eye—or palate—for game that Gostling has. Fortunately the surrounding countryside of Kenya is ready to satisfy his passion. His specialty is wildfowl, but he does not disdain such plains delicacies as gazelle, and a Gostling hunter's luncheon is a great event. The one shown here required roughly a week of shooting, one and a half days of cooking and six hours of eating. Twenty-eight different species of beast and bird, to say nothing of local fruit, vegetables, coffee, cheeses and liqueurs, went into the meal (along with several good French wines). Because of the press of time Gostling had to call upon several sportsman friends to contribute, but he did all the cooking himself, from recipes of his own devising. His repertoire includes, incidentally, a special post-hunt dinner for the hunter's faithful dog—game liver, meat and vegetables cooked, according to the words of Gostling's own recipe, in "1 pint of rainwater" and then served "in his favorite place."

With a connoisseur's nose, Lance Gostling savors the fragrance of a freshly opened cantaloupe, cooled outdoors in the shade.

Having soaked a haunch of Thomson's gazelle in a marinade of vinegar, wine and spices, Gostling arranges the meat and game birds in a pan and tops them with more seasoning before roasting. "Fresh, unmarinated venison *can* be eaten," he says, "but why cook a crown roast from fresh venison?" Below, helped by his wife, Violet, he serves up roast fowl to his guests.

I already mentioned my belief that East Africa has developed an indigenous beef equal in quality to almost anything the Western world can produce. It is not surprising, therefore, that one encounters veal in restaurants and hotels in all forms—from *saltimbocca* and *paillettes* to the immortal schnitzels of Vienna, and in some distinctly East African creations as well. For instance there is a sauté of veal that I consider a real contribution to world cuisine. Veal fillets are sautéed in oil in the usual manner and a sauce is prepared in the same saucepan with sliced shallots, grated fresh coconut, butter, curry powder, peanut oil, pepper, salt and lemon juice. The most important ingredient is sliced fresh mangoes, which are first separately sautéed, juice and all, in butter. Native South African brandy or imported Calvados (I prefer the brandy because it is of Africa) is poured into the sauce and set alight; then the mixture is simmered to thickness. At this moment the hot mangoes are added to the saucepan and the sauce poured over the fillets.

After one enjoys the classic perfection of such a dish, it is sometimes difficult to remember how deep a paradox of past and present East Africa still remains. Side by side with the feverish urge to join the contemporary world, there is still the old Africa that has lain for so many thousands of years unknown and unknowing in the sun. That old Africa was very much in the forefront of my mind not long ago when I traveled to Lake Rudolf, in northern Kenya. There, one day, I encountered a band of pastoral East African nomads, already on the move at dawn. The tall men, fine-boned and with large, vivid eyes, walked in a long line at the head of a technicolor cavalcade. They carried staffs and long throwing spears gripped firmly together in long-fingered brown hands. Behind them came fat-tailed sheep, and behind the sheep came goats and humpbacked cattle, with little boys, crackling with energy like a bush fire, urging them along. Behind the boys came camels, and the girls and women of the band sat on the camels like statues of uncrowned queens of history. They wore long gowns colored with bright vegetable dyes, of the kind in which the young Henri Matisse loved to pose his models.

I spent a day with these people, and at nightfall saw them approach a water hole in utter and terrifying uncertainty of what they might find there. This was their moment of greatest danger, for their enemies knew that they could not defend themselves while their cavalcade got the water it so badly needed before the quick darkness fell. When they saw the water already in possession of other men, I shared their suspicion and fear —and then their relief when they found that these were clans of kinsmen, also on the march. The life of these people was harsh and dangerous, yet not without delicacy and a noble hospitality. I drank camel's milk with them, and ate the hump of a camel superbly roasted on a wood fire. The scene might have been set 2,000 years before the birth of Christ.

A few days later I was back in Nairobi, at a hotel where I first stayed more than 40 years ago. I remembered a dinner I had eaten there in those remote days—an English meal unworthy of a second-rate boardinghouse. I remembered, too, how startled I was by a sudden clatter of horse's hooves and the sight of a woman on horseback bursting into the room. She was dressed in a khaki riding habit, with a leather belt round her

waist and a pistol in a holster at her hip. She took off her hat and threw it at the startled housekeeper in charge of the dining room, gave her horse to a frightened waiter to hold, and called for champagne all round. The champagne was tepid, but it was real, and to this day I remember the incident as a kind of allegory of the strange beginnings of Western "civilization" in this remote and beautiful land.

On my recent return to the hotel I had to shove my way to the reception desk, so crowded was the foyer with Greek, Mexican, Spanish and Italian tourists. They were due to start out in the morning, in minibuses painted in the zigzag patterns of a zebra skin, to stare goggle-eyed at the wild animals of the land. The two-storied building I knew 40 years before had grown into a miniskyscraper. The dining room was transformed out of all recognition, and I could get not one of the African foods I have mentioned, because the hotel was having a "French Week." Chefs, maîtres d' hôtel, waiters and pretty young Parisian guides and hostesses had been flown in from Paris for the occasion. I might have been dining in the Place Vendôme instead of in the heart of East Africa.

The extremes I have described express not only the paradoxes of a changing land, but the danger and the opportunity that confront African man on his road to a style of living and eating of his own. The danger, I hope and believe, will ultimately give way to the opportunity.

On the terrace of the Summit Restaurant, overlooking the harbor of Dar es Salaam, a waiter serves a well-to-do Tanzanian couple the final course of an elegant luncheon —a fresh coconut confection topped with a dome of meringue. The meal also included some of the superb local seafood dishes and a red wine produced in the nearby Congregation of the Passionist Fathers monastery in Dodoma.

Zanzibar Duck *(East Africa)*
BRAISED DUCK WITH ORANGE-AND-LIME SAUCE

To serve 4 to 6

A 5- to 5½-pound duck
¼ cup vegetable oil
2 cups chicken stock, fresh or
    canned
12 whole cloves
1 fresh hot chili, about 1½ to 2
    inches long, stemmed and seeded
    (caution: see page 76)
½ cup strained fresh orange juice
2 tablespoons strained fresh lime
    juice
½ cup finely chopped sweet bell
    pepper, preferably red
¼ teaspoon salt
Orange wedges or slices studded
    with whole cloves for garnish

Preheat the oven to 350°. Pat the duck completely dry inside and out with paper towels, and remove the large chunks of fat from the cavity. Cut off the loose neck skin and truss the bird securely, then prick the surface around the thighs, the back and the lower part of the breast with a skewer or the point of a sharp knife.

In a heavy 5- to 6-quart casserole, heat the oil over moderate heat until a light haze forms above it. Add the duck and, turning it frequently with a slotted spoon or tongs, cook for about 15 minutes, or until it browns richly on all sides. Transfer the duck to a plate and discard the fat remaining in the casserole. Pour in 1 cup of the chicken stock and bring to a boil over high heat, meanwhile scraping in any brown particles that cling to the bottom and sides of the pan. Stir in the cloves and chili, then return the duck and the liquids that have accumulated around it to the casserole.

Cover tightly and braise in the middle of the oven for 1 hour. Remove the duck to a plate, and with a large spoon skim as much fat as possible from the surface of the cooking liquid. Discard the cloves and chili.

Add the remaining cup of stock to the casserole and, stirring and scraping in the brown bits that cling to the pan, bring to a boil over high heat. Mix in the orange juice, lime juice, sweet bell pepper and salt. Return the duck to the casserole and baste it with the simmering sauce. Cover tightly and return the duck to the oven for about 15 minutes. To test for doneness, pierce the thigh of the bird with the point of a small, sharp knife. The juice should trickle out a clear yellow; if it is slightly pink, cook the bird for another 5 to 10 minutes.

Place the duck on a heated platter and pour the sauce over it. Garnish the platter with the orange wedges or slices and serve at once.

Steamed Papaya *(East Africa)*

To serve 4 to 6

1½ pounds underripe papaya,
    peeled, seeded and cut into
    ½-inch cubes
4 tablespoons butter
⅛ teaspoon ground nutmeg,
    preferably freshly grated
½ teaspoon salt

Pour enough boiling water into the lower part of a steamer to come to within 1 inch of the cooking rack (or make a steamer substitute with a supported plate as described in *yetemola cheguara, Recipe Index*). Spread the papaya cubes on the rack of the steamer or on top of the plate, and bring the water to the boil again. Cover the pan tightly and steam over moderate heat for 15 to 20 minutes. When the papaya is tender and somewhat translucent, transfer it to a sieve or colander to drain.

In a heavy 10- to 12-inch skillet, melt the butter over moderate heat. When the foam begins to subside, drop in the papaya and season it with the nutmeg and salt. Toss the papaya about gently with a spoon until it is evenly coated with the butter.

Serve at once from a heated bowl. Steamed papaya may be an accompaniment to Zanzibar duck *(above)* or other poultry, game or rich meats like lamb and pork.

An East African dish fit for a sultan, Zanzibar duck is braised in stock, seasoned with whole cloves and garnished with clove-studded orange wedges. Steamed papaya, flavored with nutmeg, accompanies the duck.

V

The World of Portuguese Africa

On their way home from
market, a group of
housewives pause before
the 16th Century Church
of the Misericórdia on
Mozambique Island. In
their baskets—and, in two
cases, on their heads—are
staples of the region:
cassava, sugar cane, coconuts,
watermelons and bananas.

Nowhere in Africa has the influence of a European culture been
so deep and tenacious as in Portugal's two huge possessions on the continent. Angola, on the west coast, is 14 times the size of Portugal; with
Mozambique, on the east coast, added to it, the Portuguese control nearly
800,000 square miles of Africa. Elsewhere on the continent, the European impact may have been more spectacular, but in its quiet way the Portuguese presence may have subtler consequences than any other.

Part of the reason for this may lie in the sheer persistence of the Portuguese. To begin with, they were the first Europeans to penetrate south of
the Sahara. With an urge that seemed strange, wasteful, even insane to
15th Century Europe, Prince Henry the Navigator year after year sent his
captains in their small ships to feel their way down the African west
coast. By 1483, Diogo Cam had set foot in the southern part of what is
now Angola. Five years later Bartholomeu Dias rounded what he called
the Cape of Storms. In 1497-1498 Vasco da Gama sailed past it (King
John II of Portugal immediately changed its name to the Cape of Good
Hope) and pressed on to India. Along the way he landed at several
points on the east coast of Africa, including the coral island of Mozambique, from which the present-day province takes its name; by 1510,
the Portuguese were firmly ashore there. In the centuries since, Portugal
has grown impoverished and militarily inconsequential, but it is still entrenched in Africa, while the great empires of the British, French and Germans have vanished.

Why did the weak and poor hang on after the proud and great de-

Like Mozambique *(opposite),* Angola is technically a province of Portugal rather than a colony. Covered for the most part by dry grassy savanna, the country has a great agricultural potential, which could be realized by extensive irrigation. The towns of Luanda, Dondo and Nova Lisboa are all Iberian in appearance and style; their restaurants serve Portuguese-inspired food almost exclusively.

parted? They stayed because of a dogged belief in themselves. There is something in the Portuguese that makes it impossible for them to stop doing something they have once begun. I saw a striking example of this trait on a recent visit to Baia dos Tigres in the extreme south of Angola. This excellent natural harbor would have been developed long ago had there been an inland region to justify development, but there is nothing behind the Baia dos Tigres but the great Namib Desert. Wind drives the Namib sands over the dunes on the shore like spume and vapor over a sea of earth. No trees, fruits or vegetables will grow around the bay, except in tubs; until recently, water was brought in by sea. Yet for a century a group of fishermen from the Algarve, the southernmost province of Portugal, have lived there. It has never occurred to these men to abandon their barren settlement. When I asked if they ever hankered to go to Portugal or to visit the cities of Angola itself, they looked at me as if I was mad. They seemed, in fact, as contented as any people I have ever known.

The captains who began the Portuguese adventure overseas may have been violent, cruel and rapacious; the men who carried on were the humble of Portugal. The overlords and overseers may have represented a remote government, corrupted by power and impelled by greed, but most of the settlers themselves were helpless and poor. There was, I think, little social distance between them and many of the Africans, and from the start this nearness produced an absence of color prejudice. This fact helps to explain their continued presence in Africa. And the will to remain has been reinforced by the Portuguese policy of governing their overseas possessions as integral parts of Portugal. They speak of Angola and Mozambique not as colonies but as provinces of the motherland.

It was Portuguese initiative that created some of the greatest revolutions in African food and cooking. Indigenous man in the Portuguese empire, like his counterparts elsewhere, apparently had little to offer the newcomers in the way of food. His own ideas of cooking, particularly in Angola, resembled those of the peoples of East Africa. Like theirs, his was a largely pastoral economy. Cattle and sheep were currency; meat was rarely eaten; milk, curds and whey, and cereals formed the main diet. At the same time, this indigenous man supplemented his diet by gleaning bush and jungle, plain and desert for fruits and vegetables, and in the process he became a remarkable natural botanist.

Two recent experiences of my own attest to this fact. In the mountain clefts and gorges of the Mozambique highlands I found Africans harvesting what I can only describe as a sort of tree tomato. In its shape and orange color it looked more like an unwrinkled passion fruit than a tomato, but it tasted more of the tomato than anything else—a pagan and unrepentantly savage tomato, fierce and vivid in flavor. My imagination was instantly excited by what could be done to so ardent a vegetable with selective cultivation and judicious grafting. It could even rescue the tomato from being the tame foodstuff that it so often is on our tables today.

A fortnight later, in the north of Angola, I encountered some African coffee farmers coming in from the bush for their noonday meal. They all carried branches thickly clustered with at least three different kinds of golden fruit. When I asked if I could taste them, I was immediately given

114

more fruit than my hands could hold. All the varieties were delicious and of a unique savor, cutting through my thirst, particularly on that hot day, like a knife. One of the fruits could well have been a member of the mango family; all of them, if taken seriously and developed scientifically, could become authentic African additions to the tables of the world.

In neither case could the official who accompanied me give me the botanical or even the local name of these happy discoveries. Historically, none of the European invaders of Africa have ever taken as much interest in the potentialities of the African earth as of the minerals below it. But the Portuguese, though they failed to exploit indigenous alternatives to their own foods, did the next best thing. From lands with similar climates and soils they imported an amazing variety of vegetables and fruits. It is in this respect that Portuguese influence on the food of Africa has been strongest, extending far beyond the areas under their control.

A noted contemporary traveler and observer, Sir Harry Johnston, is worth quoting on the Portuguese contribution in this regard. Harry Johnston knew his Africa as few others have, and he was a devoted historian of food. In one of his books, he says: "So early in the history of their African exploration that it is almost the first step they took, the Portuguese brought from China, India and Malaysia, the orange tree, the lemon and the lime which . . . they planted in every part of East and West Africa. From their great possession of Brazil, overrun and organized with astounding rapidity, they brought to East and West Africa, the Muscovy duck . . . chilies, peppers, maize, tobacco, the tomato, pineapple, sweet potato, manioc from which tapioca is made, and other less known forms of vegetable food. [He could have added that the Portuguese also imported the banana.] The Portuguese also introduced the domestic pig into Africa and on the West Coast the domestic cat, possibly also certain breeds of dogs. The Englishman has brought with him the potato and has introduced into most of the colonies the horse, and in places improved breeds of cattle, sheep and goats, a good many European vegetables and fruit trees, the tea plant, the coffee plant (which has however only been transported from other parts of Africa) and many shrubs and trees of special economic value, but what are these introductions—almost entirely for his own use—compared in value with the vast bounty of the Portuguese?"

In short, it was the Portuguese, with their gardeners' souls and their capacity to endure, who led an entire continent into a new range of food. In the process, they created two distinctive styles of cooking. One is South American in origin, more specifically Brazilian, and is most evident in Angola. The other, which prevails in Mozambique, reflects the Portuguese experiences of the East, from Arabian outposts in Zanzibar to India and China. The two styles of cooking borrowed freely from one another, yet to this day they retain nuances of their own.

In Angola's original capital, Luanda, life was once like life in a Brazilian city. A Brazilian dialect was favored over the pure Portuguese of the motherland, and one historian reported that Angolan ladies were Brazilian in their "ostentation and indolence." They and their menfolk were everywhere accompanied by a mass of slaves, for slaves and slavery set

Lying on the Indian Ocean just south of Tanzania, Mozambique has proved relatively inhospitable to European settlement. The Portuguese administer it, however, and their influence is felt in the coastal cities. Moreover, like much of the East African coast, Mozambique reflects contacts with Arab merchants and slave traders who brought with them the spicy cooking styles of the East.

the tone of the place. The slave traders shrewdly culled Angola for the best of the indigenous population, creating a scarcity of manpower that still afflicts the country.

I first went to Angola before World War II. On my last visit there, only a few months ago, I hardly recognized the country. For centuries it consisted of little more than a few ports linked to fortified outposts and trading posts in the interior. Now it looks like one of the most purposeful parts of Africa. No area of the continent has changed so dramatically in my own lifetime. Deposits of oil have been discovered and others are being found over an ever wider area. Broad roads have been built where there were no roads before. A policy of settlement by new immigrants from Portugal is being zealously pursued.

To be sure, only a fraction of Angola's ultimate potential has been realized as yet. For one thing, the country still has one of the lowest population densities in Africa. (A Portuguese statistician despairingly wrote of one of the most promising districts: "There is only half an inhabitant per square kilometer.") Angola also has the greatest reserves of unused land in all of Africa. Beyond its coastal belt, it soars in a series of plateaus to highlands of great beauty, where anything can be grown.

A growing awareness of Angola's resources is reflected in the eating habits of both the new Portuguese and the indigenous inhabitants of the land. There are, of course, vast, remote areas where indigenous man still tends to live as he did of old. The milk of cows and goats remains part of the basic diet, still churned in gourds and eaten with great quantities of *funge,* the Angolan version of the cassava-flour porridges of West Africa, the *posho* of East Africa and the mealie-meal porridge of Zululand. Yet on a journey in the interior I noticed that while curds and whey were eaten in the morning, smoked fish imported from the coast would be eaten at nightfall. Other changes are on the way, for there is hardly a man in the interior who has not had some experience of a Westernized diet on plantations or in towns. *Funge* is increasingly displaced by bread, and the Portuguese everywhere make excellent bread. I found that even in the smallest outpost the early-morning air would be filled with the wonderful smell of bread from the oven of some small bakery or inn, and one was automatically served, along with the delicious Angolan coffee, rolls that were still warm from the baking. I would not have exchanged them for the best of Parisian *croissants.*

The most notable changes in eating habits, however, have taken place among the Portuguese themselves, particularly in Angola's cities and larger settlements. Ten years ago the food in the better hotels and restaurants was mediocre; one ate well at the homes of high officials and the richest merchants, but nowhere else. Today it is different. Almost everywhere one goes, there are hotels or inns that serve the traveler well, and one can eat superbly at the homes of new Portuguese totally committed to living in Angola. Of the thousands of these recent arrivals, many are young men who first knew the country as military conscripts sent out from Portugal, and who found on their return home that they had fallen in love with Africa. In the highlands of the far northern interior, for instance, I met a young Portuguese who was starting a local newspaper. When I asked him why he was there, he said simply: "When I went back to Portugal after my army service, I found I was no longer happy to be just a European man. Africa had made me into something different—half Portuguese, half African—and I thought I could make the two into one only by coming to live in Angola." He had so practiced what he preached that he married a charming lady of the country.

In this couple's home I ate food that owed as much to Africa as to Portugal. I remember a noonday meal of prawns that had been caught by local fishermen in a nearby river. The prawns were browned with diced onions in a mixture of butter and olive oil (the olive tree, too, has found its way from Portugal to Angola), then were simmered in a mixture of coconut milk, tomatoes, chopped red chilies, black pepper and ginger. Meanwhile, the meat of the coconut was pounded in a mortar, salted, and mounded on a plate with parsley and lettuce. Two minutes before serving, the prawn mixture was laced with a glass of dry Madeira wine, and was then poured over the mound on the plate and served with rice. Later I ate a variant of the same dish at a hotel in Lobito, in the south; the prawn mixture was served in the coconut shells themselves, brandy was poured over it and, in the inevitable style of modern headwaiters, set alight before serving. Of the two, I preferred the version of the interior.

At a dinner at this same couple's house I relished an excellent chicken dish in Angola's great *muamba* style, cut up and cooked with thick palm oil, garlic, onion, hot red peppers, okra, pumpkin and sweet-potato leaves. The secret of the dish, I learned, was to cook it very slowly over a low fire so that the liquid of the pumpkin both helped to stew the sweet-potato leaves and blended with all the other ingredients. On this occasion we also had a Mozambique-style papaya dessert called *ovos moles de papaia (Recipe Index)*, sweet enough for the sweetest tooth, yet not so sweet that all other nuances of taste were suppressed. For this dish the papaya was puréed and blended with an equal quantity of sugar and a stick of cinnamon. The mixture was simmered until the juice dropping from a wooden spoon dipped into it started to thread. Then the whisked yolks of a dozen eggs were added to the saucepan and constantly stirred over the slowest of fires until the mixture began to thicken. It was served with the heady addition of powdered cinnamon.

We capped our meal with Angolan coffee, and until that evening I had never realized how good it was. Indeed, I had not realized how seriously the Portuguese in Africa took their coffee or how well they grew it. (It was very remiss of me, for there was always the stupendous Brazilian example to enlighten me.) In any case, it had never occurred to me that here in the far northern interior of Angola I would discover a coffee flavor to rival the best. Conventionally enough, the beans were roasted and ground fresh in a little cast-iron hand mill just before the making. What was novel to me, however, was that the ground coffee was suspended in a muslin bag down the inside of an ordinary enameled coffee-pot. Freshly boiled water—my hostess stressed the point that the water had to be used the moment it boiled—was slowly poured straight into the enameled pot until it was two thirds full. The pot was then placed on a low fire and the liquid poured out of it, strained, and repeatedly passed through the muslin bag without being allowed to boil again. The result was triumphant, but this was not the cause of my amazement; it was that the method was precisely the one we follow in the interior of southern Africa. I had always thought of it as an original South African technique, but now I realized that in its small way it was eloquent testimony of how much all of Africa owes to Portuguese ways of eating.

So seriously do the Portuguese in Africa take their coffee that they tend to judge hotels, restaurants and even a wife's housekeeping in terms of coffee making alone. I was told in all earnestness that no matter how good a hotel's service might be or how comfortable its accommodations it was to be avoided if its coffee was bad. I had this in mind when I visited some of the most beautiful coffee plantations I have ever seen, those of Uige in northern Angola. Deep in the forests in which the coffee is cultivated (the best coffee must have plenty of shade) one has the feeling of being in a kind of coffee cathedral, so dedicated, tall and solemn are the trees. I would enter the forests straight from the white heat of the tropical day and walk down long aisles between lofty pillars of trees that threw Gothic arches of shade over a vast congregation of coffee bushes. At the time I thought that the efficiency and order of Uige might be exceptional, but later I saw the same degree of meticulous cultivation in other coffee areas in the highlands and toward the south.

I remember a noonday dinner with the energetic governor of Uige at his unpretentious villa, unguarded and open to informal callers throughout the day. We began again with prawns, on this occasion flown in from the sea, and a good deal larger and fleshier than those I had eaten from the fresh water of a river. They had been grilled on thin bamboo skewers over a charcoal fire and basted with a sauce of oil, lemon juice, garlic, salt and crushed peppers. A bowl of the sauce and the drippings accompanied the prawns so that one could reflavor them while eating. This dish was followed by a main course of marinated and fried pork with an accompanying dish of extraordinary yellow rice. The rice had been browned in olive oil, then cooked in a thick cast-iron skillet along with saffron and a stock made from the blood of a pig. The meal ended with slices of fresh pineapple covered with pomegranate juice and sweetened with brown Angolan sugar, a touch of cinnamon and a dash of port wine.

To complete my report on Angolan food, I must describe each dish in its own particular setting, for looking back on my last visit there, I find that food and place are intertwined in my memory. For instance, there was the old interior city of Dondo, once the hub of a thriving trade in coffee, palm oil, peanuts, rubber, ivory and hides. The Portuguese concept of a city calls for a square with public gardens, and Dondo has them, with dazzling flower beds, a little bandstand in the center and a rim of faded 17th Century houses all around. I think of Dondo and at once remember a good honest dinner dish I had there—a dish of mutton, pot-roasted and finished off in a sauce of the sheep's own blood, and served with white rice dotted with chopped red peppers.

There was also Nova Lisboa, with its solidly built houses and tree-lined avenues. I remember thinking I had never seen a town with so many umbrellas, because the rain came down almost every afternoon so regularly that one could set one's watch by it. The sun would come out after the rain and start the landscape steaming, but the night would be cool and damp. I recall how grateful I was for a hotpot that contained meat, blood sausages, bacon, chicken, sweet potatoes, white potatoes, carrots, cabbage and beans.

Luanda, the capital of Angola, was memorable for many dishes but above all for a chicken *muamba* I had in the splendid dining room of the Hotel Continental, with artichoke leaves instead of the sweet-potato leaves of the similar dish I had in the far interior. I would begin my dinners in Luanda with papayas, the largest I have ever seen in Africa, with flesh of so deep an orange that it touched on being red, and a flavor of the most delicate sweetness. I would eat the fruit with the juice of an Angolan lime, sweetened by a few drops of port. There were first-rate restaurants in Luanda, such as the Club Naval, with its view over the harbor and a choice of crustaceans and fish to be found nowhere else in the continent. I especially remember the club for a fine *açorda* soup, a combination of cooked shrimp, eggs, tomatoes and bread, seasoned with fresh coriander, red pepper and garlic. The shrimp were browned in oil and garlic and simmered in a stock made with the shells of shrimp and the heads of fish. Then the stock was strained and the liquid joined with the other ingredients; the eggs were poached in this soup and served with another sprinkling of coriander, surrounded by hot cooked shrimp.

One of my most enduring memories of Angolan food is linked with the town of Sá da Bandeira in the melodramatically beautiful highlands of southern Angola, where the escarpments rise like a bravura aria of operatic earth straight out of deserts to the south. The area was developed nearly a century ago by people from the island of Madeira, off Africa's northwest coast. They began their life on the mainland in grass huts. For the pigs and cattle they brought with them they built enclosures to guard against lions and leopards. They built irrigation channels in strict geometric patterns, certain that one day they would have a town with a square and gardens at its heart. They planted the vegetables, the fruit trees and the flowers they had brought from Madeira, and in time created gardens that were copies of those they had left behind. They even sent back home for an image of the Virgin, so that in a cleft of a rock that resembled one of the foothills of Madeira they could have a shrine to which they could make pilgrimages. Now, on feast days, a band plays in the square of Sá da Bandeira, and people swim in one of the most beautiful pools in the world, made from a natural lake and surrounded by terraces of flowers and trees. The odds had all been against the survival of these people, but in fact they have built a bustling city surrounded by green settlements.

The meat dish that goes with this memory is not of pork or beef, but of goat. The goat was always neglected in French and British Africa, but the Portuguese brought with them the respect that cooks of the Iberian peninsula have always had for this Pan-like creature. In Sá da Bandeira it is cooked in several ways, but when I had it as my main dish on my last night there, it was made of the meat of the youngest of kids, cut in slices. A layer of meat is placed in a cast-iron pot on a bed of bacon, onions, bay leaves, garlic, cloves and powdered red chilies, all sautéed in lard. The same mixture is then placed over the layer of kid, and the process is repeated until the pot is full. In the hotel, dry white Madeira was poured over the top; but farmers of the area find this too costly an indulgence, and instead use ordinary dry Portuguese wine for the purpose. In both cases, the stew is covered and simmered slowly over a low flame until tender. Meanwhile, potatoes are boiled, allowed to cool, cut in slices and added to the stew just long enough for them to heat before serving.

I had the best version of this dish not in my hotel but at the home of a local farmer. The house was small, square and clean, with a roof of red tiles. It had a kitchen that also served as a sitting room, because in the winter and at night it turns cold in these highlands. But it also had a parlor, used only for visitors, with a small square table covered by a homemade crocheted cloth, and with waxed and polished chairs. Family portraits hung on the wall, along with a calendar of feast days and a lithograph of Christ on the Cross. In these modest surroundings I was treated like an emperor and felt like one, particularly when to my surprise the meal was crowned with a dish of fresh strawberries—strawberries not flown from Europe but grown in the soil of Angola, their savor positive and uplifting, to fit the character of their native earth.

Mozambique is farther from Portugal than Angola, but it is in some ways closer psychologically. For one thing, it has received more attention from Portugal than Angola has. For another, it possesses the finest harbors on the east coast of Africa. This coast made Mozambique a natural outlet for the interior lands that were developed by the Dutch and British in southern Africa. Through its capital of Lourenço Marques, linked by rail to Pretoria, and through Beira, the principal port for Malawi and Rhodesia, it kept pace with progress in a way that Angola never did. Moreover, its lovely coastline and its yellow sand beaches became a favorite holiday playground for Europeans of the interior. At the same time, it retained close ties with the Far East; thousands of immigrants from the former Portuguese province of Goa, on the coast of India, settled in Mozambique, adding a permanent Indian element to the culture of the province.

Geographically, Mozambique lacks the vast healthy highlands of Angola. Most of it is comparatively low-lying country, haunted for centuries by fever and sleeping sickness; its climate is more intensely tropical, its agriculture and animal husbandry totally different. Only in the northwest are there plateaus and mountains on the Angolan scale, above all in purple, cloud-scraping peaks on the eastern shores of Lake Nyasa. The Portuguese have not settled Mozambique on the same scale as Angola, and the pattern of life is far more traditionally colonial than in Angola.

Mozambican cooking reflects these factors. Usually the traveler is presented with food that is no more than a pale, vapid reflection of international cuisine. But there is one notable exception: the so-called *piripiri,* or hot-pepper dishes, utilizing the tiny, ferocious peppers of Mozambique. *Piripiri* is Mozambique's national favorite, and its major contribution to the art of cooking in Portuguese Africa. Though it has spread as far as Portugal itself, it is nowhere so constantly and ardently

Opposite: Morning mist blankets one of the coconut groves near Quelimane as a herd of long-horned cattle ambles placidly toward pasture. A city on the Mozambique coast just north of the mouth of the Zambezi River, Quelimane was a famous slave trading center well into the 19th Century; today its major business is coconut farming.

On a quiet Sunday morning a brother and sister peddle *doce de coco*—coconut candy—through the streets of Mozambique Island. In the square behind them stands a statue of Vasco da Gama, the great 15th Century Portuguese explorer who found an all-water route from Europe to India and in the process colonized this little coral outcropping. From here the Portuguese extended their power over all the mainland region that is now called Mozambique.

eaten as in Mozambique, particularly in Beira and Lourenço Marques, where *piripiri* feasts—or *piripiri* orgies—are regularly organized for holidaymakers from the interior.

It is difficult to say which city is best at *piripiri*. On the whole, I think I would choose Lourenço Marques, though my choice may also be influenced by the setting. This clean, well-ordered city glories in flamelike plants and flowering trees that seem to go with the taste of *piripiri*. There are the flamboyants, which make even the tropical sunlight look pale, and the jacaranda, brought by the Portuguese from Brazil along with the *piripiri* chilies themselves. Somehow, such plants prepare one's senses for a meal based on their fierce fellow traveler from South America.

After a day of swimming from one of the beaches or sailing along a coast with fringes of feathered palm, a lover of *piripiri* hungers for it like an addict for his heroin. I truly believe that a person who acquires a taste for the chilies of Africa, as for the curries of India or the spices of the Orient, becomes a kind of addict. My French and Chinese friends sometimes tell me that *piripiri* and spice cooking are ruinous to a sensitive palate, and boast that they have created the world's two reigning academies of cuisine without recourse to such extremes of the kitchen. I can only say that as a result of eating these dishes in the context of their own cultures and climates my admiration for them has increased over the years. And many gourmets must share my feelings, for restaurants and hotels like Mozambique's great Polana, which is a sort of Shepheard's Hotel of Portuguese Africa, are always full of *piripiri* voluptuaries.

Every Mozambican cook has her own way of preparing a *piripiri* sauce. One housewife of Lourenço Marques begins by sieving lemon juice, warming it in a pan, and adding red, freshly picked chilies. The mixture is simmered on a low fire for exactly five minutes, then the peppers are removed, salted and pounded to a smooth paste. This pulp is returned to the pan with the original lemon juice and simmered for a while longer. This sauce can be eaten over steak, mutton, fowl, fish and shellfish, preferably with rice of some kind to provide the civilized corrective to the pagan incitement of the sauce.

On my last visit to Lourenço Marques I asked the chef at the Polana what he considers the best subject for *piripiri*. He answered without any hesitation: shrimp, prawns and chicken. To make his own grilled shrimp (for an alternate recipe, see broiled marinated shrimp, *Recipe Index*), he uses four crushed peppers to four pounds of shrimp, the juice of one lemon, a cup of butter or oil and four sprigs of chopped parsley. He cuts open the shrimp lengthwise and rubs them well with salt and the crushed peppers, then grills them over a charcoal fire, and serves them with a dip of melted butter, more lemon juice and parsley. For a spring chicken he uses peppers, lemon juice and parsley, much as for the shrimp, but he also uses two cups of coconut butter. He splits, seasons and grills the chicken like the shrimp, but while the chicken turns on its spit he bastes it continually with half the coconut butter. When it is done he serves it with a sauce made from the rest of the butter and some lemon juice and chopped parsley. On one occasion he sent this dish to my table with fried potatoes and a salad. I protested against the fried potatoes and pleaded for the

fluffy rice they cook so well in Mozambique. The chef shrugged and exclaimed: "What can I do? I would much rather serve the rice, because I am an artist—but your countrymen from the interior get homesick if I give them anything without fried potatoes!"

On cool, damp nights in the highlands of Angola, I had been confronted by elaborate hotpots at dinner; on much warmer nights along the coast of Mozambique seafood hotpots were equally common. Again, recipes vary delightfully though slightly from place to place, but the minimum requirements include fresh sweet peppers, powdered chilies, tomato, onion, fresh coriander, fresh filleted fish and shelled prawns or shrimp, coconut milk, some olive oil, salt and peanut oil. Long ago, at Vila Cabral in the great mountains near the edge of Lake Nyasa, I had a hotpot of lake fish and, instead of fresh shrimp or prawns, cured and smoked ones shipped from the coast; and in some way these ingredients gave the dish more savor than their cousins of the sophisticated ports. For both dishes, the peppers, chilies, coriander, onion and tomato, with salt and olive oil added, are chopped up together. The fish and shrimp or prawns are salted and peppered, then placed in a layer at the bottom of a casserole, the vegetable mixture is put on top of it, and the seafood and mixture are laid down alternately until the casserole is full. The coconut milk is then poured over all these ingredients and the casserole is cooked in a moderate oven. When the dish is done, the peanut oil is warmed in a saucepan and poured over it, and the whole is eaten with a plain rice.

Mozambique also has its own equivalents of the shrimp fritters of Angola, a kind of shrimp popover that illustrates the differences between

Bearing a cluster of plantains on her head, a woman passes a fleet of fishing boats at a sun-dappled beach on Mozambique Island. Beyond the water—and looking quite unmilitary—gleam the whitewashed barracks of Fort Saint Anthony.

these two styles of cooking. In the Mozambican dish the spices of the East figure far more prominently than in the fritters of Angola. Not only garlic, parsley and onions, but also mint, cinnamon, cloves, saffron, coriander, cumin and red peppers give the dish its characteristic flavor. The shrimp are first mixed with all the seasonings except the cinnamon. Diced onions are browned in peanut oil, and the seasoned shrimp are added and sautéed. They are then taken from the fire and mixed with the cinnamon and more diced onions. Meanwhile, circles of thin pastry are prepared. These are filled with the shrimp mixture, folded over and secured with the thinnest of bamboo skewers, then deep-fried in peanut oil until they are crisp and brown. Accompanied by a salad, this was one of my favorite Mozambican dishes.

In the hot and feverish valley of the Zambezi River, where chicken is a common substitute for meat, there is an unexpectedly delicate and tasteful way of grilling it. The chicken is cut up, rubbed with salt, pepper, garlic and chili powder, and marinated in lemon juice. Coconut milk and olive oil are poured into a heavy cast-iron pot, the chicken pieces are added, a tight-fitting lid is placed in position, and the whole is slowly pot-roasted. For *galinha cafreal à zambeziana (Recipe Index)* the marinated chicken is simply grilled over a fire of wood coals, but the same mixture of coconut milk and oil is used to baste it; the drippings are used again and again in the basting, and are finally served as a sauce. I have had this dish with sweet potatoes baked in their jackets and thought the combination especially successful.

Mozambique is a growing producer of cashew nuts, and in some ways chicken with cashew nuts *(Recipe Index)* is to Mozambique what chicken *muamba* is to Angola. Since Mozambican chickens, like their cousins farther north, tend to be marathon runners, the chicken is often parboiled with fresh lime juice and an onion studded with cloves. Peanut oil is heated in a frying pan and the parboiled chicken is cut up and fried to a golden brown. At this moment shelled cashew nuts and coconut milk are added to the stock, the stock is poured over the chicken, and the chicken simmered until it is cooked; the whole is served with plain boiled rice.

Thanks to the link with the Far East, curry plays a substantial role in the cooking of Mozambique. To my mind, most of the many variations that are served are either straightforward derivatives of the curries of India or pale imitations of those of South Africa, particularly Natal. Yet I have eaten both superb curries and rice in its most original forms on the island of Mozambique. I especially remember a coconut rice *(see arroz de coco, Recipe Index)* flavored with onion, tomatoes and fresh red peppers. The onions and tomatoes were cooked in peanut oil until the onion was brown; the rice was cooked in double its own quantity of coconut milk, and the onions, tomatoes and peppers were stirred into the rice before serving. Not long ago I had this form of rice with some fish fresh from the coral sea around the island. The fish was barbecued, scales and all, and basted with a sauce made with finely chopped onion, a touch of garlic, fresh lemon juice and thick peanut oil. An intriguing follow-up to this dish was a dessert made from peanuts, egg yolks, sugar and cinnamon. The sugar for the sweet was dissolved over a low fire in just

enough water to make a smooth syrup. It was then removed from the heat, the other ingredients were stirred in carefully, and the mixture was returned to the heat and stirred constantly until it thickened; it was served with a sprinkling of powdered cinnamon.

Like the food of Angola, this sort of food must be thought of in its own setting, and there is no setting quite like Mozambique Island. Since I first saw it from the deck of a Japanese tramp steamer, it has developed enormously, but a fortress built by the Portuguese at the beginning of the 16th Century still dominates the shining shore and its fringe of palm. There are still many of the old Portuguese houses left, and I have one in particular in mind: a faded pink house of beautiful proportions, with a graceful curving gable on its roof. Down at the Cape of Good Hope we think of the curving gable that graces so many old Dutch and Huguenot houses as our own invention. But here it was in Mozambique, a mute symbol of the intermingling and interdependence of our histories and cultures in their African beginnings. I think of this building on the island of Mozambique as a sort of border station, where I can cross the frontier between the world of Portuguese Africa and my native world to the south.

Piri-piri is an African term both for chilies and for a ubiquitous dish of broiled shrimp or prawns marinated or basted with a hot chili sauce *(Recipe Index)*. In Mozambique, where the dish is widely known and enjoyed, the seafoods of choice are the huge prawns of Africa's east coast, usually grilled over an outdoor fire and served as shown here with lemon butter.

To serve 4

1 pound uncooked medium-sized
    shrimp (about 21 to 25 to the
    pound)
8 four-ounce sea bass or red snapper
    steaks, about 1 inch thick
1½ teaspoons salt
3 tablespoons olive oil
1½ cups finely chopped onions
2 medium-sized bell peppers,
    seeded, deribbed and finely
    chopped
2 medium-sized firm ripe tomatoes,
    peeled, seeded and finely chopped
    (see diced tomato salad, page
    84), or substitute ⅔ cup
    chopped drained canned tomatoes
1 tablespoon finely chopped fresh
    coriander
1 teaspoon crumbled dried hot red
    chilies (caution: see page 76)
½ cup fresh coconut milk made
    from ½ cup coarsely chopped
    coconut and ½ cup hot water
    (see Recipe Booklet)

To serve 4

2 tablespoons peanut or vegetable
    oil
½ cup finely chopped onions
1 small bell pepper, seeded,
    deribbed and finely chopped
1 cup uncooked long-grain white
    rice
1½ cups fresh coconut milk made
    from 1½ cups coarsely chopped
    coconut and 1½ cups hot water
    (see Recipe Booklet)
2 medium-sized firm ripe tomatoes,
    peeled, seeded and finely chopped
    (see diced tomato salad, page
    84), or substitute ⅔ cup
    chopped drained canned tomatoes
1 teaspoon salt
2 teaspoons finely chopped fresh hot
    chilies (caution: see page 76)

Peixe à Lumbo (Mozambique)
FISH-AND-SHRIMP STEW

Shell the shrimp. Devein them by making a shallow incision down their backs with a small, sharp knife and lifting out the black or white intestinal vein with the point of the knife. Wash the shrimp under cold running water and pat them dry with paper towels. Pat the fish steaks dry and sprinkle them on both sides with ½ teaspoon of the salt. Set the shrimp and fish aside.

In a heavy 10- to 12-inch skillet, heat the olive oil over moderate heat until a light haze forms above it. Drop in the onions and peppers and, stirring frequently, cook for about 5 minutes, until they are soft but not brown. Watch carefully for any sign of burning and regulate the heat accordingly. Add the tomatoes and, stirring frequently, cook briskly until most of the liquid in the pan evaporates and the mixture is thick enough to hold its shape almost solidly in a spoon. Remove the pan from the heat, then stir in the coriander, chilies and the remaining teaspoon of salt, and taste for seasoning.

Arrange 4 of the fish steaks in a heavy saucepan large enough to hold them in one layer. Scatter half of the shrimp over and around the fish and spoon half the vegetable mixture over them. Add the remaining fish steaks and shrimp, and cover them with the rest of the vegetables.

Pour in the coconut milk and bring to a simmer over moderate heat. Reduce the heat to its lowest point. Cook partially covered for about 10 to 12 minutes, or until the shrimp are firm and pink and the fish flakes easily when prodded gently with a fork.

To serve, transfer the entire contents of the saucepan to a deep heated platter or bowl. Peixe à Lumbo may be accompanied by arroz de coco (below) or hot boiled rice.

Arroz de Coco (Mozambique)
RICE WITH TOMATOES, CHILIES AND COCONUT MILK

In a heavy 10- to 12-inch skillet, heat the oil over moderate heat until a light haze forms above it. Drop in the onions and bell pepper and, stirring frequently, cook for about 5 minutes, or until they are soft but not brown. Watch carefully for any sign of burning and regulate the heat accordingly. Add the rice and stir for 2 or 3 minutes, until the grains are evenly coated. Then stir in the coconut milk, tomatoes and salt, and bring to a simmer over moderate heat.

Cover the pan tightly, reduce the heat to its lowest point, and simmer for about 20 minutes, or until all the liquid has been absorbed and the rice is tender but still slightly resistant to the bite. Remove the pan from the heat, stir in the chilies, and taste for seasoning. Cover again and let the rice rest at room temperature for about 10 minutes before serving.

Serve the rice directly from the skillet or mounded in a heated bowl. Just before serving, fluff the arroz de coco with a fork.

Milk extracted from coconut meat adds richness to such seafood dishes as a delicate fish-and-shrimp stew (foreground) with coconut rice.

Ovos Moles de Papaia (Mozambique)
PAPAYA-AND-EGG YOLK PUDDING

To serve 4

Combine the papaya, lime or lemon juice, and water in the jar of an electric blender and blend at high speed for about 30 seconds. Turn off the machine, scrape down the sides of the jar with a rubber spatula, and blend again until the mixture is a smooth purée. With the back of a spoon, rub the purée through a fine sieve into a 2- to 3-quart enameled or stainless-steel saucepan.

Mix in the sugar, cinnamon stick and cloves and, stirring constantly, bring to a boil over high heat. Stirring occasionally, cook briskly until the syrup reaches a temperature of 230° on a candy thermometer or a few drops spooned into cold water immediately form coarse threads. Remove the pan from the heat and, with a slotted spoon, remove and discard the cinnamon and cloves.

In a deep bowl, beat the egg yolks with a wire whisk or a rotary or electric beater for about 1 minute, or until the yolks thicken slightly. Beating constantly, pour the hot syrup into the yolks in a thin stream and continue to beat until the mixture is smooth and thick and is a bright, deep yellow color.

Divide the mixture among four 4-ounce heatproof dessert dishes and cool to room temperature. The dessert will thicken further as it cools. Serve at once, or refrigerate for at least 2 hours and serve the *ovos moles de papaia* chilled.

1 medium-sized ripe papaya (1 to
    1½ pounds), peeled, seeded and
    coarsely chopped
¼ cup strained fresh lime or lemon
    juice
¼ cup water
2 cups sugar
1 piece of stick cinnamon, 3 inches
    long
4 whole cloves
5 egg yolks

Cocada Amarela (Angola)
YELLOW COCONUT PUDDING

To serve 8

Combine the sugar, water and cloves in a 4- to 5-quart saucepan. Stirring constantly, bring the mixture to a boil. Then continue to boil briskly without stirring until the syrup reaches a temperature of 230° on a candy thermometer, or a few drops spooned into cold water immediately form coarse threads.

Reduce the heat to low and with a slotted spoon remove and discard the cloves. Add the coconut, 1 cup at a time, stirring well after each addition. Continue to cook, stirring frequently, for about 10 minutes, or until the coconut becomes translucent. Remove the pan from the heat.

In a deep bowl beat the egg yolks with a wire whisk or a rotary or electric beater for about 1 minute. When they thicken slightly, stir in 1 cup of the coconut syrup, then pour the mixture into the remaining syrup and stir together thoroughly.

Stirring almost constantly, cook over moderate heat for about 10 minutes longer, or until the pudding thickens enough to pull away from the bottom and sides of the pan in a solid mass.

Pour the pudding into a large heatproof platter at least 1 inch deep, or into 8 individual dessert dishes.

Serve the *cocada amarela* at room temperature or refrigerate the pudding for about 2 hours to chill it thoroughly. Just before serving, sprinkle the top lightly with ground cinnamon.

2 cups sugar
6 cups water
4 whole cloves
4 cups finely grated fresh coconut
    (*see Recipe Booklet*)
12 egg yolks
Ground cinnamon

African nuts and fruits lend distinctive touches to three desserts: a
cake containing chopped cashews *(foreground)*, a yellow coconut pudding
(center) and a papaya pudding *(top)*. The drink is hot chocolate.

VI

East and West Meet at the Cape

I do not know what the Portuguese called the mountain. They were the first Europeans to see it, looming over the Cape of Good Hope, but they may not have given it a name. At the time they were wholly absorbed by the fact that they had rounded one of the southernmost tips of Africa and found a new way to the East. With their minds aimed eastward, they remained curiously impervious to the attractions of the Cape itself.

It remained for the Dutch to see the possibilities of the place. Like the Portuguese, the Dutch made long voyages to the Far East—voyages that often lasted six months or more. By 1620 sailors of the Dutch East India Company were anchoring regularly at the Cape to refill their water barrels and search the countryside for fresh green vegetables. Gradually the idea came to them that this land, almost exactly halfway to their outposts in the Far East, might be ideal for raising vegetables and meat animals to revictual their ships. In 1651 the Dutch made a vital decision: to establish a settlement at the Cape—but a settlement with a difference. It was not to be a colony; its only purpose was to be to produce food for Dutch ships sailing between Europe and the East.

The Dutch have always been a food-conscious people who have known how to cook and eat well. It is probably no accident that they came to call the mountain that dominates the Cape of Good Hope "Table Mountain." The long summit of the mountain looks as flat as a table top; a white cloud often drapes itself around the precipitous slopes like an overhanging sheet of white linen. To the food-loving Dutch the temptation must have been irresistible: they called the cloud the tablecloth of Table

Mountain. In their homely way, the names symbolize all that was involved at the beginning of the first European settlement at the Cape, for the necessities and the obsession all had to do with food. It is not surprising that the richest, most complex and civilized contribution to the art of cooking in Africa evolved here.

The Cape country was peculiarly suited to make that contribution. It lay well within the temperate zone of the southern hemisphere, with the soil, the climate and the rainfall to grow anything that could be grown in Europe. Equally important, its halfway position between Europe and the East gave it access both to the cultures of the West and to those of Arabia, Persia, India and the lands beyond—as a sort of gigantic inn on the long road between East and West, a natural place for them to meet.

And meetings there were. From their empire in the Far East the Dutch brought Javanese and Malay slaves to work on the new farms established at the Cape. This traffic in slaves grew rapidly because, against all the intentions of the founders of the settlement, the men sent from Europe by the Dutch East India Company were soon building permanent farmsteads. These resolute men—the Free Burghers, they called themselves—soon had all the arable land around the Cape firmly in their possession. Despite official discouragement and decrees, they began to spread northward.

Then there came an explosion of population that led to further expansion: suddenly large numbers of French refugees arrived in the land. They were the famous Huguenots—Protestants who, after 1685, fled from France in search of religious freedom. Many of them came from the Bordeaux area, bringing with them not only French cooking but also a stock of their native vines to start the great vineyards of the Cape. Later they were joined by Germans and other Europeans, and eventually by the British, but of all European influences apart from the Dutch, the French was most important. At one time, in fact, this influence was so great that it offended the sober Dutch administration. One sour Dutch governor solemnly tried to prohibit French fashions, going so far as to prescribe the height of heel and length of dress that women could legally wear.

Since the slaves brought by the Dutch from the East were the Cape's first gardeners, fishermen and laborers in the vineyards, and soon became the cooks as well, historical justice demands that their contribution to South African cooking should have priority. The descendants of these people are called the Cape Malays, which is something of a misnomer. Though many of their forefathers were indeed Malayan, the term was also loosely applied to slaves brought from Sumatra, Java and other islands of the East Indies. All were called Malay because all spoke Malay, the universal language of their world. All were Muhammadans, too, and their common language and faith held them together.

In time, another world of colored people grew up around them on the Cape: the people called Cape Colored today, and of so mixed an origin that it is impossible to sort out the different strands of human material that went into the weaving. They were begotten by European fathers who married or had illicit relationships with nonwhite women—Malay, Hottentot, Bushman and the Bantu of the interior. As slaves and workers they followed the same occupations as the Malays, but they never became

Southern Africa contains the richest and best developed territory south of the Sahara—along with some of the most desolate and primitive. A number of peoples live in close proximity with little intermingling —Europeans (mainly Dutch, French and English), Indians, Malays and blacks. Descendants of European settlers rule Rhodesia and the Republic of South Africa and control South-West Africa; Botswana, Lesotho, Swaziland and Transkei are indigenously African.

an integral part of the Malay community. The Cape Colored tended to identify with their European masters: they adopted Dutch as their language, most of them became Christian, and many accompanied the Dutch and Huguenot French on their drive into the interior. The Malays themselves clung to their religion, their language and their original homes at the Cape. They retain an identity of their own, and it is with their contribution to cooking that the rest of this chapter will deal.

To this day, in Cape Malay homes, one can eat the sort of food they brought to South Africa nearly 300 years ago. The best time to visit such a home, I think, is at the end of the great Muslim fast called Ramadan and the beginning of the feast called Lebaran that follows it.

The Cape Malays compare Lebaran to both Christmas and Easter, and it is no less festive. On the day before the feast every female in a household is busy preparing scores of different dishes, and the bustle is frantic. As a visitor, I have been stunned by the movement, the sounds of pestles ringing out in iron mortars, the heightened voices rising to an almost hysterical pitch as they issue orders and instructions, and the fever of conversation. The names of the dishes—names that today are a mixture of Afrikaans, English and pure Malay—are like a litany of the Cape Malay kitchen: *sosaties, bobotie, bredie, koesisters, kerries,* pickled fish, yellow rice, *blatjang, atjar, sambal.* These dishes are prepared in such quantities that family kitchens often prove too small, and some cooking is done on primus stoves and wood fires in narrow backyards.

For another great feast, Moulidu-n-nabi, the "feast of the orange

133

South Africans of Malayan origin, a high-spirited people with a flair for festive occasions, delight in a wedding celebration like this one in Athlone, a suburb of Cape Town. Newlyweds Fuad Carr and the former Giva Abrahams, at the center of the happy assembly, are meeting here for the first time in their marriage. Their Muslim wedding ceremony took place in a mosque shortly before the celebration, but according to their religious custom the bride did not attend; instead, she was represented by a male proxy.

leaves," the women gather in one another's houses to drink cups of tea laced with their favorite spices, eat brightly colored cakes à la Javanese, and sample the many varieties of delicious homemade Malay preserves. The preparation of the Moulidu-n-nabi feast is, in fact, one of the rare occasions when Malay women are not at work in the kitchen—for it is a male duty to prepare *buriyani,* the prescribed dish for the feast.

A *buriyani* is usually made in three stages. First, rice is cooked in a little salted water. Then a boned, diced leg of mutton is simmered in another pot with sliced onions, pounded green ginger, fennel, garlic, cumin seeds and sliced tomatoes until the meat is nearly cooked. Finally, most of the rice is taken out of its pot, with a thin layer left in the bottom. Some of the meat mixture is placed on this layer of rice and the pot is filled with alternate layers of the mixture and the rest of the rice, often with some sliced hard-boiled eggs placed between, and the pot is tightly covered. The more slowly this dish cooks the better; most men cook it over a slow charcoal fire, letting it simmer in its pot for many hours. Nothing will ever persuade them to unseal their dish before the moment when they know it is done. But how do they know when that moment has come? My own guess is that it is partly by intuition—the intuition of the inspired cook that many men have deep down in them—and partly by a change in the faint incense that rises from the simmering pot.

134

It was probably not through dishes like these that the Malays first influenced cooking in South Africa. It was rather through their skill in preserving and pickling vegetables and fish for the scurvy-ridden sailors of the Dutch East India Company. The Malays were expert fishermen in a fisherman's paradise. The peninsula of the Cape is a kind of geological breakwater that divides the Indian from the Atlantic Ocean. To the west flows the deep and icy Antarctic current, a sort of Gulf Stream in reverse, bringing with it all the fish that live in cold waters. On the east, barely 15 miles away, the warm waters of the Indian Ocean wash against yellow sands and purple cliffs, and these waters contain a very different but equally rich marine life of their own.

The local demand for fresh fish was easily met; the bulk of the catch was preserved. And the Malays set about preserving their fish in two distinct ways. One was by splitting the fish open and salting and drying the flesh; such fish not only filled the needs of the East Indiamen, but in time became the basis of *smoor-vis,* one of the national dishes of South Africa. The other method produced the far more famous pickled fish *(Recipe Index)* called *ingelegde vis,* which soon became a popular export to Europe.

Every Cape Malay household—and, for that matter, every Afrikaans household, too—has its own ideas on preparing *ingelegde* fish, but the

Just as the bride and bridegroom are separated during a Cape Malay marriage ceremony, the wedding banquet is separated into two parts. The bride dines with her own party *(above)* while the bridegroom and his party have their meal at a separate table. Here Mrs. Carr helps herself from a bowl of curry. Other Cape Malay foods on the table include roast fowl, *bredies* (Malay stews), *biriyani* (saffron rice with meat), various rice and pasta dishes, fruits, gelatins, custards and sweet puddings. The ornate wedding cake, at left rear, is strictly Western.

best way is still the original way. Any firm and fleshy fish (the Malay favorite is the snoek, a kind of sea perch) is sliced and washed. The slices are then dried and fried in oil. Meanwhile, thinly sliced onions are placed in a dish with just enough wine vinegar to cover them. Salt and pepper, thinly sliced chilies, turmeric, one's favorite mixed curry powder, green ginger, a little brown sugar and a few bay leaves are added to the dish. The mixture is then brought to a boil as slowly as possible, the golden-brown fried fish is drained and placed in a jar or other receptacle, and the mixture is poured over it.

Snoek is not only the Cape Malays' fish of choice for *ingelegde vis;* it is also their favorite fish for salting, smoking and curing in the sun. When I was a boy, the white walls of fishermen's cottages were always festooned with lines on which split snoek dried and danced like laundry in the offshore breeze. And dried snoek is by far the finest of all fish for *smoor-vis,* or *gesmoorde vis (Recipe Index).* In Afrikaans the word *smoor* means both "smothering" and "braising," and both meanings enter into the cured snoek prepared by the Cape Malays. They first smother the dried fish in water to remove the salt; then they skin and bone it, and flake the flesh. Next they braise sliced or diced onions in oil, along with red chilies and diced raw potatoes. When these are almost cooked, the fish is added and the mixture is braised until brown.

Both *ingelegde vis* and *smoor-vis* played important roles in the battle for survival of the men who settled the Cape. When the battle was won the Cape Malays came up with other dishes—dishes that are all so a part of the South African way of life that they have become almost sacramental substances. Among them are *bobotie (Recipe Index), sosaties (Recipe Index)* and *bredie. Bobotie,* a kind of minced-meat pie, is to South Africa what *moussaka* is to the Greeks. *Sosaties,* or skewered and grilled meats, are what *shashlyk* is to the people of the Caucasus and shish kabob to the Turks. The stew called *bredie* is what goulash is to Hungarians.

A basic *bobotie* begins with minced lamb or beef, a little soaked bread, eggs, butter, finely chopped onion, garlic, curry powder and turmeric. All are mixed together, put in a pie dish with meat drippings, and baked in a low oven for a time. The moment the mixture begins to brown, the dish is taken from the oven and some eggs beaten up with milk are poured over the top; then the dish is put back into the oven and baked very slowly to a deep brown. The pace of the cooking is important: if the oven is too hot the *bobotie* will be dry, and that should never happen, for an ideal *bobotie* is eaten moist, over rice.

What I have described is (I believe) *bobotie* as it was in the beginning, but it is no longer the *bobotie* eaten in South Africa, except in Malay homes. In my own home, for instance, we added a handful of finely chopped blanched almonds and some raisins to the mixture. The simple egg-and-milk mixture poured over the *bobotie* halfway through the baking (a mixture that can easily turn into a stodgy baked custard) was scorned by our cooks. At a late stage in the cooking, they would beat bread crumbs fried in drippings into the mixture and bake it quickly in a hot oven. In her famous book *Where Is It?* Hildagonda Duckitt, the Fannie Farmer of South Africa, says that a teaspoon of sugar should be added to the meat mixture, and that an ounce of tamarind water gives the dish an exceptionally pleasant, tart flavor. But these are only a few variations, and there are almost as many as there are homes in South Africa.

The word *sosatie* is derived from two Malay words: *saté,* which means "spiced sauce"; and *sésate,* which means "meat on a skewer." This second great standby of the South African diet is usually made of mutton cut into small cubes suitable for spiking on thin wooden skewers. Originally the Cape Malays marinated the meat in a mixture of shredded fried onions, curry powder, chilies, garlic and a generous quantity of tamarind water. They usually did this early in the afternoon and left the meat in the marinade until the next day. They would then skewer the cubes of meat with alternate pieces of mutton fat, and roast them on an open fire or fry them in a heavy skillet. Just before the *sosaties* were ready the cook would boil the marinade in a saucepan until its ingredients were cooked and the liquid reduced, and he would serve the *sosaties* with rice and this sauce. But I have had Malay *sosaties* in which green ginger also went into the marinade and during the simmering stage the cook added a few bay leaves, an orange leaf or two and another spoonful of curry. Again, the variations are endless; the Olympian Miss Duckitt rounds out her marinade with either vinegar or the juice of lemons (we always used lemon juice at home), sugar and milk. Because of the Muslim proscription against pig products, the Malays never skewered bacon with their *sosaties,* but it is quite common among other Cape residents nowadays to do *sosaties* with alternate cubes of mutton and squares of bacon, all conventionally marinated.

The last of the three great Cape Malay main dishes is the stew called *bredie.* Almost every country in the Western world has its meat stew. The Irish, of course, have Irish stew; the English, Lancashire hotpot; the Dutch, *hutspot;* the Germans, *Eintopf;* and the Hungarians, goulash. But only in South Africa is the dish of Oriental origin. The very word *bredie* is significant: it is a Malagasy word from Madagascar, and between the east coast of Madagascar and the world of India and Malaya there has been a steady coming and going since recorded history began. To this day, the *bredies* are a culinary reminder of that traffic.

A Cape Malay cook starts a *bredie* by browning thinly sliced onions in mutton fat, butter or oil, in that order of preference. Meat or fish is then laid over the onions and gently braised. The chosen vegetables, sliced or cubed, are placed on top of the meat with various seasonings, but always with chilies. Curiously, the vegetable used in one of the earliest forms of *bredie* was pumpkin, even though the Dutch regarded it as food fit only for slaves. Today, pumpkin *bredie (Recipe Index)* is one of South Africa's almost mystical dishes, and if the pumpkin is firm and crisp it can be excellent. Some Cape Malay cooks add a little salt, a few chilies and a potato or two to the pumpkin; others flavor it with green ginger, cinnamon sticks, a few cloves and a little chopped garlic. The variations are endless, and pumpkin *bredies* are only a subdivision of them. I have had wonderful cauliflower *bredies,* and others made with green beans *(Recipe Index),* curried beans, turnips, kohlrabi, celery, carrots, peas, button turnips, and a spinach *bredie* enlivened by the addition of sorrel.

Continued on page 140

A Classic Game Pie without the Game

Maria Jacobs, far better known as Cookie, is a fixture at Lanzerac, a lovely country-house-turned-hotel in the old Cape city of Stellenbosch. Of Malay descent, she has been employed there as long as anyone can remember. One of Cookie's major culinary accomplishments is a minced-meat dish that now goes by the Afrikaans name of *bobotie,* though it, too, is of Malay descent. Several generations ago, when *bobotie* was introduced into South Africa, it gained popularity as an effective way of cooking the game of the region. Today, Cookie's *bobotie* lacks game, but it is still unmatched for succulence and flavor.

The makings for a *bobotie (left)* are eggs, onions, tomatoes, lemons and lemon leaves, sugar, curry, milk and minced meat. Below, midway through the preparation process, Cookie sets halved hard-boiled eggs in the cooked meat. Next she will spread over the top a coating of eggs beaten with milk and bake the whole pie very slowly. At right, Cookie proudly displays the result.

The variation that most stimulates the South African palate, however, is unquestionably tomato *bredie (Recipe Index)*. I know about a dozen recipes for cooking tomato *bredie,* and all of them are good; the one in Miss Duckitt's *Where Is It?* is probably as good as any. All *bredies* begin roughly in the way I have described, but in this recipe boneless mutton is cut into small pieces and browned with onions over a fairly hot fire. Large tomatoes are cut into slices or passed through a mincing machine; if the tomatoes are not quite ripe, sugar and salt as well as the traditional chilies are added. The braised meat, crisp fat and tomato are then stewed as slowly as possible until the liquid in the pot is reduced to a rich, thick gravy. Upcountry, we often added some peeled, cored and sliced quinces to the mixture, cutting the razor edge of the quince flavor with a small addition of sugar. To my mind there is no stew, goulash or hotpot to equal *bredie* cooked this way and eaten with a simple but perfect rice.

To accompany great main dishes there must be great salads and condiments—and the Cape Malays have them. As a counterpart to the Western salad, they offer a sliced or shredded vegetable dish called the *slaai;* more adventurously, they grate and spice cold fruits and vegetables in a dish called a *sambal*. Their condiments include *blatjang,* a form of chutney, and *atjar,* a generic name for a great variety of pickles. Progressing from the most esoteric to the most nearly familiar, I will discuss them in reverse order.

Of the many kinds of *atjar* the oldest, I expect, is mango *atjar* as made in Java. Every Javanese district has its own variety, and I have eaten it there as an ingredient of a complex pickled mixture with several kinds of chilies. The earliest Cape Malay green mango *atjar (Recipe Index)* differed from the Javanese in that the fruit was dressed with oil and curry. In the most sophisticated form of mango *atjar* the flesh is sliced from the stone and soaked in salt water for several days, then removed and dried; garlic, fenugreek, turmeric and chilies are cooked in oil, curry powder is stirred in, and the mixture is spread between layers of sliced mango in a screw-top jar. Alternatively, lemons, green beans, onions, cauliflower and other vegetables can be pickled as *atjars,* but the variety most popular with the Europeans of the Cape is the mixed-vegetable *atjar.*

In our household, this was a wildly miscellaneous affair. All the babes and sucklings of the vegetable kingdom went into it: tiny cobs of corn, barely an inch long; the youngest of cucumbers; minute walnuts; the hearts of young cabbages; all manner of green, yellow and purple beans, immature and thinly sliced; the florets of snow-white young cauliflower; celery, tiny carrots, radishes and button turnips, along with lemons, apricots, peaches and a thin, light-skinned tangerine called a *naartje.* To all this we added green ginger, the roots of wild aniseed, turmeric, saffron, garlic, coriander, peppercorns, nutmeg and almost all the spices of the East, and we simmered the vegetables and spices together until the vegetables were tender. At this point we separated the ingredients from the liquid, picked out and rejected the inferior ones, and pickled the rest in oil and curry. Such a mixed *atjar,* we used to say as children, was the only pickle we didn't mind getting into.

Then there is *blatjang.* This chutneylike condiment also had its origin in Java, and acquired its name from a prawn-and-shrimp mixture that was sun-dried, pounded in a wooden mortar, and shaped into masses resembling large cheeses. In this form it was imported to the Cape. From these beginnings *blatjangs* evolved into more complex forms. They are now made with apricots *(Recipe Index)*, dates *(Recipe Index)*, quinces and raisins. A typical modern *blatjang*—if any can be called typical—appears in Miss Duckitt's *Where Is It?* Her recipe calls for a handful of finely ground red chilies, 40 sweet almonds, a tablespoon of apricot jam, two onions baked in an oven and mashed in a mortar, two cloves of garlic and two lemon or bay leaves, all mixed together with a teaspoon of salt and two tablespoons of lemon juice. But the importance of *blatjang* is not in its modern complexities but in the fact that it became for South Africa what Worcestershire sauce became for the English.

As vital as *atjars* and *blatjangs* in the life of the Cape Malays is the *sambal,* a condiment made of such grated vegetables and fruits as carrots, cucumbers, apples and quinces, salted and seasoned with fresh lemon juice or vinegar and the inevitable chilies. No Malay feast is complete without a *sambal* of some kind. Quince *sambal* is a favorite with roasts, since it is a wonderful corrective for anything with a hint of grease or fat. Carrot *sambal* *(Recipe Index)* goes well with fried fish or roasted chicken, and the apple variety is a Jack-of-all-trades that goes with any dish. But the *sambal* loved above all others, and the perfect accompaniment for a curry, is cucumber *sambal* *(Recipe Index),* which cools the tongue and protects the palate against the fires of the fiercest chilies or spices.

As for the *slaais,* or salads, to which the *sambal* is related, I will mention only *dadel-slaai,* or date-and-onion salad *(Recipe Index),* a great favorite as a side dish with a Malay pot roast. The Malays eat dates in many ways and use them a great deal in baking and cooking, but this salad is perhaps the form they most enjoy. To make it, they stone and slice the dates and add young onions sliced as thin as tissue paper. Boiling water is poured over the mixture and it is left to stand for 15 minutes. The ingredients are then separated, and alternate layers of dates and onions are arranged in a bowl or dish. As a dressing, brown sugar and salt are dissolved in vinegar or diluted lemon juice and poured over the salad.

To complete a Cape Malay meal there are often baked goods, and the Malays of the Cape are as good at baking as they are at other cooking. They are particularly good at pancakes and pastries, not only as sweets, but also as wrappings for minced fish, lobsters, crayfish and meats, and as toppings for chicken or seafood pies. But they have made one contribution to South African sweet pastry that is part of the mystique of national taste: the *koesister (Recipe Index),* a spiced braided cruller dipped in rich, cinnamon-flavored syrup. It is one of the most fattening pastries ever invented, and enough to make a diet-conscious diner blanch with horror—but it is delicious.

Finally, there is a kind of Cape Malay candy called *tameletjie.* It is one of the simplest of foods, but its role in the imagination of generations of South Africans demands that it should be the last word on Malay cooking, just as it was the first in most of our South African lives. Brought to the Cape by the first Malay slaves, *tameletjie* is so old that nobody is

Continued on page 145

Among the Cape Malays of South Africa, a main dish is often accompanied by a number of spicy side dishes, following a custom brought to the region by cooks of Malay origin. Shown here are examples of four distinct kinds of such side dishes: *atjar* (pickles)—lemon (1), green bean (2), mango (3); *slaai* (conventional salads)—tomato (4), date and onion (5); *sambal* (grated salads)—cucumber (6), carrot (7); and *blatjang* (chutneys)—apricot (8), date (9). Recipes for all the dishes are listed in the Recipe Index.

quite certain of its origin; some specialists in these matters suspect that it originally came from China. But whatever its origin, it remains essentially a caramelized sugar, made of coarse brown sugar and water in equal proportions. Some Malays add dried ginger to the mixture; others add cinnamon, crushed walnuts, almonds, peanuts and even a little butter, which puts the sweet on the road to becoming a rudimentary marzipan.

In all these forms *tameletjie* used to be hawked in the streets of Cape Town, among the white-walled, gabled houses and along avenues of oaks planted back in the 17th Century. The Malay peddlers have vanished, and most of the houses of gable and grace have made way for ugly concrete ones. *Tameletjie* itself has been overwhelmed by an avalanche of mass-produced sweets. But I am certain that wherever there is a garden large enough to hide them, and wood enough to make a secret fire, boys still make the original *tameletjie,* just as we did as children.

We did not need money to buy our *tameletjie* from hawkers or from the shops that sold them. We could make them ourselves out of materials given to us by our Malay cooks—and if they refused us (in my childhood sugar was expensive, and a great luxury), we had no hesitation in swiping the sugar when its guardians' backs were turned. Fortunately, the gardens and orchards around our house were huge, with sheltered copses in which we could set a discreet fire without attracting attention from the house. Here we would make a syrup of our dark-brown sugar and water, pour it into a tin, set a quick fire on some flat stones and stand the tin upon it. We needed no culinary expert to tell us to boil the syrup briskly; hunger and a sense of guilt made us hurry our clandestine confection. As the mixture frothed and bubbled we would stir it with a wooden stick, and from time to time let a drop of the syrup fall from the stick into a can of cold water. The moment it congealed on touching the water, we knew the *tameletjie* was ready. If we were brave enough, we would leave it on the fire a moment longer to let it caramelize a little more, then pour it straightaway onto the greased lid of a cardboard box. Miraculously—to us—it would set almost at once, and we would carry it off to let it cool in some safe hiding place. Our final product was hard and translucent; held against the African sun, it glowed like amber.

When I stayed with friends on the Cape, we would make a somewhat more elaborate form of *tameletjie.* We would cull pine cones from the dense pine forests and extract the seeds, then pour a thin layer of *tameletjie* into our container, sprinkle the pine seeds densely upon the congealing mixture and pour the rest of the mixture over that. In the interior, our favorite variation was based upon the stones of a special variety of apricots. Our families all grew apricots of many varieties, and as children we learned to choose the ones that had sweet stones, not only palatable but far more to our liking than almonds bought in the shops. With these we made our favorite and most subtle form of *tameletjie.* It could not rival the complex variations on the simple theme that were produced from time to time by our cooks, but nothing ever equaled our surreptitious, do-it-yourself *tameletjies,* which contained a spice not to be found in any kitchen or pantry—the spice of breaking with authority and launching an adventure of one's own.

Opposite: Half a million Indians live in South Africa today, descendants of laborers who came to work the sugar fields of Natal in the 19th Century. Close-knit and seclusive, they cleave to their traditions and ancestral foods. At the home of Mrs. Fatima Meer in Durban, for example, high tea includes the Indian delicacies shown here: *samosas,* small meat-stuffed turnovers; *sev,* noodlelike squiggles of chick-pea dough pressed through a sieve and deep-fried; and *vade,* ground lentils flavored with herbs, shaped into balls and fried.

To pickle a snoek: vegetable oil, vinegar, brown sugar, turmeric, onions, whole peppercorns, bay leaves—and one fresh fish.

A Fine Pickle of Fish Borrowed by South Africa from Asia

Centuries ago Malay seamen plying the trade routes of the Indian Ocean developed a distinctive and delicious technique for preserving fish to make their long months at sea more bearable. The technique has been naturalized (along with a large number of the Malays themselves) in South Africa. Today, the finished dish even has an Afrikaans name: *ingelegde vis*. Almost any firm-fleshed fish may be used in making Malay-style pickled fish, but the favorite is the barracudalike snoek, a species in good supply in the offshore waters of South Africa. Strong in taste and texture, snoek requires some cooking before it can be pickled; the preferred method is to fry it in vegetable oil. Then the fillets are soaked in a mixture of vinegar and spices. Without needing refrigeration, *ingelegde vis* is edible for months—on land or sea.

146

Hussein Philander, a Malay cook who has worked 26 years for the Bernard Muller family in Cape Town, is an expert at making *ingelegde vis*. At left he fries fillets of snoek in vegetable oil. The cooked fish is transferred to a waiting bowl and wine vinegar, chopped onions and spices are added. The completed dish, ready to be packed in jars, is shown in the picture below.

Pickled Fish *(South Africa)*

Starting at least 2 days ahead, heat ½ cup of the vegetable oil in a heavy 10- to 12-inch skillet over moderate heat until a light haze forms above it. Pat the halibut completely dry with paper towels and place the steaks in the hot oil. Turning the fish with a slotted spatula, fry the steaks for 3 or 4 minutes on each side, or until they are golden brown. As they brown, transfer them to paper towels to drain and cool.

Prepare a marinade in the following fashion: Pour off and discard the oil remaining in the skillet and wipe the skillet dry with paper towels. Pour in ¼ cup of vegetable oil and heat it until a light haze forms above it. Drop in the onions and, stirring frequently, cook for 8 to 10 minutes, or until they are soft and golden brown. Watch carefully for any sign of burning and regulate the heat accordingly. Add the sugar, chilies, curry powder, ginger root, crumbled bay leaves, coriander and salt, and stir over low heat for 2 minutes. Stirring constantly, pour in the vinegar and water in a slow thin stream. Bring to a boil over high heat, reduce the heat to low, and simmer the marinade uncovered for 10 minutes.

Remove the skin and bones from the halibut and cut the meat into 1½-inch squares. Spread about a third of the halibut evenly in a glass or enameled serving dish about 8 inches in diameter and 4 inches deep. Cover the fish with a cup or so of the marinade, then add another layer of halibut. Add a second cup of marinade, the remaining fish, and finally the rest of the marinade left in the skillet. Place the 2 whole bay leaves on top and cover the dish tightly with plastic wrap.

Marinate the pickled fish in the refrigerator for at least 2 days. Serve it with the onions from the dish in which it has marinated, moistening each portion with a spoonful or so of the liquid.

To serve 8 as a first course

¾ cup vegetable oil
2 pounds halibut steaks, sliced about 1 inch thick
3 large onions, peeled and cut crosswise into slices ⅛ inch thick
½ cup light-brown sugar
3 tablespoons finely chopped fresh hot chilies *(caution: see page 76)*
3 tablespoons curry powder, preferably Madras type
1 tablespoon scraped, finely chopped fresh ginger root
2 large bay leaves, crumbled, plus 2 large whole bay leaves
1 teaspoon ground coriander
2 teaspoons salt
2 cups malt vinegar
1 cup water

Green Bean Atjar *(South Africa)*
GREEN STRING BEANS PRESERVED IN SPICED OIL

Starting several days ahead, place the beans in a deep bowl and pour in enough boiling water to cover them completely. Let the beans stand for 2 minutes, drain them in a sieve or colander, and run cold water over them to set their color. Return the beans to the bowl, add the salt, and stir until the salt dissolves. Cover tightly with plastic wrap and set aside at room temperature for 2 hours. Drain the beans and squeeze them gently to remove any excess moisture; then pack them into a 1-quart jar or crock.

In a small skillet or saucepan heat ¼ cup of the oil over low heat until a light haze forms above it. Add the curry powder and turmeric, and stir until the spices dissolve in the oil. Add the chilies, garlic and fenugreek. Stirring constantly, pour in the remaining 1¼ cups of oil in a thin stream and cook until the mixture begins to splutter. Reduce the heat to low and simmer for 2 or 3 minutes. Pour the hot oil mixture over the beans. Let the beans cool for about 1 hour, then place them in the refrigerator uncovered to pickle for 2 or 3 days before serving them.

To make about 1 quart

2 pounds fresh green string beans, trimmed, washed and cut lengthwise into quarters
2 tablespoons salt
1½ cups vegetable oil
2 tablespoons curry powder, preferably Madras type
2 teaspoons ground turmeric
2 tablespoons finely chopped fresh hot chilies *(caution: see page 76)*
1½ tablespoons finely chopped garlic
1 teaspoon fenugreek seeds, pulverized with a mortar and pestle or in a small bowl with the back of a spoon

Halibut chunks, in a marinade seasoned with bay leaves, curry powder and other spices, are a subtle version of South African pickled fish.

Parsley and lemon wedges garnish a spicy version of *gesmoorde vis,* made with salt cod, tomatoes and boiled potatoes.

Gesmoorde Vis *(South Africa)*

SALT COD AND POTATOES WITH TOMATO SAUCE

To serve 4 to 6

1 pound salt cod
3 medium-sized boiling potatoes
   (about 1 pound)
4 medium-sized firm ripe tomatoes
3 tablespoons vegetable oil
3 small onions, peeled and cut
   crosswise into slices ⅛ inch
   thick
1 tablespoon plus 1 teaspoon finely
   chopped fresh hot chilies
   (caution: see page 76)
1 teaspoon finely chopped garlic
1 tablespoon light-brown sugar
1 lemon, cut lengthwise into 4 or 6
   wedges
Parsley sprigs

Starting a day ahead, place the cod in a glass, enameled or stainless-steel pan or bowl. Cover it with cold water and soak for at least 12 hours, gently squeezing the cod dry and changing the water every 3 or 4 hours.

Drain the cod, rinse it thoroughly under cold running water, and cut it into 1-inch pieces.

Drop the potatoes into enough lightly salted boiling water to cover them completely and cook briskly, uncovered, until they are almost tender and show only slight resistance when pierced with the point of a sharp knife. Drain and peel the potatoes and cut them into 1-inch cubes.

Place the tomatoes in a pan of boiling water and let them boil briskly for about 10 seconds. Run cold water over them, and peel them with a small, sharp knife. Cut the tomatoes crosswise into ⅛-inch-thick rounds.

In a heavy 10- to 12-inch skillet, heat the oil over moderate heat until a light haze forms above it. Drop in the onions and, stirring frequently, cook for 8 to 10 minutes, or until they are soft and golden brown. Watch carefully for any sign of burning and regulate the heat accordingly. Add the tomatoes, 1 tablespoon of the chilies, the garlic and sugar, and cook briskly, uncovered, stirring from time to time, until most of the liquid in the pan has evaporated and the mixture is thick enough to hold its shape lightly in a spoon.

Stir in the cod and potatoes, reduce the heat to low, and cover tightly. Simmer for 20 to 25 minutes, or until the fish flakes easily when prodded gently with a fork. Taste for seasoning.

Serve the *gesmoorde vis* at once, mounded on a heated platter or in a large bowl. Sprinkle with the remaining teaspoon of chopped chilies and arrange the lemon wedges and parsley sprigs decoratively on top. Serve accompanied, if you like, by hot boiled rice and lemon or green bean *atjar (Recipe Index)*.

Tomato Salad (South Africa)

Overlapping the tomato slices slightly, arrange them attractively in a ring or rows on a large platter or four individual serving dishes.

Sprinkle the tomatoes evenly with the salt and sugar, and scatter the strips of chili on top. Dribble the vinegar over the tomatoes and let them rest at room temperature for about 15 minutes before serving.

To serve 4

2 large firm ripe tomatoes, washed, stemmed and cut crosswise into slices ⅛ inch thick
½ teaspoon salt
¼ teaspoon sugar
1 fresh hot green chili, stemmed, seeded and cut lengthwise into strips about ½ inch long and ⅛ inch wide *(caution: see page 76)*
2 tablespoons red wine vinegar

Bobotie (South Africa)
BAKED GROUND LAMB CURRY WITH CUSTARD TOPPING

Preheat the oven to 300°. Combine the bread and milk in a small bowl and let the bread soak for at least 10 minutes.

Meanwhile, in a heavy 10- to 12-inch skillet, melt the butter over moderate heat. When the foam begins to subside, add the lamb and cook it, stirring constantly and mashing any lumps with the back of a spoon, until the meat separates into granules and no traces of pink remain. With a slotted spoon transfer the lamb to a deep bowl.

Pour off and discard all but about 2 tablespoons of fat from the skillet and drop in the onions. Stirring frequently, cook for about 5 minutes, until the onions are soft and translucent but not brown. Watch carefully for any sign of burning and regulate the heat accordingly. Add the curry powder, sugar, salt and pepper, and stir for 1 or 2 minutes. Then stir in the lemon juice and bring to a boil over high heat. Pour the entire mixture into the bowl of lamb.

Drain the bread in a sieve set over a bowl and squeeze the bread completely dry. Reserve the drained milk. Add the bread, 1 of the eggs, the apple, raisins and almonds to the lamb. Knead vigorously with both hands or beat with a wooden spoon until the ingredients are well combined. Taste for seasoning and add more salt if desired. Pack the lamb mixture loosely into a 3-quart soufflé dish or other deep 3-quart baking dish, smoothing the top with a spatula. Tuck the lemon, orange or bay leaves beneath the surface of the meat.

With a wire whisk or rotary beater, beat the remaining 2 eggs with the reserved milk for about 1 minute, or until they froth. Slowly pour the mixture evenly over the meat and bake in the middle of the oven for 30 minutes, or until the custard is a light golden brown.

Serve at once, directly from the baking dish. *Bobotie* is traditionally accompanied by hot boiled rice.

To serve 6

1 slice homemade-type white bread, 1 inch thick, broken into small bits
1 cup milk
2 tablespoons butter
2 pounds coarsely ground lean lamb
1½ cups finely chopped onions
2 tablespoons curry powder, preferably Madras type
1 tablespoon light-brown sugar
1 teaspoon salt
½ teaspoon freshly ground black pepper
¼ cup strained fresh lemon juice
3 eggs
1 medium-sized tart cooking apple, peeled, cored and finely grated
½ cup seedless raisins
¼ cup blanched almonds, coarsely chopped
4 small fresh lemon or orange leaves, or substitute 4 small bay leaves

VII

Great Cooking from Rich Farms

At the edge of a tidal pool on the shore of Table Bay, near the southern tip of Africa, two University of Cape Town students assemble their catch of crayfish in readiness for a picnic. In the distance Table Mountain, for centuries the eagerly awaited halfway mark for voyagers from Europe to the Far East, looms as a backdrop for Cape Town.

The officers of the Dutch East India Company who founded the first settlement at the Cape of Good Hope in 1651 envisioned it as a glorified farm supplying fresh food for their seafarers to and from the Orient. They tried to discourage the small group of their employees who set about farming on their own, but the Free Burghers, as they called themselves, were soon growing more food than was needed to victual the company's ships. The settlement's gradual transformation into a colony was given impetus by an influx of French Huguenots seeking haven from religious persecution. The separate yet interacting customs of Dutchmen and Frenchmen thousands of miles away from their homelands helped produce a new way of life among the white settlers at the Cape.

I like to date the start of that way of life from 1685. That was the year when the Huguenots began fleeing France. It was also the year when Simon van der Stel, the governor sent by the East India Company to rule at the Cape, decided that after his retirement he would live out the rest of his days there. He obtained the grant of a large tract of land lying in a wide and gentle curve of fertile earth on the eastern slope of Table Mountain. Van der Stel called the imposing homestead he built there Groot (Great) Constantia, and by the time he retired to it in 1699 Constantia had already begun to win fame in Europe. As the first gentleman farmer in the land, Van der Stel set a seal of respectability upon the expansion of the farming activities of the Free Burghers and their French Huguenot allies. From his day on, the Dutch word for farmer, *boer,* became a word carrying the highest social cachet.

Groot Constantia itself became a model that every farmer did his utmost to copy. Its buildings exemplified a beautiful new architectural style called Cape Dutch, characterized by a gracefully curved form of gable. Van der Stel (and later his son, who succeeded him as governor) literally shanghaied architects and craftsmen from ships bound for the East and set them to work with slaves as apprentices. Soon there were indigenous builders, cabinetmakers and silversmiths, many of them Cape Malays skilled in the crafts of the East, and all sorts of greater or lesser Constantias began to rise. They can still be seen in meadows folded away among the mountains north of the Cape, bearing names charged with the dreams of their founders: Rustenburg (Fortress of Rest), Schoongezicht (View of Beauty), Vrede-en-Lust (Peace and Contentment). La Gratitude, one of the most beautiful of all, was built in a valley called Fransch Hoek (French Corner) for the Huguenots who congregated there.

Van der Stel did more than provide the Cape with a model for elegant homes filled with handsome furniture and table refinements. With the help of Huguenots newly arrived from the world's most celebrated wine-producing country, he laid the foundation of a great wine industry. The wines of Constantia led all others of South Africa from the early 18th Century on and gained an increasing reputation in Europe. When a young lady in a novel by Jane Austen fainted, no reader of that day was surprised to learn that she was restored to her senses with a drop of Constantia. The French poet Charles Baudelaire, a guest at Groot Constantia in the mid-19th Century, was so charmed by the hospitality, the food and the wine that he composed a poem containing these lines:

> *Je préfère au Constance, à l'opium, aux nuits,*
> *L'élixir de ta bouche où l'amour se pavane;* . . .
> I prefer to Constantia, to opium, to nights,
> The elixir of your mouth where love luxuriates; . . .

Alas, that rare Constantia has vanished, along with the secret of its making. The very grape from which it was made disappeared in the 1890s, killed off by the dread pest phylloxera, which also destroyed many other species at the Cape.

The subsequent revival of South Africa's wine industry is one of the more remarkable feats of agriculture in the past half century. Between the two World Wars the winegrowers of the Cape abandoned a policy of producing imitations of the centuries-old wines of France, Germany, Spain and Portugal and bottling them with such European labels as claret, Burgundy, hock, sherry and port. Today, even when the wines carry names reminiscent of great European wines, they do so only because the names are associated with the type of grape from which the South African wines are made. Thus, there are South African white wines made from Riesling, Sauvignon and Clairette Blanche grapes, and red ones made from the Cabernet, Hermitage, Pontac and Pinot varieties.

Whatever their names or classification, the white wines of the Cape compare well with good wines from anywhere in the world. One of my favorites, Nederburg Hochheimer, made from Clairette Blanche grapes, is a light white wine with a delicious fugitive bouquet; when its subtle flavor is grasped at last, it is as though one is possessing not merely a wine

but the quarry of a hunter who has prevailed against all the odds of a difficult chase. A somewhat heavier wine called Witzenberg is made from French grapes grown at the foot of the mountain of that name. Witzenberg spends at least 18 months in casks of French oak before it is bottled but, like all the best white wines of the Cape, should be drunk young to appreciate its aromatic freshness. It is particularly good chilled on a hot summer day. At the top of all the Cape's white wines, however, I would place the various Rieslings, particularly Nederburg Hochheimer.

Good as the Cape white wines are, the red wines are better. One that comes close to achieving greatness is Alto Rouge, which has a claret flavor but is slightly stronger than a conventional claret. There is not much of it about, but a single bottle will prove its quality. It is made from three grapes, Cabernet, Shiraz and Hermitage, in proportions determined after a long process of trial and error. In France even the heavier Burgundies will hold their quality in casks for only a year or two; for Alto Rouge, the maturing process lasts three years, and the bottled wine has a long life for its type. I have drunk 21-year-old Alto Rouge and found it superb.

Best of all the red wines, I think, are the heavier and still stronger Burgundy types, which have an alcohol content as high as 15 per cent. One of my favorites is Stellenrood, perhaps because its fine bouquet and flavor are matched by its color, one of the loveliest I have ever seen in a wine—a

Rays of a westering sun slice through the mountains enclosing the vineyard-rich Hex River Valley near Stellenbosch. The valley, which runs northeastward about 75 miles to the edge of the bleak Karroo Desert, once grew many kinds of fruit, particularly citrus. Today it is given over almost entirely to viticulture. Some wine is produced, but choice table grapes make up the bulk of the valley's output.

sort of Homeric red purple. In this list, too, the name Constantia reappears, with an excellent full-bodied wine.

Another triumph of South Africa's wine industry has been that of the producers of sherries. The list of sweet, medium-dry, dry and extra-dry sherries produced at the Cape is now so long that I doubt that any Spanish wine dealer's catalogue could equal it. Each of these Cape sherries has something uniquely its own and many are to my mind as good as anything obtainable in Spain. If I had to pick a favorite among the South African sherries, it would be Gezellen. There is, unfortunately, not much of it available on the market, but it is well worth looking for.

Finally there is Cape brandy. South Africans sip brandy in preference to any other spirit, and have become as discerning about it as the Rhinelanders are in matters of wine or the Scots in whiskies. Both as a pre-dinner beverage and as a liqueur, South African brandy holds its own, in my opinion, with the best brandy of Europe. One, which bears the name K.W.V., is comparable to the finest Armagnac. There are South African brandies available today that have spent 40 years in casks of French Limousin oak. From the oldest of these brandies is made the great liqueur of the Cape—tangerine-flavored Van der Hum. One of the best of all Van der Hums, it is pleasant to report, is made at Constantia; and so my story of the renaissance of Cape wines ends where it began, at the great estate founded almost 300 years ago by old Simon van der Stel.

As for solid fare, one of the most notable French-Dutch contributions to Cape cooking was in the preparation of fish. Surprisingly, the Huguenots never introduced *bouillabaisse,* nor did they attempt to enhance fish with their homeland heritage of sauces. Possibly the overwhelming riches of the seas around the Cape posed a challenge all their own; in any case the settlers evolved some highly enterprising ideas about dealing with the creatures they found in South African waters, particularly the shellfish, from little periwinkles and mussels to magnificent crayfish.

At the Cape periwinkles are eaten raw, with or without an astringent sauce, and they are also combined with spices and herbs in a superb soup. Hildagonda Duckitt directs her readers to collect periwinkles from rocks just below ebb-tide level, immerse them in fresh water to kill them and remove the sand, and pound the flesh in a mortar. The flesh is simmered in a beef or mutton stock flavored with onions, lemon, peppercorns and a mixture of spices. Flour is used to thicken the soup and a touch of burnt sugar is stirred into it before it is poured into a tureen; then a tumbler of dry white wine and a handful of crisp croutons bring it to perfection.

Mussels, too, are used to make a potent and delicious soup; but perhaps out of respect for their higher standing in the crustacean world the stock contains not only meat but also milk and cream, spiced with nutmeg and flavored with a sprinkling of grated cheese. For those who prefer mussels in more solid form, they are minced and made into croquettes, flavored with wine, pepper, saffron and turmeric or curry powder. There is also a mussel *bobotie,* developed by the Cape Malays, made in the same manner as a meat *bobotie,* but with ginger, bay leaves, parsley, *atjar,* raisins, almonds and lots more pepper stirred into the mixture.

Far outshining the mussel or periwinkle, however, is the Cape cray-

Napoleon is said to have asked for a glass of Constantia on his deathbed, and this great South African dessert wine, beloved among winebibbers as long ago as the 18th Century, is still produced on the estate of Groot (Great) Constantia near Cape Town. Built in 1684 by Simon van der Stel, first governor of South Africa, and named for his wife, Groot Constantia has the scrolled gables, shuttered windows and brilliant whitewashed walls that are typical of the best Cape Dutch architecture.

fish, also renowned as South African rock lobster. The ways of preparing this choice food are legion. Some pioneers were content to follow the Cape Malay example of braising the crayfish with onions and chilies, or using them in a crayfish curry *(Recipe Index),* or of mincing the crayfish, mixing it with soaked bread or cooked rice, binding the mixture with whisked eggs and forming one version of the *rissoles* known all over the country as *frikkadels.*

But there are even better ways of doing these great shellfish. One fascinating recipe has come down to me from an anonymous 19th Century housewife who lived in a valley deep in the Hottentots-Holland Mountains. This lady would extract the meat of tender young female crayfish from the tail and claws, particularly the fatter flesh that lies against the shell, and pound it fine in a mortar with an equal amount of beef marrow and some pepper, salt, bread crumbs, egg yolks, whipped cream, a pinch of red chilies and fresh lemon juice. This mixture was reinserted into the empty shells and baked in an oven until done.

One might have expected Cape cooks to develop as much skill with meat as with shellfish, for the original settlers were charged with providing the ships of the Dutch East India Company with fresh meat. But meat could be safely salted and smoked at home in Holland, so animal husbandry never became a Cape specialty. Still, there are two kinds of meat that did stimulate culinary inventiveness—fowl and pig.

Chicken was always a great favorite at the Cape on Sundays when the main meal was eaten in the middle of the day, after church. In its most exalted form it was pot-roasted with a few slices of bacon, its juices sealed within the skin by a light browning in lard and its flavor enhanced by a little dry white wine. The chicken was roasted for about an hour and a half. It would often go into the pot with its liver tucked under one wing and its gizzard underneath the other, and it would cook for the first hour or so breast down, like an infantryman under fire; then it would be turned over so that more fat could be spread on it and, if necessary, the wine increased. At this stage the heavy lid of the pot would have coals of fire heaped upon it. Despite the wine, which gradually changed from an alcoholic substance to a natural gravy, the chicken would emerge crisp, brown and so tender that it would fall apart at the touch of the knife.

Such a chicken could be filled with what the English call the "usual stuffing," but the best Cape stuffing (and to my mind the perfect one) is the grape we call Hanepoot—literally "cock's foot," or in South African English, "honey pot." Hanepoot is one of the finest, most versatile grapes of the world. It is eaten as a fruit for its delicate aromatic flavor and makes wines, like Constantia Berg, of a velvet texture and a warm amber color. It is superb as a raisin and first-rate as jam—and it is an incomparable stuffing for chicken roasted the old Cape way. Thus stuffed, the chicken is normally served with rice made yellow with turmeric, saffron or a judicious combination of both.

When even Hanepoot-stuffed chicken is not considered impressive enough for a Cape occasion, there is roast suckling pig. This dish is prepared with the utmost reverence. The pig is washed, scraped and scrubbed again and again in boiling water, until it is as clean and without blemish

Afrikaner housewives believe in preserving some part of the abundance of the South African harvest for themselves and their families. Here, before shelves laden with preserved fruit and vegetables, Mrs. Miemie Steyn of Ceres, in Cape Province, shows off her jars of pears and pickles. She also preserves some fruit in the "planked" Voortrekker style, in which peaches or figs are cooked with sugar, mashed to a pulp and spread on planks to dry, then cut in strips to be eaten at leisure.

as a Japanese Samurai after his ritual Bath of Purification before battle; then it is rubbed down until completely dry. No question of dusting the skin with flour has ever arisen in the minds of our best cooks; they have quarreled a great deal about the choice of a stuffing, but even in this matter, they tend to be purists and to permit the sweet, tender flesh to go to the table unaided and alone. Their one concession is to rub the skin well with fresh lemon (a corrective to fat) along with the usual salt and pepper. They then roast the suckling in a baking pan, basting it constantly until the crisp skin crackles like static electricity at the touch of a probing fork. To my taste the dish goes best with rice or baked sweet potatoes and a tart quince jelly.

I myself love suckling pig most when it is grilled in the open over wood coals plied with mountain herbs that impart a wild savor to the meat of the young animal. One of my earliest memories is of eating such a grilled piglet on a farm near the Cape, served with a quince sauce and the finest of young turnips, each hardly bigger than a button, braised in a little white wine and butter. I never knew where the combination of turnip and pork came from, for I had encountered it only at the Cape, but many years later, in a small restaurant in the South of France, I ate wild boar with exactly this vegetable accompaniment. Immediately I realized that it made good cooking sense to serve a root vegetable with an animal so expert at rooting, so in love with the roots and tubers of the earth. I should have guessed that only the French would have fastened on so felicitous a reflection of the facts of life to make a perfect dish.

Not unexpectedly, in a place that began as a vast fruit and vegetable farm, the range of Cape fruits and vegetables is an impressive one. There was hardly a vegetable raised in Europe or the New World that was not successfully duplicated at the Cape, along with many an Oriental variety. Vegetables were not only raised, but also loved. With certain exceptions, such as Sunday chicken and roast suckling pig, the main dish of a Cape meal would be accompanied by four to eight different vegetable dishes, and on hot days in my youth I would have thought a summer dinner table poor indeed if it did not offer half a dozen different kinds of salad.

The tomatoes of South Africa deserve a special word, for they are, I truly believe, the finest-tasting tomatoes in the world. They range from a tomato hardly bigger than a berry, through a medium-sized elongated tomato, fragrant to nose and palate, up to the large tomato of the Mediterranean type, naturalized by generations of growth in the African soil. All have their different uses, but all share one quality: like the people who grow them, they are full of a definite character of their own, with a fine, sharp, assertive flavor. One of my own preferred uses for the tomatoes of the Mediterranean type is in a fish sauce. A number of these tomatoes are first skinned and thinly sliced. About a quarter the number of onions are diced and browned in butter, the tomatoes are added along with a little pepper and salt, and the whole is simmered slowly together until both onions and tomatoes merge in one glowing red sauce.

Another noteworthy Cape way with a vegetable is its unique approach to cooking the common cabbage. A firm young cabbage is cut into slices about three quarters of an inch thick and placed in a deep, heavy dish

158

over a generous layer of bacon; the remainder of the dish is filled with alternate layers of cabbage and bacon, then sealed at the top with several rashers of bacon. The dish is tightly covered and baked in a moderate oven until the cabbage turns a light green gold; then the lid is removed and the top rashers of bacon are crisped under the broiler. Cabbage and bacon *(Recipe Index)* is of such high repute in South Africa that it gave Afrikaans a unique expression: *kool sonder spek*—cabbage *without* bacon —a term used to describe anything lacking in character or flavor.

South African fruits are no less a source of pride and care. Only the other day, walking with a friend through one of the wine and fruit farms established at the Cape nearly three centuries ago, I was delighted to see once again how well the colony's founders had planned their farming. They harvested their first apricots, for example, in early spring. I well recall how in my boyhood, after the austerities of winter, the yellow fruit would tempt me and my schoolmates to raid the orchards and eat and eat until we slunk away, suffering from a well-known indisposition of the Cape called apricot tummy. Almost into the autumn, these first apricots were followed by other varieties of their kind, maturing later and later; but by Christmastime—which is to say, by South Africa's early summer —the new plums were supplanting apricots in our affections. One by one crops of figs, peaches and grapes would appear in ordered succession, followed at the first hint of autumn by quinces and pomegranates, which could be stored in our gabled attics almost indefinitely. Autumn itself brought medlars and persimmons, large and aglow, like lamps in the darkening groves, along with crops of amber loquat and the guava. Sliced open, the guavas were rich with the colors of a Gauguin painting, and their jams, jellies and bottled forms were exciting elements of Cape fare. To round out the cavalcade of fruit there were melons—muskmelons, watermelons and winter melons—and strawberries. These strawberries, above all the kind from the hills around the Stellenbosch—named after the great Simon van der Stel—were a saga in themselves. On hot summer days hawkers used to carry them through the streets of Cape Town, loaded in great wicker baskets, from which smaller baskets tenderly tucked between quilts of oak leaves threw off delicious intermingled scents. The street cry that announced their coming was more melodious than any cry I ever heard in the streets of London, and it brought a rush of perspiring citizens out of the big white houses to their gates.

One fruit, the Cape gooseberry, merits special mention. It is not a native of the Cape; according to an old legend, it came from the Crimea in one of the Russian ships that used to drop anchor in Table Bay. Whatever its origin, it is now stabilized in a single variety. When ripe, it is a green-gold berry topped by a straw-colored hood, or *kappie* (sunbonnet). All refined tastes in fruit, I think, are highly ambivalent, and a Cape gooseberry combines tartness and sweetness, creating a tension that makes music on the tongue. It can be used to play the role that cranberries do in the roasts of America, but to us it is most popular as a jam—not a jam in the mass-produced form that does its reputation so much injury in the world outside, but as we made it at home.

In the category of preserves, however, perhaps the greatest honor

Continued on page 162

The cook counts the crayfish. Several days of bad weather cut down on the catch, and the party bought a few from a fisherman.

Sun, Sand and Crayfish on Blouberg Strand

For these University of Cape Town students the white sands of Blouberg Strand, just across Table Bay, make an ideal site for a picnic on a sunny and relatively calm day. Not far from the city, Blouberg offers a wealth of crayfish for the catching. (Also known as spiny or rock lobsters, these crustaceans are the source of South Africa's meaty, delicious and widely exported rock lobster tails.) A few hours of skin diving, while a jug of Lieberstein wine cools in the sand at the water line, are usually capped by a lobster or two per picnicker. Boiled *(right)* and served with mayonnaise, the result is a simple yet sophisticated meal.

The silverware at a Blouberg Strand picnic is generally limited to a single hunting knife to stir the pot and split the cooked crayfish; eating is done with the fingers *(left)*. The wind whistling off the bay tends to sprinkle sand over everything liberally, and the fire had to be protected by a windbreak built of sand and driftwood. But a copious supply of inexpensive Lieberstein wine *(below)* helped to set an agreeable tone for the proceedings.

should go to the Cape form of tangerine, the *naartje,* with its thin, closely fitting skin of citrus satin. It is to the Cape what the kumquat is to China, and I suspect that the Cape way with the *naartje* is a local application of good kumquat principles borrowed from the Far East. A *naartje* preserve contains two pounds of sugar for every pound of fresh fruit. The *naartjes* are scraped (preferably with a knife of bone or glass, for all good Cape cooks believe that metal imparts an unpleasant flavor to the fruit), two slits are cut across the bottom, and the fruit is soaked in several changes of water for as long as three days. At the end of that period the sugar is made into a syrup, in which the fruit soaks for one more night. The process of turning it into a preserve, which finally starts the next day, consists of simmering the syrup slowly until the *naartjes* within it are almost translucent. Almost any citrus fruit, even a huge grapefruit, is preserved in this way and used instead of marmalade to bring a special glow to a South Africa breakfast table.

The final branch of cooking in which the Cape colonists achieved distinction was in the baking of breads, cakes, biscuits, tarts and pastries. The earliest Cape cookbooks devote the major portions of their texts to the arts of baking, as if the cooking of meat, fish and vegetables was so inbred a skill that it could be taken for granted, while every home baker required guidance and new points of departure.

The spirit of invention was strong. Cookies, for example—particularly the *soetkoekie (Recipe Index),* or sweet cookie—multiplied like rabbits at the Cape. Indeed, Cape cooks conjured up so many different kinds of cookies that they were hard put to find names for them. Some are named after national events or historical faces—for example, Bond cookies ("Bond" refers to the first great political party formed at the Cape to reconcile the conflicting interests of the English and the Dutch). Other labels include uncle's cookies, auntie's cookies, bachelor's cookies, spinster's cookies and snatched-kisses cookies.

All this variety was possible because, early in its history, the Cape discovered near the site of what is now the thriving country town of Malmesbury a great stretch of black earth ideal for growing wheat. This earth was as dark as the famous *chornozem* of Russia, and as fertile as any land in the Ukraine. Indeed, several hardy breeds of wheat were imported from the Ukraine, because Malmesbury endured Ukrainian extremes of climate: cold winters, with cold winds; long, rainless summers, with a heat so intense that the air seemed to run like molten glass, and rains that, when they did come, were fickle and unpredictable. But the wheat throve and so from earliest times the Cape colony had the material to support the art of baking and cultivated it diligently and well.

For me, the supreme place in this section of the national kitchen is occupied by something we call *mosbolletjie. Mos* is the Afrikaans word for grape juice in the first stage of fermentation; *bolletjie* is both a diminutive and a form of endearment of the Dutch word *bol,* which means a sphere, ball or bun. And a grape "bunlet" is a great pastry.

There are almost as many Cape versions of *mosbolletjie* as there are of cookies. A good example of its more sophisticated form is given by Miss Duckitt in a recipe that suggests the vast quantities of the pastry that used

Opposite: Crayfish curry, like many other dishes popular at the Cape of Good Hope, was originally a creation of immigrant Malay cooks who brought their traditional Far Eastern foods to South Africa. In the version shown, modifications of their recipe—such as the addition of tomatoes to the sauce—reflect European tastes *(Recipe Index).*

162

to be baked in an average household once a day or every other day. The recipe calls for 16 pounds of flour, three and a half pounds of sugar, two pounds of raisins, eight eggs, one and a half pounds of butter, a pound of animal fat, two tablespoons of aniseed, two grated nutmegs and a tablespoon of ground cinnamon. Freshly fermented grape juice is normally used to activate all of this mixture, except for the butter, fat and eggs, and produces the best buns. The *mosbolletjie* mixture is then placed in a large pastry basin, a depression is made in the center and the fermented raisin juice is strained through a sieve to join it. Some flour is sprinkled over the top of the juice, and the basin is set aside in a warm place for several hours while the mixture rises. This is the critical stage in the making of the bunlets. All good Cape cooks believe that the banging of a kitchen door or even a loud noise can make the rising mixture loose its spirit and collapse. I have never known our kitchen so silent as in those hours of the six days of the week on which *mosbolletjies* were baked. Nor can I forget the chastening I received at the hands of one of our cooks when I once burst into the kitchen at the height of the rising. I never did it again.

When the mixture had properly risen, the butter and fat were melted, the separated yolks and whites of the eggs were briskly whisked, and the whole was mixed together with enough warm milk to enable the cook to knead the ingredients into a stiff dough. All this had to be done by hand and no self-respecting cook would consider it done in less than three quarters of an hour. Once more the dough was set aside and tenderly covered like a infant, with a special blanket of its own. In the morning the buns were shaped from the dough, set side by side in buttered baking pans, and left in the same warm place for a final half an hour of rising. Then they were brushed with the yolk of an egg and a mixture of milk and sugar and baked for half an hour in a hot oven.

To this day I cannot say which of two great aspects of *mosbolletjies* I find most exhilarating. One is the sight of them coming out of the oven, joined together shoulder to shoulder like a battalion of guardsmen trooping the colors, their heads covered in deep dark brown like that of Attic honey. The other is their scent, which spread from the kitchen and pantry to our nursery tea room like a perfume. When the buns were separated, one was amazed that a headgear so dark brown could cover a body so fluffy and so white. Eaten warm with the freshest of butter and tea or coffee, there was nothing more appetizing for us in the bleakness of a cold winter's afternoon.

But that was not the end of the enormous service *mosbolletjies* performed for us. Next morning the leftover bunlets were cut in half, set in another baking pan and baked into the brown rusks we call *mosbeskuit,* a word derived from the French Huguenot *biscuit,* or twice baked. *Mosbeskuit* introduced us to the Cape form of the French *petit déjeuner,* or breakfast. It consisted of a cup of the hottest coffee and milk and a small plate of *mosbeskuit,* usually brought to our bedside just at the break of the fierce impatient day of Africa. We would eat the hard biscuit as the French peasant used to eat his twice-baked bread, dunked first in the coffee and swallowed along with sips of the hot liquid. If there is a better way to begin a strenuous working day, I do not know it.

Opposite: Three South African pastries reflect their Dutch ancestry in Afrikaans names. The almond-topped *soetkoekies (bottom)* are rich with spices; *koesisters,* the intricate braided crullers at center, can be assembled easily by following the illustrated directions in the recipe; *krakelinge,* the crisp figure-8 cookies at top, are dusted with sugar and chopped nuts.

To serve 4

1 cup dried apples
½ cup dried pitted prunes
½ cup seedless raisins
1½ cups water
1½ pounds boneless lamb
   shoulder or 1½ pounds beef
   chuck, trimmed of excess fat and
   cut into 1-inch cubes
1 teaspoon salt
2 tablespoons vegetable oil
1 cup finely chopped onions
2 tablespoons curry powder,
   preferably Madras type
2 tablespoons red wine vinegar
1 tablespoon strained fresh lemon
   juice
¼ cup salted peanuts, coarsely
   chopped
2 medium-sized bananas

Dried Fruit Curry *(South Africa)*

Combine the apples, prunes and raisins in a bowl, pour the water over them and let them soak for at least 1 hour, turning the fruit occasionally.

Pat the cubes of lamb or beef completely dry with paper towels and sprinkle them with the salt. In a heavy 10- to 12-inch skillet, heat the oil over moderate heat until a light haze forms above it. Brown the meat in the hot oil in 2 or 3 batches, turning the cubes about frequently with kitchen tongs or a slotted spoon and regulating the heat so that they color richly and evenly without burning. As they brown, transfer the cubes of meat to a plate. Set aside.

Pour off all but about 2 tablespoons of the fat from the skillet and drop in the onions. Stirring constantly and scraping up the browned bits clinging to the bottom of the pan, cook the onions for 3 or 4 minutes, or until they are soft.

Reduce the heat to low, add the curry powder, and stir for 2 minutes or so. Then return the meat, along with any liquid that has accumulated around it, to the skillet. Stir in the apples, prunes and raisins and their soaking water, the vinegar and the lemon juice. Bring to a boil over high heat, then reduce the heat to low.

Partially cover the skillet and simmer for about 1 hour, or until the meat is tender and shows no resistance when pierced with the point of a small, sharp knife. Check the pan from time to time and, if the mixture looks too dry, add up to ¼ cup water, a few tablespoons at a time. When the curry is done, however, most of the liquid in it should have cooked away.

Taste for seasoning and mound the curry on a heated platter. Just before serving, sprinkle the peanuts over the curry. Peel the bananas, cut them into ⅛-inch-thick slices and arrange the slices around the curry. Dried fruit curry is traditionally accompanied by hot boiled rice.

To make about 30 cookies

1½ cups all-purpose flour
1 teaspoon double-acting baking
   powder
1 teaspoon ground cinnamon
⅛ teaspoon salt
8 tablespoons butter (1 quarter-
   pound stick), softened
¾ cup sugar
1 whole egg, lightly beaten
1 egg white combined with 2
   teaspoons water and beaten to a
   froth
½ cup blanched almonds, finely
   chopped or pulverized in a
   blender or with a nut grinder

Krakelinge *(South Africa)*
FIGURE-8 COOKIES

Sift the flour, baking powder, cinnamon and salt together onto a strip of wax paper and set aside.

In a deep mixing bowl, cream together 7 tablespoons of the butter and ½ cup of the sugar, beating and mashing them against the sides of the bowl with the back of a large spoon until they are thoroughly blended.

Beat in the whole egg, then add the sifted flour mixture, about ½ cup at a time, stirring well after each addition. With your hands vigorously knead the dough in the bowl until it can be gathered into a somewhat firm, compact ball.

On a lightly floured surface, roll the dough into a rectangle at least 6 inches wide, 15 inches long and about ¼ inch thick. With a ruler and a pastry wheel or small, sharp knife, trim the rectangle to exactly 6 by 15 inches, and then cut it crosswise into 30 strips each ½ inch wide and 6 inches long.

Dried apples, raisins and prunes are cooked with meat in a dried-fruit curry; the banana slices and peanuts are garnishes.

To shape each *krakelinge,* gently pinch and fold the long edges of one strip of dough together and roll the strip lightly into a pencil-like cylinder about 6 or 7 inches long and ⅓ inch in diameter. Lift one end of the cylinder in each hand, cross the ends over one another, and loop them together to make a figure 8. Pinch the ends together tightly and lay the cookie on a wire cake rack set over wax paper.

When all of the *krakelinge* have been shaped, spread the beaten egg-white mixture lightly over the tops with a pastry brush. Stir the almonds and the remaining ¼ cup of sugar together and sprinkle the mixture evenly over the cookies.

Carefully transfer the racks of cookies to the refrigerator and chill them for at least 30 minutes, which will firm the dough and set their shape before baking.

Preheat the oven to 400°. With the pastry brush, spread the remaining tablespoon of butter evenly on 2 large baking sheets. Carefully transfer the cookies with a metal spatula to the buttered sheets, arranging them 1 inch apart. Bake the cookies in the middle of the oven for about 12 minutes, or until they are delicately browned.

With a spatula, transfer the *krakelinge* to wire racks to cool. The cookies will keep up to 2 weeks in a tightly covered tin.

To make about 4 dozen 3-inch-long
  crullers

SYRUP

4 cups sugar
2 cups water
3 pieces of stick cinnamon, each 2
  inches long
2 tablespoons strained fresh lemon
  juice
2 pieces lemon peel, each 3 by 1
  inch
A pinch of salt
¼ teaspoon cream of tartar
  combined with 2 teaspoons cold
  water

CRULLERS

4 cups all-purpose flour
4 teaspoons double-acting baking
  powder
½ teaspoon ground cinnamon
½ teaspoon ground nutmeg,
  preferably freshly grated
½ teaspoon salt
2 tablespoons butter, chilled and cut
  into ¼-inch bits
2 tablespoons lard, chilled and cut
  into ¼-inch bits
1½ cups buttermilk
Vegetable oil for deep frying

HOW TO BRAID A KOESISTER
Each tiny 1-by-3-inch rectangle of
dough is braided into a separate
koesister as shown in the drawings
at right: With a pastry wheel or
small, sharp knife, divide the
rectangle lengthwise into three
equal strips cutting from the narrow
bottom end to within about ½ inch
of the top edge. Starting at the top,
interweave the strips into a tight
three-plaited braid (*center*). Pinch
the loose bottom ends together and
tuck them snugly under the braid.

Koesisters (South Africa)
BRAIDED CRULLERS WITH CINNAMON-AND-LEMON SYRUP

First prepare the syrup in the following fashion: Combine the sugar,
water, stick cinnamon, lemon juice, lemon peel and a pinch of salt in a 2-
to 3-quart saucepan. Cook over moderate heat, stirring constantly until
the sugar dissolves. Stir in the cream of tartar mixture, increase the heat
to high, and cook briskly, uncovered and undisturbed, until the syrup
reaches a temperature of 230° on a candy thermometer or a small amount
dropped into ice water instantly forms a coarse thread.

Remove the pan from the heat at once and place it in a large pot of ice
water. Stir gently until the syrup cools to room temperature. Remove and
discard the cinnamon sticks and lemon peel, and refrigerate the syrup for
at least 2 hours, or until it is thoroughly chilled.

To make the *koesisters,* sift the flour, baking powder, ground cinnamon, nutmeg and ½ teaspoon of salt together into a deep bowl. Drop
in the butter and lard and, with your fingertips, rub the flour and fat together until the mixture looks like fine, dry meal. Stirring constantly with
a large spoon, slowly pour in the buttermilk in a thin stream, and continue to stir until all the ingredients are well combined. Then knead the
mixture with your hands until it forms a soft, pliable dough. Divide the
dough into two balls and drape a dampened kitchen towel over them
loosely until you are ready to roll them.

On a lightly floured surface, pat one ball of dough into a rectangular
shape about 1 inch thick, then roll it into a rectangle at least 12 inches
long and 6 inches wide and no more than ¼ inch thick. With a pastry
wheel or small, sharp knife and a ruler, trim the rectangle to exactly 12
by 6 inches. Cut the rectangle crosswise into four 3-inch strips and divide
each of these into six 1-inch-wide pieces to make a total of 24 rectangles
each 3 by 1 inch. Following the diagrams, cut and braid each of these
small rectangles into a *koesister*. Set them aside on wax paper and cover
them with a dampened kitchen towel, then roll, cut and shape the remaining ball of dough similarly.

Pour the vegetable oil into a deep fryer or large, heavy saucepan to a
depth of 2 or 3 inches and heat the oil until it reaches a temperature of
375° on a deep-frying thermometer. Fry the *koesisters* 4 or 5 at a time,
turning them occasionally with a slotted spoon, for about 4 minutes, or
until they are richly browned and crisp on all sides.

As they brown, transfer them to paper towels to drain briefly. While
they are still hot, immerse them in the cold syrup for a minute or so.
Then, with tongs, transfer them to a wire rack set over paper towels to
drain completely. Serve the *koesisters* warm or at room temperature.

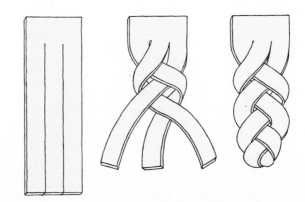

Soetkoekies *(South Africa)*
SWEET WINE AND SPICE COOKIES

To make about 30 two-inch cookies

Preheat the oven to 350°. With a pastry brush, spread 1 tablespoon of the softened butter evenly on two large baking sheets. Sift the flour, baking soda, cinnamon, ginger, cloves and salt together onto a strip of wax paper and set aside.

In a deep bowl, cream the remaining 4 tablespoons of butter and the dark-brown sugar together, mashing and beating them against the sides of the bowl until they are thoroughly blended. Beat in the egg, then add the flour mixture ½ cup at a time, stirring well after each addition. Beat in the wine and the chopped almonds.

With your hands vigorously knead the dough in the bowl until it can be gathered into a somewhat firm, compact ball. If the dough then seems too soft, knead in up to ¼ cup more flour, adding it a tablespoon or so at a time.

On a lightly floured surface, roll the dough into a rough circle about ¼ inch thick. With a cookie cutter or the rim of a glass, cut it into 2-inch rounds. Arrange the rounds about 1 inch apart on the buttered baking sheets. Then gather the scraps of dough into a ball, roll it out into another circle, and cut out rounds as before.

Press a blanched almond half lightly into the center of each *soetkoekie* and brush the entire top surface of the cookie with the beaten egg white-and-water mixture.

Bake the *soetkoekies* in the middle of the oven for 15 minutes, or until they are crisp and firm to the touch. With a wide metal spatula, transfer the cookies to a rack to cool. The cookies will keep up to 2 weeks in a tightly covered jar or tin.

5 tablespoons butter, softened
2 to 2¼ cups all-purpose flour
1 teaspoon baking soda
1 teaspoon ground cinnamon
½ teaspoon ground ginger
¼ teaspoon ground cloves
¼ teaspoon salt
1¼ cups dark-brown sugar
1 egg, lightly beaten
¼ cup port, Madeira or sweet sherry
½ cup blanched almonds, finely chopped or pulverized in a blender or with a nut grinder, plus 15 whole blanched almonds, split lengthwise into halves
1 egg white combined with 2 teaspoons of water and beaten to a froth

Rough Puff Pastry *(South Africa)*

Sift the flour and salt into a large chilled mixing bowl. Drop in the butter and lard and, working quickly, rub the flour and fat together with your fingertips until the mixture looks like flakes of coarse meal. Pour 4 tablespoons of ice water over the mixture all at once and gather the dough into a ball.

If the dough crumbles, add up to 2 tablespoons more of ice water, 1 teaspoon at a time, until the particles adhere. Dust lightly with flour, wrap the dough in wax paper and chill for 30 minutes.

Place the pastry dough on a lightly floured surface and press it into a rough rectangle about 1 inch thick. Dust a little flour over and under it, and roll it out into a strip about 21 inches long and 6 inches wide. Fold the strip into thirds to form a three-layered rectangular packet, reducing its dimensions to about 7 by 6 inches.

Turn the dough around so that an open end faces you and roll it out once more to a 21-by-6-inch strip. Fold it into thirds as before and roll it out again to a similar strip. Repeat this entire process twice more, ending with the dough folded into a packet.

Wrap the dough tightly in wax paper, foil or a plastic bag, and refrigerate it for at least 1 hour. The dough may be kept in the refrigerator for 3 or 4 days before it is used.

2 cups sifted all-purpose flour
¼ teaspoon salt
8 tablespoons (1 quarter-pound stick) unsalted butter, chilled and cut into ¼-inch bits
¼ cup lard, chilled and cut into ¼-inch bits
4 to 6 tablespoons ice water

Old-fashioned Dutch Chicken Pie (South Africa)

In a heavy 3- to 4-quart casserole, combine the chicken, onion, allspice, cloves, mace, salt and peppercorns. Pour in the 3 cups of water and bring to a boil over high heat.

Reduce the heat to low, cover the casserole tightly, and simmer until the bird is tender but not falling apart. (A roasting chicken should be done in about 1 hour; a stewing fowl may take as long as 2 hours, depending on its age.)

Transfer the chicken to a plate and strain the stock through a fine sieve set over a small saucepan. There should be about 3 cups of stock. If necessary, add fresh or canned stock to make that amount, or boil the cooking liquid uncovered over high heat to reduce it to 3 cups. With a small, sharp knife, remove the skin from the chicken and cut the meat away from the bones. Discard the skin and bones and cut the meat into 1-inch pieces. Set the chicken aside.

To prepare the sauce, skim as much fat as possible from the surface of the chicken stock. Stirring constantly with a wire whisk, add the wine and gradually pour in the Cream of Wheat in a thin stream, stirring over low heat until the mixture thickens lightly and comes to a boil.

In a small bowl, break up the egg yolks with a table fork, add the lemon juice, and when they are well mixed stir in 2 or 3 tablespoons of the sauce. Whisk the heated egg yolk-and-lemon mixture into the simmering sauce. Bring to a boil again and boil for 1 minute, whisking constantly. Remove the saucepan from the heat, taste the sauce for seasoning, and set it aside.

Spread half the chicken pieces evenly in a heavy 1½-quart casserole or baking dish at least 2 inches deep. Scatter the ham dice on top and arrange the egg slices over them. Then arrange the rest of the chicken over the eggs, and pour the sauce evenly over it.

Preheat the oven to 400°. On a lightly floured surface roll out the puff pastry into a rough rectangle about ¼ inch thick. Then, from the edge of the rectangle, cut 2 or more strips, each about ½ inch wide and long enough when placed end to end to cover the rim of the baking dish. Lay the strips around the rim and press them firmly into place. Moisten them lightly with a pastry brush dipped in cold water.

Drape the remaining pastry over the rolling pin, lift it up, and unfold it over the baking dish. Trim off the excess with a small, sharp knife and, with the tines of a fork or your fingers, crimp the pastry to secure it to the rim of the dish. Cut a 1-inch round hole in the center of the pastry covering to allow the steam to escape as the pie bakes.

Gather the scraps of pastry into a ball, reroll and cut it into simple leaf and flower or berry shapes; moisten one side with the egg-and-water mixture and arrange them decoratively on the pie. Then brush the entire pastry surface with the remaining egg-and-water mixture.

Bake the pie on the middle shelf of the oven at 400° for 15 minutes. Reduce the heat to 350°, and continue to bake for about 45 minutes longer, or until the crust is a delicate golden brown. Serve the chicken pie at once directly from the baking dish.

A 5-pound stewing fowl or roasting chicken, cut into 6 or 8 pieces
1 large onion, peeled and quartered
6 whole allspice
4 whole cloves
¼ teaspoon ground mace
1 teaspoon salt
6 whole black peppercorns
3 cups water
½ cup dry white wine
¼ cup Cream of Wheat
2 egg yolks
2 tablespoons strained fresh lemon juice
½ pound smoked ham, trimmed of excess fat and cut into ½-inch dice
2 hard-cooked eggs, cut crosswise into slices ¼ inch thick
1 recipe rough puff pastry (page 169)
1 egg combined with 1 tablespoon cold water and beaten lightly

Ornamental cutouts of pastry dough decorate an old-fashioned Dutch chicken pie. The old spice boxes contain the medley of spices that go into the pie: cloves, allspice, peppercorns and ground mace.

VIII

On the Track of the Voortrekkers

Often, in the heart of Africa, I have watched wild geese placidly afloat on some flashing hippopotamus water, as still as painted geese on a painted pool, looking as if they would be there forever, when suddenly, without even a honk at one another, just as if some common electrical current had conveyed an urgent warning, they would all together take wing and vanish over the bush into the blue. Something of this sort happened in the collective subconscious of great numbers of colonists at the Cape of Good Hope, mostly of Huguenot-Dutch descent, in 1835. With one accord, they decided they had had enough of Europe, as personified in the British administration that had won control of the Cape from the Dutch in 1795, and took off northward for the high and dangerous interior.

They loaded their long covered wagons with all the provisions and goods space would allow, hitched the wagons to their teams of oxen, put their women in the driving seats with their children alongside and their few servants within, gathered their cattle and mounted their horses. Leaving behind their well-established farms and comfortable homes, they forsook the colonial Cape and embarked on what history knows as the Great Trek. In time they settled in what are now the provinces called the Orange Free State, Transvaal and Natal—the springboards for later, equally adventurous leaps farther north into what later became Southern Rhodesia, Zambia and Malawi.

Just as their French and Dutch forebears had made the Cape a fertile and civilized colony in commemoration of the culture of the Europe they had abandoned, so these men took with them the memory of what was

Wearing the traditional bright blankets of their people, two Xhosa women carry corn and melons to market. The Xhosas are the most numerous tribe in South Africa; more than half live by cattle raising and by a rudimentary agriculture in the Transkei, a windswept region on the Indian Ocean below Natal.

good in the way of life of the Cape. Yet, under new and grimmer circumstances, they evolved something more authentically African than the oddly Mediterranean colony they left behind, and soon this was reflected in their way of cooking. In the process of their pioneering, they made greater contact with Bantu Africa than ever before in the history of southern Africa. In the vast areas to the north of the Cape, the Bantu was safe from slave traders, and his societies were relatively stable and organized. He owned cattle, and their milk was his most valuable and plentiful source of food. Cultivation of the land—the responsibility of Bantu women—concentrated on cereals, particularly millet, or "Kaffir corn." The women pounded it with pestles like long, heavy cudgels, in mortars carved out of wood and standing on pedestals three to four feet high. Even now, the sound of the pounding of corn evokes an acute vision of the whole of Africa before the coming the European.

The porridge the Bantus made from millet, as well as their millet beer (which many Europeans still believe contains healing properties for flagging stomachs and rheumatic joints), were their major contributions to the food of everyone in the interior. Today in southern Africa porridge made from millet is still the favorite, and this holds true despite the introduction of a great rival: the porridge made from the meal of American Indian corn, or maize, or, to give it its South African name, mealie. The pioneers planted mealie wherever they found suitable earth. Soon it was also as much a Bantu crop as a European one and was established as a basic feature of Bantu diet, so that it is hard to say which of the two sectors of the population gained more from the swap. But had it not been for millet and mealie, the new pioneers transplanted from the Cape would have found their harsh life even more precarious.

174

Though it is possible to argue over which of the two cereals produces the better of our national porridges, there is no doubt that mealie was for a host of reasons the more important. It is impossible even to whisper the word to South Africans of any color without evoking the subtlest associations of childhood and inherited history. The mealie even appears in the most popular of all South African folk songs. This was written by a Boer prisoner of war on the island of Ceylon at the beginning of the century, yearning as all good folk songsters do for his native land, and particularly the girl for whom the song is named. Each stanza of the song is made effective as a national tear-jerker by ending the chorus with lines noting that it is "Down by the mealies and the green-thorn tree where my Sarie [Sarah] lives."

On the pioneer's march into the interior there was a brief period when his attitude to his livestock resembled that of the Bantu: suddenly he found them too valuable to be used as food except in dire extremities, for they were the precious seeds of future plenty in the promised land he hoped to settle. As far as possible he got his meat by hunting game, as abundant in the interior as fish were in the seas of the Cape. In due course he evolved a set of skills in cooking venison and wild fowl. As a people on the move for months and even years on end, the Boers could not afford to linger overnight in camps waiting on elaborate processes of cooking. They had to rely mostly on foods they prepared in bulk during one prolonged stopover, foods that could last until a suitable time and place arrived for the supply to be renewed again.

The role that pickled fish played at the Cape colony was played on the Great Trek by meat that was salted, spiced and cured. It was hung in strips from ropes suspended between the trees of thorn and spreading acacias

On Major Piet van der Byl's backlands farm in Cape Province, two farmhands break open bales of alfalfa to feed a flock of sheep. The season is winter and grazing is sparse; the best of the fields and most of the alfalfa are reserved for lambing ewes. Wool from sheep like these Merinos is South Africa's principal export commodity.

175

or the wild willows and poplars that marked some stream or natural spring where camp was pitched for longer than usual. The pioneer and soon the national South African word for meat prepared in this way was *biltong.* The English people of the towns have always expressed a horror of *biltong,* regarding it as proof of the lack of culture of the interior. Yet *biltong* is just another aspect of the honored, universal way of preserving meat or fish. It is akin to the Parma prosciutto of Italy, the *jambon de Bayonne* of France, the smoked salmon of Scotland, the *carne seca* of Mexico, the *tassajo* of South America, and the *déndéng* of the jungles of Java. But the country that comes closest to producing an equivalent of *biltong* is Switzerland. I have met it there as *Bündnerfleisch,* or the famous *viande de Grisons.* Delicately carved in ruby-red slices, it appears without the slightest hint of an inferiority complex on the menus of the best Swiss restaurants and hotels.

The secret of good *biltong* is the fact that initially it was made out of the best meat of the animal killed for the purpose. At a period when there was no refrigeration and life was constantly one of movement and uncertainty, the game shot for food was never wasted. What had to be eaten fresh was eaten soon after the killing. Thus, liver and kidneys went almost warm from the animal onto the portable grill, were cooked on wooden coals, and were consumed as one of the greatest of delicacies; they remain so to this day. The meat that could be pot-roasted over camp-fires—and eaten cold for some days afterwards—formed only a small proportion of the meat of animals as big as the buffalo or eland. When game of this size was killed, the camp if at all possible would be pitched long enough to convert what could not be immediately eaten into *biltong.* Most of the fat was rendered for invaluable items like soap or candle wax. The skins were salted, dried and tanned to make leather for what we call *velskoens*—veld shoes—as well as for clothes for the men, whips, bridles, halters, saddles and harnesses for the horses, thongs for the yokes of oxen, and strips for cross-woven bases of chairs and beds. Everything was used because all was a matter of life and death.

Once the pioneers took to permanent farming, the cattle slaughtered for food were dealt with exactly as the game had been, and *biltong* made out of the best beef became a prized food. The meat was cut into solid strips, each weighing from three to eight pounds. The strips were rubbed with a little salt and left for an hour or so before another good rubbing with a mixture of half a pound of brown sugar to an ounce of saltpeter. The meat was then left for one to three days, according to the heat and climate in which the animal had been killed, and from time to time was rubbed with the same mixture. After that it was hung in a cool, dry place and left to cure. Done this way, *biltong* could last for years. Though the outside would look hard, dry and unyielding, the inside would still be ruby-red, moist, fragrant and delicious. Indeed the meat within could be so fresh that if it was thinly cut one could grill it or even fry it as a kind of bacon. It made a delicious supper dish. One of our great outdoor pleasures as children on the farms in the interior was to sit on winter nights huddled close by a wood fire, with a dish full of thinly sliced beef *biltong* by our sides; each of us, armed with a little wooden skewer, would grill

the *biltong* on the fire and eat it as if it were some new kind of Arabian delight. At home, I preferred it cut in the thinnest of slices or grated, and eaten piled thick on slices of whole-meal bread warm from the oven and well covered with fresh butter.

A fellow traveler of *biltong* was our friend the *mosbolletjie,* or grape bunlet, of the Cape, grown into robust, manly form and rebaptized *boerbeskuit*—farmer's rusks. For long periods these rusks took the place of bread. They proved so vital that, along with *biltong,* they became the subject of legislation. A law compelled every male from 14 to 65 to be prepared to serve his country, and part of the preparedness required that he have on hand *biltong* and *boerbeskuit* enough for one month, plus 50 rounds of ammunition and two horses for riding into battle. The rusks and *biltong* were chosen not only because they were excellent sustenance, but also because they were light and easy to carry in saddlebags. As late as 1914, when civil war broke out in South Africa and my older brothers were called up, I remember what a flurry of cooking and baking followed since we had enough *biltong* but not enough *boerbeskuit* to send with them into battle.

None of the people who took part in the Great Trek had the time or indeed the facility to put in writing the account of the life on the uncharted

In a mud-walled hut in the Transkei, a Xhosa woman grinds mealie meal for porridge in a stone "mill." The girls in the background have daubed their faces with white powder as part of the lengthy initiation ceremony marking their passage into womanhood. In the Transkei cooking is generally done indoors over an open fire, because the wind is too strong outside.

The Afrikaner *braaivleis* (literally, "grilled meat") is something between a large-scale American outdoor barbecue and a patio cookout; the picture above shows a relatively modest *braaivleis*. In the garden of his farm near Pretoria, Dawie van Heerden *(left)* places onions, potatoes and coils of a type of sausage called *boerewors* on a charcoal grill, while a friend grinds corn to make mealie meal porridge and the ladies prepare side dishes.

road into the interior. Almost all we know about this incredible episode has come down to us in the same way as the history of Bantu Africa, by word of mouth from generation to generation. In my family, fortunately, this word was loud and clear, because my grandmother was a survivor of one of the foremost treks. Her eldest daughter—my mother was the youngest—was closest to this period, and whenever she visited us, she would have to sit up with us night after night trying to satisfy the infinite curiosity we had as children about that melodramatic event in our history. As a special treat this aunt would take charge of our kitchen and cook the delicacies of the pioneers—things like the *voortrekker-koekie,* a rough descendant of the cookie, or *vetkoekies,* an adaptation of the doughnut.

The pioneers made *voortrekker-koekies* only on the rare occasions when they had enough cream to make a little butter. For baking powder they used "cream of tartar," their name for the extract they made from the fruit of the baobab tree. The dough was rolled out as for biscuits, but in shapes according to the cook's fancy. The more the consumers were children, the more fantastic the shapes. The *vetkoekie,* according to my aunt, was made in the proportions of one whisked egg to a breakfast cup of meal, two tablespoons of sugar, half a cup of milk and two teaspoons of baking powder. The meal and baking powder were mixed dry, the whisked egg, sugar and milk were added to form the dough, and the ingredients were dropped into boiling fat until they turned dark brown. They were eaten as they were or, if possible, dusted with sugar.

The making of the pioneers' all-important bread was a far more serious proposition because of the longer preparation and greater heat required. In the time of my youth, bread was best baked in ovens outside the house, built of good red firebricks. These ovens were usually near the great loam pots or coppers used for the making of soap. Both were sources of wonder to us as children. The loam pots were built into the top of a large square brick pedestal about four feet high, with room underneath for a grate in which a fierce fire could be maintained. One of my earliest memories is the vision of one of our maids standing by the copper with a long wooden ladle stirring it as it bubbled and chortled like the witches' cauldron in *Macbeth*, while she crooned a strange song over it until the loam for soap was done. The bread oven, close by, was twice as tall as the pedestal for the loam pot and about eight feet long, with a domed roof made of layers of brick laid as closely together as the planking of a boat and in the pattern of a succession of perfect Norman arches.

Some hours before the dough for the bread was kneaded and left to rise in the warm kitchen, one of the men would lay the brick oven with dry wood and light it. Whenever he opened the iron gate of the oven, one looked straight into a world of flame after flame dancing and leaping in an intricate pattern. By the time the bread was ready for baking, the bricks could be no hotter and only live coals were left of the wood, their glow swiftly fading on the oven floor. Then the loaves would arrive from the kitchen, borne aloft under a canopy of damp, snow-white cloth, like the remains of a distinguished person being conducted on a bier toward a state cremation. The loaves would be solemnly inserted in the oven, and the iron door clamped to and locked. Although the coals within were either dead or dying, the heat contained in the bricks was enough to produce bread, each loaf with its head high and browned to perfection.

For safety's sake the bread oven and loam copper were built in a far corner of the courtyard outside our kitchen, where the air would be full of scents coming over the white walls from the gardens and orchards that lay beyond. But the wonderful smell of fresh bread would dominate all others as the resurrected loaves were carried back triumphantly across the courtyard into the house.

Our huge old-fashioned kitchen range had an oven too, large enough for baking bread, but this oven was reserved exclusively for more finicky, delicate substances like *mosbolletjies,* cakes, tarts, pastries and the proliferating race of *soetkoekies.* Curiously, the oven was never used for roasting even the biggest joints of meat. All our meat was pot-roasted, and the size of some of our cast-iron pots used to roast a baron of beef or a leg of mutton had to be seen to be believed. The cooking of the interior assumed, almost as an 11th commandment, that *all* meat had to be pot-roasted to give of its best.

The chief source of meat in the interior was and is mutton. From the moment the pioneers settled down to permanent farming, sheep raising became the mainstay of their economy. In crossing the escarpment that separated the Cape Colony from the interior, they had traversed a wa-

Overleaf: With a few extra touches, the foods traditionally served at an outdoor *braaivleis* can become an elegant indoor dinner. The *sosaties* of skewered lamb *(top left)* were marinated in a curry-tamarind sauce and broiled in the oven. The *boerewors,* or beef and pork sausage, at bottom left, can be grilled or fried. Accompanying the meats are green mealie "bread" (actually a steamed corn pudding), a salad and baked potatoes.

terless sort of wasteland known as the Little and the Great Karroos. The Little Karroo had a slightly more reliable climate and accordingly was settled first. Many of the features of Cape farming were reproduced there, including even the growing of grapes, fruit and vegetables.

The Great Karroo, which stretched for hundreds of arid miles into the heart of what became the Orange Free State, posed the real problem. But the pioneers soon unlocked the secret of this apparently intractable earth. First they based themselves at some rare fountain of water or fickle stream and slowly spread outward from it; they dammed clefts and depressions to catch rain water when it fell and so secured permanent watering places for their sheep and cattle. On the Great Karroo a strange, gnarled little shrub grew, with fantastically deep and intricate roots that enabled it to survive the longest periods of drought. At the end of what looked like a dead twig it put out a green, fragrant and glutinous leaf on which sheep thrived as they had never thrived even on the grass of the Cape; moreover, it gave their meat exceptional savor. Once the sheep had water to drink, this region turned into one of the greatest sheep-rearing and wool-growing areas of the earth, comparable to the best sheep lands of Australia and New Zealand.

Soon the water collected behind dams was reinforced by the erection of windmills and the sinking of wells to pump out water for the sheep to drink and to fill reservoirs to irrigate kitchen gardens and orchards. This for me was always one of the most moving aspects about the pioneers: although they had rejected the Cape forever and there never was any thought of turning back, they were pursued by a dream of all that they had left behind. Wherever they went and as soon as they could, they reproduced in miniature the gardens that had been the main purpose of the original Cape settlement. They also planted orchards and ornamental trees. As their water supplies improved they expanded the pattern and were soon sending back to the Cape for greater and more varied supplies of plants and seeds to make each farm a surprising green oasis.

The best houses of the pioneers were built on secure stone terraces called *stoeps,* with the house itself in the center. On the sunny side of the *stoep,* the house beams were intertrellised with lighter cross timber to support grapevines. In the summer one could sit in the shade of the dense leaves and by just reaching up pick one's own bunch of grapes at the end of a meal. These vines reached proportions that were not exceeded even at the Cape. By some law, which makes fruit wrested from Cinderella earth and desert sweeter and lovelier than any other kind of fruit, their grapes were far better for eating and for turning into jam or jelly than their colonial prototypes. The same law governed the orchards. The Cape grew and continues to grow fruit for the world; the interior could only grow fruit for its own consumption, but of incomparable flavor. The peaches and the apricots were bigger, crisper, less woolly and ultimately better subjects for canning and jamming.

The fig trees alone seemed a whole chapter of Revelation, so Biblical in their appearance and abundance that one thought of them instinctively as offshoots of the garden from which Adam and Eve were ejected. In our childlike imaginations we divided our figs into two kinds. The thin-skinned, extremely sweet white varieties were known as Eve's figs, while the large purple pear-shaped ones, growing in trees so big that we could play in them, were obviously male, and known as Adam's figs. We applied the same imaginative fancy to the grapes we grew. One kind grew in clusters so dense and large that we called them Canaan grapes, because to pioneers in search of a new promised land they were like the grapes of which they read in the Old Testament around their campfires at night, the grapes that Joshua's spies, returning across the Jordan, had to carry suspended across a wooden stave held by two men, so heavy were they. To the parched Israelites, after 40 years of wandering in the deserts of Sinai, the grapes of Canaan were final proof that their land of divine promise had been found at last.

Our gardens and orchards, like those at the Cape, were designed to produce something most of the year. In the winter, citrus fruits like the ubiquitous *naartje,* or tangerine, and the bitter kind of grapefruit used principally for jam, called *pompelmoes* (obviously a corruption of the French word for grapefruit, *pamplemousse*) helped us over the worst of the season when no other fruits or vegetables were available. Nonetheless there were long periods to be faced without either, and despite the fact that we had fresh meat and fresh milk, this lack was a health hazard. Without refrigeration, the only means of creating some kind of substitute was by canning or making jam. The scale on which this was done in a well-founded household was immense. In the process of getting the household shipshape for the voyage from autumn into summer, vegetables like peas and beans and fruits from the smallest plums to the largest peaches were bottled on a titanic scale. Jam making, however, surpassed all other efforts because jam was not restricted just to a winter role. Among a people who relied so much on their daily bread, jam was consumed three or four times a day, all year round.

For some reason the apple, which did well at the Cape, never thrived in the interior. Its place was taken over by the quince, and quince jam was easily made. The quinces were peeled, cored and sliced fairly thick and placed in either a copper or enamel pot that had been scrupulously cleaned and oiled. Just enough water to float the last layer of quinces was poured in, and the quinces were boiled with an amount of sugar equal in weight to the peeled fruit until the mixture was clear but not mushy. This was one of our favorite jams with bread and butter, but it was also often served instead of a jelly with roast venison, particularly a roast leg of springbok, by far the most appetizing game to be found in Africa.

Quince was also made into a *sambal* that we considered a must with curries and *boboties.* This *sambal* was very simply made. The quince was peeled and grated, a little salt added, and the "quince mince" squeezed to free it from moisture. The pulp was then put into a china bowl, mixed with some finely chopped chilies and a little lemon juice but never any vinegar, even wine vinegar, which only made it harsh and crude. This *sambal* was delicious with smoked and dried fish dishes and to my taste nicer than horseradish with a heavy roast. Sometimes the whole quince, cored and baked and only slightly sugared, was used as an accompaniment to roast pork and, usually, fat mutton or beef roast dishes; and of course

Continued on page 187

For an Ostrich Omelet: One Egg and a Big Pan

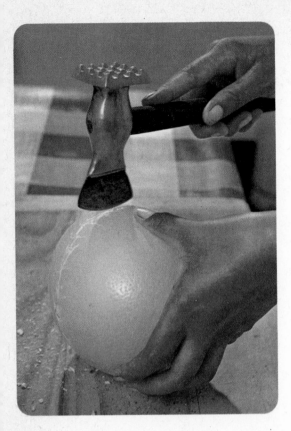

Ostriches once roamed from the Cape of Good Hope to Syria, in the Middle East. Now they are almost extinct outside Africa, and even on that continent they have become a rarity. The birds simply had too much to offer to man—especially during the period around the turn of the century, when their plumes were in fashion and though on open ground with a following wind the flightless ostrich can run 40 miles an hour, it is not hard to kill. Today, ostriches are raised commercially in thatched lean-tos *(opposite)*, mainly near the town of Oudtshoorn in Cape Province, and about 60,000 pounds of feathers are collected annually. The eggs, however, are far more useful than the feathers. An ostrich egg weighs about three pounds, and a single clutch may contain 15 eggs. The one being split open at left made an omelet big enough to feed a dozen people *(below),* and the taste was comparable to that of the best hen's egg.

there was quince sauce, made exactly as apple sauce is made. Recalling all this, I am amazed at the disappearance of the quince from so many modern kitchens and its neglect in Western European orchards.

But the unique feature of a home garden in the interior was the mulberry fruit tree, an emigré from China. As a child I watched with growing excitement as the mulberry began to appear, swell from a startling, phosphorescent green-white shape into a large red fruit, and finally turn into deep purple to show that it was imperially ripe for eating. One tree in our garden produced more berries than we could possibly use, and the whole village was invited to come and fill baskets with berries destined for pastries, pies and puddings.

We would eat the mulberry raw by itself in the garden, or at table on a hot day with cream and sugar or as a thick syrup made by adding three cups of sugar to every cup of mulberries and cooking them until they gained the required thickness; the syrup was strained but the tiny mulberry seeds remained behind, and it could be preserved in jars like any other confection. One ate it as jam—and mixed with clear honey as a cough mixture for sore throats or bronchitis.

One reason why our jams were so good was that an effort was made to prevent the original fruit from being overcooked and in the slightest degree mushy. Whenever possible, the fruit was preserved whole or just halved so that the stones, which could make some jams unpleasantly bitter, could be removed. Figs were always made into jam whole, even the green fig, which next to the Cape gooseberry makes perhaps the most beloved of all jams in South Africa; also preserved whole were the *naartje,* or tangerine, oranges and grapefruit—in particular the powerful *pompelmoes.* This last, used in place of marmalade, was a majestic feature of our breakfast table. One extra-large jam jar would just about hold a single *pompelmoes* and its surrounding syrup. Even in the bright light of an early African morning, it glowed on the table like a lamp. Fortunately or not, the fruit has never lent itself to mass production in this form, I suspect because its preparation is too much trouble. I meet it nowadays only on farms in my own part of Africa where people still believe as I do that its taste is well worth the trouble of making it.

If I have dwelt so lovingly on jams and preserves, it is because of their affinity for bread. Next to *biltong,* bread was traditionally the life-supporting food of the interior. This role was so dramatic that old people, in telling us of the trials of their early history, always used one phrase to sum up the periods when they did not have enough to eat. It was a simple phrase, yet one that filled our hearts with horror: *Daar was dikwels brood gebrek*—"there was often lack of bread." To us children, it seemed the ultimate in deprivation.

Such periods gradually dwindled, and once the pioneer communities became permanent settlements, sheep and cattle could be bred in such quantities that they could be slaughtered liberally for food. First, as I have indicated, came the sheep. Black-nosed, fat-tailed African sheep thrived in the interior, their fat providing "butter" long before we had herds of dairy cattle. As the pioneers moved from the Karroo, which proved so unexpectedly kind to sheep, to the great grasslands of the high

Opposite: Frikkadels, the seasoned hamburgers of South Africa, may be braised as spicy patties or used to stuff cabbage rolls. Both forms are shown here, surrounding a mound of yellow rice cooked with raisins; the salads at top are cucumber and chili, and beet and onion.

Terts, or tarts, are a South African specialty. The ones shown here are *(from left)*: *melk tert,* a custard tart, the national favorite; sweet potato; raisin; and coconut. The sour-cream sauce is usually served with a raisin *tert.*

veld to the north, they found the country increasingly suitable for rearing cattle. Although mutton retained first place, beef began to appear more often in the diet. For a long time this meant the meat of the ox. The main aim of the frontiersmen was to grow the most powerful and hardy breed of oxen possible, so that their lifeline with the Cape as well as the thrust forward into the interior could be securely maintained, no matter what the lack of roads or what the barrier of mountain and river. The quality of the meat, milk and butter were all subsidiary considerations, and on the whole cooks had to be content to use the meat of oxen that had grown too old to haul the heavy wagons to and from the Cape.

Away from the towns, a slaughtered ox or cow produced far more meat than one family could use. As a result, beef was slaughtered only in the cold of winter when one could be certain that the meat would not go bad in the days needed for preserving it, either as *biltong* or in another form that quickly joined *biltong* as a favorite food: the *boerewors (Recipe Index),* or Boer sausage. The original *boerewors,* like the original *biltong,* was made out of the best of the meat that could not be eaten immediately. Even by the time of my childhood, with all the amenities of a well-equipped farm and kitchen on hand, the slaughtering of a single beast was the signal for a kind of general mobilization in which all our manpower—and female power—were thrown into battle. It took the entire household working from dawn to sunset before the beef had been properly disposed of. The bones were set aside for soup and above all for their marrow. Such meat as could be used over the next few days as roasts, steaks or the boiled beef we loved was stored in the coldest larder. But this formed only a small part of the animal. All the rest was turned either into *biltong* or *boerewors.*

Moreover, we never slaughtered an ox without killing a pig too. The gut of the pig was by far the finest envelope for sausage meat; the lard, as well as a small amount of the pork, went into the filling along with the beef. Before the arrival of hand mincing machines, the selected meat was finely carved up on wooden boards with heavy butchers' knives. The sausages formed in this manner looked like coils of garden hose—not at all like the bedraggled chain of fragments of pallid meat pulp and bread one sees in meat shops in Britain and America. The sausages we made, redolent of crushed spices, were strung across beams in cool, dry, dustproof outhouses, where we also hung our *biltong.* In time *boerewors,* like *biltong,* cured itself, and once cured could be taken on the longest of journeys, cut into slices with a knife and eaten by itself, far more delicious than any salami I have ever met. But well before it was cured it could be wonderfully responsive to grilling on live coals. One long unbroken coil of sausage would fill the biggest cast-iron frying pan in my family and provide food enough for some dozen people at a sitting.

With the emergence of the *boerewors,* the great southern African institution known as the *braaivleis* came into being. *Braaivleis* is the Afrikaans version of the American barbecue. It started, I believe, as an annual commemoration of all that southern Africa owed to the pioneers of the interior. The day normally chosen for this was December 16; on that day in 1838 a few hundred white pioneers, greatly aided by the Cape Colored servants who accompanied them into the interior (for political convenience this part of the story is ignored in our popular histories) defeated the armies of the Zulu king Dingaan who had massacred hundreds of pioneers. To celebrate the victory, farmers would load their families, bedding and food on covered wagons and make for some well-watered place deep in veld or bush. There, with hundreds of other families, they would pitch camp and for some days live life as it was lived on the trek.

These extraordinary gatherings were part prayer meetings run by the local *predikant,* or priest, and part political rallies; the speechmaking would start up as soon as prayers were ended in the morning and finish only before the last text in the Bible was read and the last prayer said at night. As a young boy I found the speechmaking a bore, but as an adventure of living and eating in wild natural surroundings, the experience was incomparable. The gatherings set the pattern for the smaller *braaivleis* of today, no longer celebrated just once a year but almost every weekend in suburban households as well as in villages and on farms —even by people who have no share in the traditions that gave it birth.

The food served on these occasions is becoming more and more elaborate, the side dishes and wines more and more refined. But only two things are essential for a good *braaivleis:* the original *sosatie* of the Cape Malays, and *boerewors.* Pancakes usually serve as a sweet to cap the re-

A couple of jiggers of tangerine-flavored Van der Hum liqueur *(left)* are used in making *chippolata (Recipe Index),* a molded dessert dominated by the rich textures of custard and ladyfingers. Van der Hum is a South African invention dating from the early 19th Century. An old recipe for it calls for the flavoring of whole cloves, cardamom, cinnamon, nutmeg, sugar and the grated and dried peels of tangerines.

past, but at a recent *braaivleis* in my own province, the Orange Free State, we ended with a *melktert (Recipe Index)*. The *melktert* is to South Africa as apple pie is to America. As we had it, it was made in the proportions of one pint of milk to two tablespoons of sugar, a tablespoon of the finest corn flour, two eggs, a stick of cinnamon and a tablespoon of butter. The milk was boiled with the sugar and the cinnamon, a roux made of the butter and the flour, with a little milk added to make it liquid before it was combined with boiled milk. The mixture was boiled for five minutes, then poured into a basin; when it was cold the two eggs, well whisked, were folded into it. The whole was then poured into a tart dish lined with pastry made as thin as possible and baked for 20 minutes. Served with a sprinkling of cinnamon and sugar on top, it was an excellent end note. If I were organizing a *braaivleis* of my own, however, I would top it off simply with strong hot coffee, drunk in the Ethiopian manner with spoonfuls of black wild honey.

Almost as traditional as the *braaivleis* is the southern African fondness for game. Today hunting is restricted to our winter months (the middle of the calendar year), and some varieties of game like the springbok, the blesbok and the eland are protected by farmers. But in my youth there was hardly any form of wildlife that did not find its way to our table. My collection of recipes includes some that date from long before my time for cooking the great mountain tortoises, the mountain lizard called *likkewaan,* the hare, the zebra, the giraffe (highly prized for its marrow) and even the hippopotamus, equally prized for its lard.

And springbok: of some 200 kinds of antelope in Africa, it is this lovable, elegant gazelle that has become southern Africa's prime heraldic animal. Yet it could never have achieved its place in the popular imagination, and its predominance over all other forms of venison at the table, if its meat were not so sweet and tender. It provided in the past and still provides the most delicate of *biltongs,* the finest liver, the finest *tournedos* and above all the best natural roast on the whole continent.

On its arrival in the kitchen, a leg of springbok is immediately and reverently seized and well rubbed with salt, pepper, a pinch of dry powdered ginger and a slight scraping of garlic as well. It is then larded and marinated for 24 hours, preferably in red wine and wine vinegar, perhaps with a bay or lemon leaf or two. Then it is browned and a few tablespoons of lard are added, as well as half a cup of red wine, pepper, some cloves and salt to taste. From then on the joint is placed on a lower flame and allowed to braise gently in a tightly covered pot. From time to time the pot is shaken to let the sauce flow over the joint. This method is felt to be better than the conventional basting process because the quintessential of good pot-roasting on this scale is to keep the cover sealed in order to ensure that no moisture or fragrance escape from within. After about two and a half hours the cook raises the cover and quickly probes with a skewer to see whether the roast is done; in fact, it is better that roast venison be somewhat overdone than not done enough. At the end, it is placed on a platter and put in an open oven to keep it warm while the sauce is made from the natural gravy or the marinade. Or the venison may be cut up for a savory stew *(see jugged venison, Recipe Index).*

Opposite: At dawn, barely touched by the sun, the Zambezi River rumbles over Victoria Falls, on the Zambia-Rhodesia border. David Livingstone, traveling down his "glorious river" in 1855, became the first white man to set eyes on the falls, and named them for his queen. Long before that, however, they had been known by another, far more descriptive name—Mosi-oa-Tunya, "Smoke That Thunders."

By the time the Boer pioneers were well established in the interior, the waning Far Eastern influences in their cooking were suddenly reawakened by the arrival in Natal of thousands of Indians imported to work on the sugar plantations set up by the British. Indian curries soon became a regular feature of life in the interior. No week would go by without the appearance of one or two main curry dishes in the average household. Even such orthodox pioneering dishes as *kop en pootjies* (sheep's head and trotters) and *hoofkaas* (head cheese and brawn) began to be done in curried form, and to this day they are regular and good homely dishes on the farms *(see curried brawn, Recipe Index)*.

Curry in all its forms, in fact, is enjoyed in homes and hotels everywhere in southern Africa. (If only the national palate could be allowed to govern for a year or two, there would be no apartheid or racial prejudice left in the land, because our cooking already is the best advertisement for a multiracial society, free of all discrimination.)

Along with their curries the Indians brought their mangoes, pawpaws (papayas), loquats, and many other Oriental fruits that began to appear in chutneys, pickles and fruit salads. They also brought with them the versatile *brinjal,* or eggplant, which became one of our most familiar vegetables, as dependable as the pumpkin, cabbage, beans and corn.

Another strong food influence on the people who turned their backs on the Cape in the 1830s, and their successors, was the German influence of South-West Africa, which emerged into the 20th Century as a German colony but is now effectively South African. As is clear from some of the recipes in this book, many good aspects of the old German colonial ways have survived. Even today, in South-West Africa, conditions approximate more closely the rugged character of our European beginnings. Some ingredients like the meat of the humpbacked ox and the fat-tailed sheep, which have largely disappeared in South Africa, are still available for the cook in South-West Africa.

I never go back there without feeling that despite the airplane and the automobile I have gone back in time to the sort of community I knew as a child. I can sum this up in an experience I had on a journey from Windhoek to the Etosha Pan in the far north. I had set out before dawn and when the sun rose was not yet in sight of any town. I asked my driver how long it would take before we would get to one.

He answered with another question: "Are you hungry?"

"Yes," I said, not troubling to explain to him that I really was much more thirsty than hungry.

"Well, why wait for the town?" he said (turning off the main road along a track as he spoke), "when there is such a clear *koffie-paaitjie* [little coffee road] right here?"

I recollected with a rush of warm emotion that when I was young, that was precisely what we called any side road that indicated that some form of human habitation might be near, where we would be warmly welcomed with coffee, food and shelter.

The custom has almost vanished in my own part of Africa and to find it still taken for granted here in the southwest was surprising and reassuring. After some miles the road brought us to a farm rearing the black-nosed sheep that produces astrakhan fur. It was owned by a family of German origin and the welcome could not have been more generous than the term *koffie-paaitjie* implied. I not only had coffee but also a breakfast of porridge made of mealie meal, served with cream and honey. This was followed by bread and a bit of the scrambled egg of an ostrich.

Although I had fully intended to move on after breakfast, I was shown such hospitality that I stayed on all day and night. The language of the house was German and we spoke in German. When we came back to the homestead from a visit to the farm, there were other touches of the German to greet us, for we sat down to tea and a superb *kartoffel-puffer*. It was made of white floury potatoes grated, buttered and baked in the fat rendered from the tail of the black-nosed sheep, until all melted and recongealed as one. It was baked a deep golden brown on both sides and turned out on our plates with a sauce of mixed dried apple and dried apricot purée. For dinner that night we had mutton braised in beer, with a dish of rice and small squashes baked in butter in the oven, as well as a bottle of dry wine, followed by one of the richest and best German walnut-and-almond cakes I have ever eaten.

But it was really the scrambled ostrich egg I had eaten at breakfast that remained in my mind. I was still thinking of it at dawn the next morning when I bid goodbye to my generous host. The morning star was already high in the eastern sky over the Kalahari Desert—the star that figures so heroically in the Stone Age mythology of my native land under the name of "The Dawn's Heart." Watching it, I knew why the ostrich egg had captured my imagination. The ostrich plays a very special role in this mythology. It is the bird that inadvertently brought the gift of fire to man and was punished for doing so by having its power to fly removed. That this greatest bird of all should have been chosen for its Promethean role is fitting, because the mastery of fire has always seemed to me the most inspired and greatest idea ever to issue from the mind of man.

I suddenly realized why, on my many expeditions to the Kalahari, I had always on the last day pitched camp near one of the many dead trees that stand upright like ghosts in the desert. That night I would make a fire around the tree, and eat my meal watching the fire climb up the dead wood until finally it burned there in the dark like a Gothic cathedral of flame. I would watch it, feeling intensely grateful for the gift of fire, for the many good and great things it had done for man. Among other boons, it released him from the bondage of having to eat his food raw. And it set him on the long way to evolving an art of cooking, converting food from a mere necessity into a source of delight and a cause for joy in being alive, however cold the day or dark the night.

To serve 4 to 6

2 pounds lean ground lamb
½ cup soft fresh crumbs made
    from homemade-type white
    bread, trimmed of crusts and
    pulverized in a blender or finely
    shredded with a fork
½ cup finely chopped onions
2 eggs
¼ teaspoon ground nutmeg,
    preferably freshly grated
1 teaspoon ground coriander
2 teaspoons salt
Freshly ground black pepper
¼ cup vegetable oil
1 cup beef stock, fresh or canned
1 tablespoon flour
1 tablespoon cold water

Frikkadels *(South Africa)*
BRAISED MEAT PATTIES FLAVORED WITH NUTMEG AND CORIANDER

Combine the meat, bread crumbs, onions, eggs, nutmeg, coriander, salt and a few grindings of pepper in a bowl. Knead vigorously with both hands, then beat with a spoon until the mixture is smooth and fluffy.

Divide the mixture into 12 equal portions and shape each one into a round, flattened patty about 1 inch thick and 2 inches in diameter.

In a heavy 10- to 12-inch skillet, heat the oil over moderate heat until a light haze forms above it. Brown the patties in the hot oil, 5 or 6 at a time, turning them with a slotted spatula and regulating the heat so that they color richly and evenly on both sides without burning. As they brown, transfer the patties to a plate.

Pour off the fat remaining in the skillet and in its place add the stock. Bring to a boil over high heat, stirring constantly and scraping in the brown bits clinging to the bottom and sides of the pan. Return the patties, along with any liquid that has accumulated around them, to the skillet. Reduce the heat to low, cover partially, and simmer for 30 minutes.

With a slotted spoon or spatula, transfer the *frikkadels* to a heated platter and drape with foil to keep them warm while you prepare the sauce.

Skim as much fat as possible from the liquid remaining in the skillet. There should be about 1 cup; if there is less, add more beef stock or, if there is more, boil the liquid over high heat until it is reduced to 1 cup. With a wire whisk, make a smooth paste of the flour and water, then whisk it into the liquid in the pan. Cook, stirring frequently, until the sauce comes to a boil and thickens lightly. Pour the sauce over the *frikkadels* and serve at once, or present it separately in a bowl. *Frikkadels* can be accompanied by yellow rice with raisins *(Recipe Index)*.

NOTE: *Frikkadels* may be made from lamb, beef or pork—or any combination of these—to suit your taste.

To serve 6

1 large head green cabbage (2 to 3
    pounds)
1 recipe uncooked *frikkadel* meat
    mixture *(above)*
2 cups boiling beef stock, fresh or
    canned
2 tablespoons flour
½ cup cold water
Salt
Freshly ground black pepper

Cabbage Rolls Stuffed with Frikkadels *(South Africa)*

Wash the cabbage under cold running water and trim off and discard any discolored or badly bruised outer leaves. Place the cabbage in enough boiling water to cover it completely, and cook it briskly for about 10 minutes. Lift the cabbage out of the pot but keep the water at a boil. Carefully peel off as many outside leaves as you can without tearing them, and set them aside. Then return the cabbage to the pot, boil for a few minutes longer, and once more peel off the softened outer leaves. Repeat the process until you have at least 12 unbroken leaves.

To make the cabbage rolls, spread the leaves on a flat surface and with a small, sharp knife trim off the tough rib end at the base of each one. Pat and shape about ⅓ cup of the *frikkadel* meat mixture into a flattened, round patty about 2 inches in diameter and 1 inch thick.

Place the patty in the center of the leaf and fold the top over, tucking it securely under the meat. Fold the sides over the top, and roll the filled leaf into a neat package. Loop kitchen string around the width and length of the roll and tie it securely. Trim, fill, fold and tie the remaining cabbage leaves similarly.

Arrange the rolls seam side down in a heavy skillet large enough to hold them snugly in one layer. Pour in the 2 cups of stock, and bring it to a boil. Then lower the heat, cover the pan tightly, and simmer for 1 hour. (Check the pan from time to time and if it seems dry, add a few more tablespoons of boiling stock—or water.) With a slotted spoon or tongs, transfer the cabbage rolls to a heated platter and drape foil loosely over them while you prepare the sauce.

With a whisk, make a smooth paste of the flour and cold water, and whisk it gradually into the stock remaining in the skillet. Cook, stirring frequently, until the sauce thickens lightly. Season with salt and pepper.

To serve, pour the sauce over the cabbage rolls or present it separately in a bowl or sauceboat.

Beet and Onion Salad *(South Africa)*

To serve 4

With a small, sharp knife, cut the tops from the beets, leaving about 1 inch of stem on each. Scrub the beets under cold running water, then drop them into enough lightly salted boiling water to cover them completely. Reduce the heat to low, partially cover the pan, and simmer for about 30 minutes, or until the beets show no resistance when pierced with the point of a small, sharp knife. The beets should be kept constantly covered with water; add boiling water if necessary.

Drain the beets in a colander and, when they are cool, slip off their skins. Cut the beets lengthwise into slices ¼ inch thick and then into strips about ¼ inch wide, or slice them into rounds ¼ inch thick.

Combine the vinegar, salt and sugar in a deep bowl and stir until the sugar dissolves. Drop in the beets and the onions and turn them about with a spoon until they are coated with the vinegar mixture. Let the salad marinate at room temperature for about 30 minutes, turning the beets and onions every 10 minutes or so. Serve at room temperature.

1 pound fresh firm small beets
¼ cup red wine vinegar
1 teaspoon salt
½ teaspoon sugar
2 small onions, peeled, cut crosswise into slices ¼ inch thick and separated into rings

Geelrys *(South Africa)*
YELLOW RICE WITH RAISINS

To serve 4 to 6

In a heavy 2- to 3-quart saucepan, melt the butter over moderate heat. When the foam begins to subside, add the rice and stir until the grains are coated with butter. Do not let the rice brown. Add the water, cinnamon, turmeric, saffron and salt and, stirring constantly, bring to a boil over high heat. Reduce the heat to low, cover tightly, and simmer for about 20 minutes, or until the rice is tender and has absorbed all the liquid in the pan.

Remove the pan from the heat, discard the cinnamon stick, and add the raisins. Fluff the rice with a fork, stir in 1 teaspoon of sugar, taste, and add more if you wish. Cut a circle of wax paper or foil and place it inside the pan directly on top of the rice. Cover the pan with its lid and let it stand at room temperature for about 20 minutes.

Just before serving, fluff the rice again with a fork and mound it in a heated bowl or platter.

2 tablespoons butter
1 cup uncooked long-grain white rice
2 cups boiling water
1 piece of stick cinnamon, 2 inches long
½ teaspoon ground turmeric
A pinch of crumbled saffron threads or ground saffron
1 teaspoon salt
½ cup seedless raisins
Sugar

To serve 8

3 teaspoons butter, softened
1 dozen best quality (or homemade type) ladyfingers, split in half
½ cup Van der Hum tangerine liqueur, or substitute any orange-flavored liqueur such as Cointreau or Grand Marnier
1 envelope unflavored gelatin
¼ cup cold water
4 egg yolks
⅓ cup sugar
2 cups milk
1 tablespoon finely grated fresh tangerine or orange peel
2 egg whites
8 tablespoons finely chopped preserved ginger
1 cup heavy cream, chilled
2 tablespoons sifted confectioners' sugar

Chippolata (South Africa)
MOLDED TANGERINE AND GINGER CUSTARD

With a pastry brush, spread 2 teaspoons of the butter evenly over the bottom and sides of a 1½-quart charlotte mold or any other plain, round 1½-quart mold 3 or 4 inches deep. Cut a wax paper circle to fit the bottom of the mold, spread one side with the remaining teaspoon of butter and lay the paper in the base of the mold, buttered side up.

With a pastry brush moisten the cut side of each of the ladyfinger halves with the liqueur. To line the mold with ladyfingers, cut a ½-inch circle out of a ladyfinger half and place it, curved side down, in the center of the paper. Cut ladyfingers into slightly tapered wedge shapes to fit and radiate around the circle—like petals in a rosette—and arrange them curved side down on the paper. Stand the remaining ladyfingers side by side around the inside of the mold, and with scissors trim off any excess rising above the rim.

Sprinkle the gelatin over the cold water and set it aside to soften. Meanwhile, with a wire whisk or a rotary or electric beater, beat the egg yolks and sugar together for 3 or 4 minutes, until the yolks are thick enough to fall in a ribbon when the beater is lifted from the bowl.

Combine the milk and the tangerine or orange peel in a 1½- to 2-quart enameled, stainless-steel or glass saucepan and cook over moderate heat until bubbles appear around the edge of the pan. Remove the pan from the heat and, beating constantly, add the egg yolks. Then stir in the softened gelatin. Return to low heat and continue to stir until the custard mixture is smooth and thick enough to coat the spoon lightly. Do not let the mixture come anywhere near the boiling point or it will curdle. Strain the custard through a fine sieve into a deep bowl and set it aside to cool.

Wash and dry the whisk or beater; then, in a separate bowl, beat the egg whites until they are stiff enough to stand in firm, unwavering peaks on the beater when it is lifted from the bowl.

Set the bowl of custard into a larger bowl filled with crushed ice or ice cubes and water. With a metal spoon, stir the custard for 4 or 5 minutes, until it is quite cold. Beat thoroughly with a whisk to be sure it is perfectly smooth. Scoop the egg whites over the custard, sprinkle in 4 tablespoons of the ginger and, with a rubber spatula, fold together gently but thoroughly.

Ladle the custard into the mold, spreading it and smoothing the top with the spatula. Refrigerate for at least 2 hours, or until the custard is firm to the touch and thoroughly chilled.

To unmold and serve the *chippolata,* run a sharp knife around the sides of the mold and dip the bottom in hot water for a few seconds. Place a chilled serving plate upside down over the mold and, grasping both sides firmly, turn the plate and mold over. Rap the plate sharply on a table and the *chippolata* should slide out of the mold. Gently remove the wax paper from the top and refrigerate the custard for an hour or so or until you plan to serve it.

Just before serving, whip the cream with a clean wire whisk or a rotary or electric beater until it forms firm peaks on the beater when it is lifted out of the bowl.

Dust the top and sides of the *chippolata* lightly with the confectioners' sugar. With a pastry bag fitted with a decorative tip, pipe whipped-cream rosettes around the base and make as fanciful a pattern as you like on the top of the custard. Sprinkle the remaining 4 tablespoons of ginger at random or in clusters over the cream.

Sosaties *(South Africa)*
SKEWERED MARINATED LAMB WITH CURRY-TAMARIND SAUCE

To serve 6

Starting a day ahead, heat the bacon fat or lard in a heavy 8- to 10-inch skillet over moderate heat until it is very hot but not smoking. Drop in the chopped onions and, stirring frequently, cook for about 5 minutes, or until they are soft and translucent but not brown. Watch carefully for any sign of burning and regulate the heat accordingly. Add the curry powder, coriander and turmeric, and stir for 2 or 3 minutes longer. Then add the tamarind water (or lemon-juice mixture), jam and sugar, and continue to stir until the mixture comes to a boil. Reduce the heat to low and simmer partially covered for 15 minutes. Pour the curry-and-tamarind mixture into a large, shallow bowl and cool to room temperature.

Sprinkle the lamb with the salt and a few grindings of pepper. Toss the lamb, lemon or bay leaves, garlic and chilies together with the cooled curry mixture, cover tightly with foil or plastic wrap, and marinate the lamb in the refrigerator for at least 12 hours, turning the cubes over from time to time.

Light a layer of coals in a charcoal broiler and let them burn until a white ash appears on the surface, or preheat the broiler of your oven to its highest point.

Remove the lamb from the marinade and string the cubes tightly on 6 long skewers, alternating the meat with the layers of onions and the squares of fresh pork fat. Broil 4 inches from the heat, turning the skewers occasionally, until the lamb is done to your taste. For pink lamb, allow about 8 minutes. For well-done lamb, which is more typical of South African cooking, allow 12 to 15 minutes.

Meanwhile, prepare the sauce. Discard the lemon or bay leaves and pour the marinade into a small saucepan. Bring to a boil over high heat, then reduce the heat to low. Make a smooth paste of the flour and 2 tablespoons of cold water and, with a wire whisk or a spoon, stir it gradually into the simmering marinade. Cook, stirring frequently, until the sauce thickens lightly. Taste for seasoning.

To serve, slide the lamb, onions and fat off the skewers onto heated individual plates. Present the sauce separately in a small bowl or sauceboat.

3 tablespoons rendered bacon fat or lard
1½ cups finely chopped onions
1 tablespoon curry powder, preferably Madras type
1 teaspoon ground coriander
½ teaspoon ground turmeric
1 cup tamarind water *(Recipe Booklet)*, or substitute ½ cup strained fresh lemon juice combined with ½ cup water
1 tablespoon apricot jam
1 tablespoon light-brown sugar
2 pounds lean boneless lamb, preferably leg, trimmed of excess fat and cut into 1½-inch cubes
1 teaspoon salt
Freshly ground black pepper
4 fresh lemon leaves or 4 medium-sized bay leaves
2 teaspoons finely chopped garlic
2 teaspoons finely chopped fresh hot chilies *(caution: see page 76)*
2 medium-sized onions, peeled, cut lengthwise into quarters and separated into individual layers
¼ pound fresh pork fat, sliced ¼ inch thick and cut into 1-inch squares
1 tablespoon flour
2 tablespoons cold water

Cucumber and Chili Salad *(South Africa)*

To serve 4

Combine the cucumbers, salt, 1 tablespoon of the vinegar and ¼ teaspoon of the sugar in a bowl and turn them about with a spoon until well mixed. Let the cucumbers marinate at room temperature for about 30 minutes, then squeeze the slices vigorously to remove any excess moisture and drop them into a serving bowl.

Add the remaining 2 tablespoons of vinegar, ¼ teaspoon of sugar and the chilies, and toss together gently but thoroughly. Serve at once.

2 large cucumbers, peeled and cut crosswise into rounds ⅛ inch thick
1½ teaspoons salt
3 tablespoons red wine vinegar
½ teaspoon sugar
2 teaspoons finely chopped fresh hot chilies *(caution: see page 76)*

Recipe Index: English

NOTE: An R preceding a page refers to the Recipe Booklet. Size, weight and material are specified for pans in the recipes because they affect cooking results. A pan should be just large enough to hold its contents comfortably. Heavy pans heat slowly and cook food at a constant rate. Aluminum and cast iron conduct heat well but may discolor foods containing egg yolks, vinegar or lemon. Enamelware is a fairly poor conductor of heat. Many recipes therefore recommend stainless steel or enameled cast iron, which do not have these faults.

Recipe Index: Foreign

General Index Numerals in italics indicate a photograph or drawing of the subject mentioned.

Abidjan, capital of Ivory Coast, *map 61*
Abrahams, Giva (Mrs. Fuad Carr), *134-135*
Abyssinia. *See* Ethiopia
Accra, capital of Ghana, *map 61,* 83; Kaneshie Market, *64*
Açorda soup (shrimp, bread and poached eggs, Angola), 119
Addis Ababa, capital of Ethiopia, 23, 28, *map 28,* 41, 46-47, *50, 51;* Maskal procession, *48-49*
Addis Ababa Restaurant, *41, 42, 43, 44-45*
Africa: *maps 20-21, 28, 61, 93, 114, 115, 133;* animals and plants same throughout continent, 22; colonialism vanishing, 23; contemporary divisive conflicts, 23; food, 23; Portuguese importations of plants and animals, 115; trees and shrubs, 28; unity in diversity of races, languages, cultures, 18; wild life, 97, *98-99,* 100, 102, *104-105, 192-194.* *See also* names of countries and regions
Afrikaans, official language of South Africa, 135, 146, 164
Afrique Noire (land of the blacks), west of the Great Rift Valley, 59, 60, *map 61*
Alecha (Ethiopian stew *not* flavored with *berberé*), 38; served for breakfast, 40
Algarve, Portugal, 114
Allspice, *34,* 170
Alto Rouge (South African red wine), 155
Amhara, Ethiopian tribe, 43
Amharic, official language of Ethiopia, 35, 49
Angola, 23, 113, *map 114,* 116-120, 123, 124, 125; Brazilian influence on cookery, 115; coffee, 117-118; Portuguese commitment to African life, 116-117
Appetizers: avocado stuffed with smoked fish, Sierra Leone, 82, *89;* quiche, Senegal, 69; shrimp pâté, Tanzania, 104
Apple *sambal,* 141
Apricot: *blatjang* (chutney, Cape Malay, South Africa, 141, *143;* varieties, South Africa, 159
Arab: culture in West Africa, 22; influence in East Africa, 92; influence in Mozambique, 115; -style cookery, Mozambique, 115
Arabia, *map 21,* 132
Architecture, Cape Dutch, South Africa, 154, *156*
Arroz de coco (coconut rice, Mozambique), 124
Ashanti tribe, Ghana, 62
Athlone, South Africa, 134
Atjar (pickles, Cape Malay, South

Africa), 133, 140; green bean, *142;* green mango, 140; lemon, *142;* mango, *142;* mango, Java style, 140; mixed-vegetable, 140
Atlantic Ocean, *map 20-21,* 135
Avocado stuffed with smoked fish, Sierra Leone, 82, *89*

Baeta, Barbara, 83
Bagamoyo, Tanzania, 92, *map 93*
Baía dos Tigres, Angola, 114, *map 114*
Banana: fritters, West Africa, *87; gin,* Uganda *(waragi),* 105; ways of serving in West Africa, 64; wine, 64
Bantu, 11, 132, 174, *175;* British-trained cooks, East Africa, 101, 104; culture of East Africa, 22
Baobab, The, Senegalese inn, 61
Baobab tree, 18, 22, 28, *95;* fruit, *94;* fruit and seeds used as food, 61, 177; uses, *94*
Barley-flour pellets, Ethiopian snack, 40
Basil, sacred, 37
Baskets for bread, Ethiopia, 30-31, *39, 41, 42*
Baudelaire, Charles, 154
Baumann, Oskar, 97
Bean(s): dried spotted (governor's), South Africa, 10; green, atjar (pickle, Cape Malay, South Africa), *142;* purées with coconut milk *(frejons),* Nigeria, 67; red, West Africa, 66
Beef: *biltong,* South Africa, 176; raw with *berberé* dip, Ethiopia, *57;* stew *(alecha),* Ethiopia, 38; stew *(wat),* Ethiopia, 35, 37, 38, 39, 41, *42, 43*
Beehive pattern of buildings, Ethiopia, 29, 46
Beekeeping, Ethiopia, 31; hives, Gojjam, *31*
Beet and onion salad, South Africa, 186
Beetles, poisonous, South-West Africa, 19
Beira, Mozambique, *map 115,* 120, 122
Belgian Congo (The Congo), 59
Benin bronzes, 59
Berberé (red-pepper mixture, universal seasoning in Ethiopia), 32; *34,* 35, 37, 40, *46, 57;* ingredients, *34*
Bereles (decanter-shaped bottles, Ethiopia), 30, *42, 43*
Berries, desert, *19*
Beverages: Alto Rouge (South African red wine), 155; banana gin, Uganda *(waragi),* 105; banana wine, West Africa, 64; chocolate, hot, Portuguese Africa, *128;* coffee, Angola, 117-118; coffee, Ethiopia, 28, 32, *43,* 192; Constantia (South

Africa dessert wine), 154, 156, 157; Gezellen (South African sherry), 156; K.W.V. (South African brandy), 156; Lieberstein (South African white wine), 160, 161; millet beer, Bantu, 174; mint tea, Senegal, *68;* Nederburg Hochheimer (South African white wine), 154; sherries, South Africa, 156; Stellenrood (South African red wine), 155-156; *talla* (beer, Ethiopia), 31, 40, 46; *tej* (Ethiopian honey wine), 30, 31, 32, *42, 43,* 52; Van der Hum (South African tangerine-flavored liqueur), 156, *191;* Witzenberg (South African white wine), 155
Bida, Nigeria, 58, *map 61*
Biltong (salted, spiced, cured meat, South Africa), 175-176, 190; compared to cured meats of other countries, 176; importance to Voortrekkers, 187; sandwiches, 177; skewered grilled, 176-177; springbok, 192
Biriyani (saffron rice with meat, Cape Malay, South Africa), *135*
Bishop's weed (Ethiopian spice), 37
Black Pot Restaurant, Accra, 83
Black Umfolozi River, 12
Blatjang (chutney, Cape Malay, South Africa), 133, 140; apricot, 141, *143;* as made in Java, 140-141; date, 141, *143*
Bloemfontein, South Africa, *map 133*
Blouberg Strand, South Africa, *160, 161*
Blue Nile, *map 21,* 28, *map 28,* 37
Bobotie (minced-meat pie with custard topping, South Africa), 133, 136-137, *138, 139;* mussel, 156
Boerbeskuit (farmer's rusks, South Africa), 177
Boerewors (beef and pork sausage, South Africa), *178, 180,* 190, 191
Boers, 12, 13, 153; victory over Zulus celebrated, December 16, 1838, 190-191. *See also* Cape Colony; Great Trek; Voortrekkers
Bond cookies, South Africa, 162
Botswana, *map 133*
Braaivleis (grilled meat, outdoor barbecue, South Africa), *178,* 190-192; food to serve, 191-192
Brazilian cookery, Angola, 115
Brazilian trees and plants, Mozambique, 122
Brazzaville, Congo Republic (Middle Congo), 67
Bread(s): baking, South Africa, 179; *boerbeskuit* (farmer's rusks, South Africa), 177; *dabo*

kolo (wheat scone or biscuit, Ethiopia), 40; importance to Voortrekkers, 187; millet, Ethiopia *(injera),* 30-31, *36, 38, 41, 42, 43,* 52; *mosbeskuit* (baked rusks, South Africa), 164; *mosbolletjie* (grape bunlet, South Africa), 162, 164, 177, 179; Portuguese, Angola, 116; used as eating utensil in Ethiopia, 38; varieties, Ethiopia, 38
Breakfast: Angola, 116; Cape Colony *(petit déjeuner),* 164; Dahomey, 72; Guinea, 72; Ivory Coast, 72; South-West Africa, 194
Bredie (meat and vegetable stew, South Africa), 133, *135,* 136, 137; tomato, 140
Brinjal (eggplant, South Africa), 194
British, 120, 133, 193; influence in East Africa, 93, 100-105; influence in Tanzania, 92; masters at Cape of Good Hope, 13, 173; settlement in South Africa, 132; slave trade, 60
Buffalo, 104
Bündnerfleisch (viande de Grisons) compared with *biltong,* 176
Buriyani (mutton-rice dish, Malay, for Moulidu-n-nabi festival), 134
Bushman, 11, 17, 18, 23, 132; in Etosha Pan region, 8, *9;* in South-West Africa, 18, *19*
Buttermilk: curds and collard greens, Ethiopia *(yegomen kitfo),* 38, *39;* soup garnished with cinnamon and nutmeg, South Africa, *14*
Byzantium, 48

Cabbage with bacon, South Africa, 158-159
Cakes and cookies: Bond cookies, South Africa, 162; cake with chopped cashews, Portuguese Africa, *128; krakelinge* (figure-8 cookies, South Africa), *165; soetkoekies* (almond-topped spice cookies, South Africa), 162, *165,* 179; *voortrekker-koekies* (cookies, South Africa), 178; walnut-and-almond cake, German, South-West Africa, 194. *See also* Desserts
Calabash containers for winnowing millet, Fadiouth, 71
Calalou aux fruits de mer (spinach, lamb and seafood stew, West Africa), 73
Cam (Cão), Diogo, 113
Camarões (prawns, Portuguese), origin of name of Cameroon, 64
Camel hump, roasted, East Africa, 108

Credits and Acknowledgments

The sources for the illustrations in this book are shown below. Credits for the pictures from left to right are separated by commas, from top to bottom by dashes.

Photographs by Richard Jeffery—Cover; pages 14, 15, 25, 33, 34, 39, 54, 57, 66, 73, 85, 87, 89, 111, 125, 127, 128, 142, 143, 148, 150, 163, 165, 167, 170, 180, 181, 186, 188, 189, 191. All other photographs by Brian Seed except: 4—Top row Walter Daran—Christopher Morris, Monica Suder. 12, 13—Eliot Elisofon. 20, 21 —Map by David Greenspan and Lothar Roth. 28 —Maps by Lothar Roth. 58—Eliot Elisofon. 61 and 93 —Maps by Lothar Roth. 95—Lynn McLaren from Rapho Guillumette. 98—Maitland Edey except top. 99 —Maitland Edey except bottom right. 114, 115, 133 —Maps by Lothar Roth. 168—Drawing by Matt Greene.

For their help in the production of this book the editors and the staff wish to thank the following: *in the United States,* South African Consul General and Mrs. O. F. de V. Booysen and members of the Consulate, including Mrs. J. Malin; Mrs. E. Paulsen; Mrs. M. Thomas; Mrs. R. Viljoen and Mrs. J. Wessels; Kathleen Brandes, TIME-LIFE BOOKS; Patricia Calvert, Calvert-Stearns, Inc. for Ethiopian Airlines; Carl du Toit, South African Information Service; Fred Hayford, Ghana Embassy, Washington, D.C.; Lisa Little, The Museum of Primitive Art; Gail Miller, Washington, D.C.; Penny Roach, Columbia University; Mrs. James Sheffield; South African Tourist Corp.; Mr. and Mrs. H. Donald Wilson; Mr. L. E. S. de Villiers, Director of the South African Information Service, and Mrs. de Villiers; *in England,* Gary Pownall, photographic assistant to Brian Seed; *in Ethiopia,* H. E. Hapte Selassie Taffesse, Administrator Ethiopian Tourist Organization; Kifle Seyoum and Elizabeth Yemane-Berhan, Ethiopian Tourist Organization; *in Ghana,* Barbara Baeta, Flair Catering; Gordon Dove; James Moxon, proprietor of Black Pot Restaurant; Nene Azu Mate Kole, Second Paramount Chief Odumasi Krobo; *in Kenya,* New Stanley Hotel; Wilhelm Schiffer; Lance Gostling, editor of *Auto News;* Begum Taj Nanji; *in Mozambique,* John Campbell, General Manager, Sena Sugar Estates; Senhor Botelho de Sousa, Centro de Informação e Turismo de Moçambiques; *in Rhodesia,* Major Alfred MacIlwaine; Mrs. Patricia Ryan, Victoria Falls Hotel; Barbara van der Wael; *in Senegal,* Henriette Berthily, Centre Culturelle Français; *in South Africa,* Adrian Boshier, Museum of Man and Science, Johannesburg; Dr. Paul Bosman and family; R. S. Immerman, J. W. Jagger Library, University of Cape Town; Etaine Erbehart, Assistant to R. S. Immerman; Brian Maguire, Potgietersus, Transvaal; Wilf Nussey, *Johannesburg Star;* Mrs. Naomi van der Merwe; *in South-West Africa,* Game Wardens of the Etosha Pan; *in Tanzania,* Mrs. Hilda Bomani; Mrs. Martha Bulango; Gordon Ferguson, Kilimanjaro Hotel; Patrick Hemingway, College of African Wildlife Management, Mweka; Skip Leavitt and Willy Wagner, Ngorongoro Crater Lodge; Mary O'Shea, *The Sunday News;* Dr. Andreas von Nagy, Mount Meru Game Sanctuary Lodge.

In New York City the following shops and galleries also contributed to the production of this book: African Modern Store; Amron Galleries, Inc.; Belgravia House; Bonniers, Inc.; Connoisseur East; Country Floors, Inc.; Cross Keys Antiques; Decor Technique; Decorative Accents; du Verrier Antiques; 18th Century Antiques; Far Eastern Fabrics, Inc.; Fisher's Antiques; Ginsburg and Levy; F. Gorevic & Son, Inc., Greek Island, Ltd.; Arthur A. Grogin Antiques; Hammer Galleries; Irish Pavilion; George M. Juergens, Inc.; H. J. Kratzer, Inc.; La Cuisinière, Inc.; Liberty House; L. Lipka Antiques; Patina Antiques; The Pottery Barn; Raphaelian Rug Co.; Dorothy Schlesinger Antiques; Edward Sporar Antiques; Tablerie, Inc.; Treasures from Portugal.

Sources consulted in the production of this book include: *A Recipe Book for Ghana Schools,* Dr. E. Amarteifio et al; *Old-Time Recipes,* E. Barnard, ed.; *Africa and Africans,* Paul Bohannan; *An Atlas to African Affairs,* Andrew Boyd and Patrick van Rensburg; *Portuguese Africa,* Ronald H. Chikote; *The Kudeti Book of Yoruba Cookery,* C. M. S. (Nigeria) Bookshops; *West Africa in History,* W. F. Conton; *Ghanaian Favourite Dishes,* Alice Dede; *Traditional Cookery of South Africa,* Judy Desmond; *Cook and Enjoy It,* J. de Villiers; *Hilda's "Where Is It" of Recipes,* Hildagonda J. Duckitt; *Portuguese Africa,* James Duffy; *Ethiopian and American Cook Book,* Ethiopian National Literary Campaign Organization; *An Introduction to the History of West Africa,* J. D. Fage; *Braai and Barbecue* and *Meat on the Menu,* Lesley Faull; *Cape Cookery Old and New* and *Traditional Cookery of the Cape Malays,* Hilda Gerber; *The Art of Charcuterie,* Jane Grigson; *A History of Ethiopia,* A. H. M. Jones and Elizabeth Monroe; *Panoply of Ghana,* A. A. Y. Kyerematen; *Africa South of the Sahara,* G. W. Kingsnorth; *The Story of South Africa,* Leo Marquard; *An Introduction to the History of East Africa,* Zoë Marsh and G. W. Kingsnorth; *Africa in the Days of Exploration,* Roland Oliver; *A Short History of Africa,* Roland Oliver and J. D. Fage; *The Land and the People of South Africa,* Alan Paton; *Recipe Book for Tanzania,* Mrs. E. Pendaeli-Sarakikya and Sister Agnesa Blaser; *Cooking and Sweets of the Portuguese Overseas Territories,* The Portuguese Government Agency of Overseas Territories; *Encyclopedia of Southern Africa,* Eric Rosenthal, ed.; *Recettes Culinaires Sénégalaises,* Anna Sagna; *Mrs. Slade's South African Cookery Book,* Mrs. H. M. Slade; *South African Traditional Dishes,* Pamela Sieff; *Africa, A Study in Tropical Development,* L. Dudley Stamp; *A History of Southern Africa,* Eric Walker.